50 Years of
Soul-Stirring Illustrations

by
Dr. John R. Rice

Sword of the Lord Publishers
Murfreesboro, Tennessee 37130

Clothbound ISBN 0-87398-266-5

Paperbound ISBN 0-87398-267-3

Printed and bound in the United States of America.

Introduction

Over the past fifty-six years Dr. Rice has developed literally thousands of soul-searching and heart-stirring illustrations. Many of his sermon stories were born out of his childhood experiences as a lad growing up in the cowboy land of West Texas. His young manhood, his college days as a debater, training as a college teacher and experience as a football coach provided many rich and colorful incidents that eventually found their way into the classic sermons delivered by Evangelist John R. Rice.

Dr. and Mrs. Rice make their home on a small farm just outside the city of Murfreesboro, Tennessee. When in town, and the weather permits, Dr. Rice enjoys horseback riding across his rocky pastureland. The Rices have six daughters, each of whose husbands is in full-time Christian service.

With over a half century of full-time Christian work, Dr. Rice has started and pastored a number of churches, and authored books and pamphlets that have been circulated in over 50 million copies printed in thirty-eight different languages. He has conducted citywide revival campaigns in many of the major metropolitan areas of this nation and since 1934 has been the founding editor of THE SWORD OF THE LORD. His syndicated nationwide radio broadcast, the VOICE OF REVIVAL, is heard every week and millions of Americans have seen him preach on television.

Out of this vast storehouse of experience has grown these best-loved and most-used illustrations. Probably nothing is more characteristic of Dr. Rice's long and fruitful ministry than his beautiful and simple sermon illustrations.

Some would say, "I best remember Dr. Rice for his tears." Yes, he weeps when he preaches and the illustrations he shares allow the listener to feel his burden and weep with him. Perhaps someone else would point out that this servant of God preaches with power and surely he knows God's fullness of the Holy Spirit. Dr. Rice's burning illustrations demonstrate by way of example how we, too, can have this wonderful power. Multiplied thousands recognize Dr. Rice as an authority on the subject of answered prayer. The casual reader leafing through his famous book, *Prayer—Asking and Receiving,* is charmed by the hundreds of illustrations proving again and again that God hears and answers prayer.

The publishers are delighted to record in this permanent form a rich treasury of the best sermon stories gleaned from the ministry of Dr. John R. Rice. This edition is sent forward with our prayers, trusting it to be used as a source of inspiration, encouragement and hope for the Christian, for the preacher, and for the Bible teacher.

Ron English

1978

Table of Contents

STEWARDSHIP

WILL OF GOD, THE

Answered Prayer

Cooperate or Quit. Years ago I was in a great church in revival services. The pastor pointed out to me a man in the church who violently opposed the pastor's leadership. This man declared that the pastor was not really a pastor, but was an evangelist; that they did not need to have revival services going on all the time in the church. He insisted that there ought to be more formal worship services, that the church ought to follow more the leadership of the denomination, etc.

The pastor suggested that I talk with this man. I said I believed that the man ought to be willing either to become reconciled to the pastor and cooperate with the pastor's leadership, and quit causing division, or he ought to move his membership to another church and not become a bone of contention and a cause of division. The pastor insisted that I talk with his member on this matter, and I did.

He was a saved man, evidently an honest man of good intentions. He saw my point. I showed him that the church felt this pastor was God's man for them, that it would be wrong to try to cause dissension and strife in the church. I urged him, if he could do so happily, to cooperate with the pastor and the people and help to build a great evangelistic church; but if he could not do that, then I urged him to move his membership to another church where he would feel more at home.

The man carefully considered my advice and then he and his daughter asked for their letters and moved their membership at once to another church. Since the man was evidently a godly man, though wrong, I think, in his opposition to the pastor, his letter was granted. And the next Sunday morning he joined another church.

But the pastor came to me somewhat disconsolately and said, "Did you know that man put $20 in the offering every Sunday?"

I thought it was funny then and I have smiled hundreds of times over it since. But it reminds me that we do not always want what we pray for.

* * *

God Answered Both Prayers!

Mrs. Rice and I have had great joy out of an incident that happened here. I often get my prayers answered and that is good. For instance, I prayed for rain and got rain more than once. And some time ago, last summer or fall, after we had had our morning Bible reading, I prayed, "Lord, the grass is getting a little dry in the pasture for the horses and cattle. Will You give us rain that the grass may be green? Other people need rain." I expected it to come that day. The truth is, later we found the weather report was that probably we would have rain that day. But in our community a little boy wanted to go, that closing Saturday, to the State Fair, and he said, "O Mother, we must go."

She said, "Honey, it is going to rain. The weather forecast says it will rain. See, it is clouding up now."

"No, it won't rain, Mother."

"Oh, yes it will," she said.

And they saw him go into his bedroom—a little fellow six or seven years old—and kneel down by his bed. After awhile he came back and said, "Mother, it is not going to rain. We can go to the Fair."

Well, when they tried to outtalk him, he said, "No, there won't be any rain. We ought to go." Well, to humor him everybody took their unbrellas and raincoats and went to the Fair. They carried their weather togs around all day and it was a fair day, and it didn't rain a drop. Then that night, after they got back home, the Lord answered my prayer and gave rain, too. And Mrs. Rice thinks that is a great joke that the Lord answered that little fellow's prayer and postponed mine until he could have his day at the State Fair! Do you believe God did that? I do.

* * *

A Boy to Be a Preacher. Pray definitely. At Bob Jones University I said, "We need some preachers. Why don't you get them like God's people got John the Baptist? They prayed and God gave a preacher." I said, "How many here will pray that God will give you a boy to train for God? Will you give him to God for a preacher and expect God to make a preacher out of him? How many will pray about it?" Several stood to pledge to God for that.

A young evangelist who had been married fourteen years had no children. He stood that night and prayed. I went back to Rev. Harold Sightler's church that October. He came to hear me. There was his wife heavy with child! He said, "We're going to have a boy. He will be born in February. His name is going to be called Joel, and he is going to be a Baptist preacher." Sure enough! Joel was born. God answered prayer after all those years.

We ought to have somebody who will be definite with God, who will pray through and get things settled.   * * *

Who Forgot? Dr. Hyles and I were in a conference a couple of years ago in Indianapolis. One night I took subscriptions for THE

SWORD OF THE LORD. I had asked the Lord for twenty subscriptions that night. When I got back to my room I found only eighteen. I said, "Now Lord, I asked for twenty."

So the next morning in the morning service I said, "Which two of you filled out a subscription blank last night and didn't hand it in?" Sure enough, two men very sheepishly held up their subscription envelopes!

People ought to get down to business with God in definite praying. They even said, "Grant unto thy servants, that with all boldness they may speak thy word, By stretching forth thine hand to heal; and that signs and wonders may be done by the name of thy holy child Jesus." They prayed for particular things, definite things. Oh, what wonderful answers to prayer! The power of God. . .souls saved. . . blessed revival. . .people healed.

* * *

$1,000 for Radio! Some years ago I was praying about the Voice of Revival broadcast. "Lord, I need encouragement. I've got such heavy bills. Oh, if you will just have someone send $500 for the Voice of Revival broadcast."

The old Devil whispered to me, "Now who is going to send you $500? Does anybody regularly send that much? Are you likely to get $500? Besides, if you got a $500 gift

it would likely be earmarked about like this: $200 for the Missionary Literature Fund, and $150 for the Ministers' and Missionaries' Subscription Gift Fund. And then you will have $150 for the radio." The old Devil insisted, "You are not likely to get $500 for the radio."

I said to the Lord, "Lord, I am not talking about what is likely, what is probable. You show the old Devil. I believe You can even send $1,000 in by tomorrow."

The next day came a check for $1,000, designated just for the radio, from a man I had never seen nor heard of!

* * *

Short Ribs of Beef! I was conducting a conference on soul winning and revival at the great Church of the Open Door, Los Angeles, along with two or three other nationally-known evangelists, when I became so dizzy that I went to see a doctor. He discovered I was anemic and insisted I must lighten my schedule, leave off some personal campaigns, and rest. He insisted also that I should have lots of beef. And my body craved the meat needed to build up my blood.

But we were in the midst of war. The best steaks and the prime rib roasts went to the boys in service and to the big hotels and expensive eating places which I did not patronize. I would not spend $3.50 for a steak.

One day at Checotah, Oklahoma, as I walked down to the little cafe where I had my noon meal each day, I was hungry for beef. Ordinarily in those war days, with rationing, the plate lunch would have pig knuckles and sauerkraut, or Polish sausage, or macaroni and cheese. But as I walked along I prayed, "Lord, if I were home and my wife should ask me today just what I wanted, and she could get it for me, I would suggest short ribs of beef. Lord, it is such a little matter, and I will love You just the same if You do not want to bother, but it would make me very happy if I could have the beef my body needs."

Immediately when I sat down in the little cafe the waitress suggested a choice of two plate lunches, and the first one included short ribs of beef! She brought me a fine serving and I had all I could eat. And for days afterward I went around with a thrill in my heart like a girl who has just gotten a letter from her sweetheart! I had a holy joy to remember that I had such a God who loved me and cared for my needs and would provide even such a little detail as the kind of meat I had requested for a meal.

*   *   *

The Lord's Bills

Once when I was preaching in the Evansville Rescue Mission, Evansville, Indiana, Dr. Ernest I. Reveal, the founder and then head of the mission, found that about $500 worth of local bills had accumulated. The heavy expense of running the mission, feeding the hungry, giving beds, baths and laundry to the unfortunate; securing jobs, sending runaway girls home, running a camp for women and children in the summer—all these had piled up debts of $500. He called for the good women who attended the mission to meet one morning at ten o'clock for a prayer meeting. Then he set himself about to pray over these $500 worth of bills.

And the way he did it seemed to me almost sacrilegious, it was so bold. I had already found that when Brother Reveal prayed, he simply chatted with the Lord in an informal but very persistent way. He got in his car one day and had difficulty finding his key and I heard his murmur, "Now look here, Lord!" When a paper was mislaid on his desk, he looked diligently for it, murmuring softly, "Lord, help Ernie! Lord, help Ernie!" So when praying about these bills, my dear brother, who had had so many prayers answered, simply spread them out on his desk, leaned back in his chair, and had an argument with the Lord. "Well, Lord, I am sure glad these bills are not mine! Lord, You know I have been in this town twenty-three years and I always pay my bills. But these are not my bills, Lord. They are Yours. And if You don't pay them, there is going to be an awful stink in this town. You know all about me, Lord, and You know that we made these bills in Your name and we believe You led in them and it looks to me like You are going to have to pay them!"

I was amazed at that prayer. It seemed to me to be too personal, too intimate, in talking to a holy God. I wondered if God was not displeased with that kind of praying. But I did not wonder long, for at ten o'clock while the good women were gathering to start the prayer meeting to pray for the money for the bills, the mail came and in one letter was a check for $500 which would pay every one of them! Brother Reveal boldly argued with God! He reminded God of His own faithfulness, of His own promises, of His own good name. And God heard him!

*　*　*

Small Praying. Once in Dallas, Texas, when a good deacon came to the office on a weekday, we discussed our needs and agreed to pray. We were to start a tent revival campaign, and seats, lights, our advertising, and financing were serious problems. We were building a great church building, paying cash for carloads of brick and loads of concrete in the midst of the depression, and the money involved serious problems. I had heavy printing bills on THE SWORD OF THE LORD and on free literature given away. We talked about people we wanted to see saved; about the daily radio program which required so much labor and broadcast fees; and when we got down to pray this good man was somewhat overwhelmed. He began his prayer something like this, "Dear Lord, it may seem like we are asking You an awful lot, but if You will just give us these things today, we'll try not to ask You so much any more."

I have laughed in my heart many times at the ridiculous idea that we could be asking so many things that God would be strained to answer them, or that God would be displeased at our boldness. But in actual truth, all of us have the same guilty frame of mind. We dare not ask things big enough for a great God, the things He has invited us to ask. We sin continually in small prayers growing out of our small faith.

*　*　*

The First $1,000 for the Sword

Let me tell you of the mercy of God in the first $1,000 gift I ever received for the work of Sword of the Lord. It was some twenty-four years ago in Dallas, Texas. I was pastor of the Galilean Baptist Church, but without any set salary. I had begun THE SWORD OF THE LORD, and God was blessing it with increased circulation. The price was fifty cents per year for this weekly paper! You may well imagine that the four large pages weekly cost much more than that. And the more subscriptions we received, the further we went in debt. When I would leave the church for two weeks to go out to hold revival campaigns and God's people gave me a love-offering, I put it on the printing bills.

But we began a great brick tabernacle, and in several ways that cut my income. First, the more money I raised for the cash payments for brick, concrete, lumber, carpenters' wages, and plumbing, the less the good church people had to put in the envelope specially marked "for the pastor." Then I was so occupied with the burdens of raising money for the church building and helping supervise construction that I could not be away as much in revival services as usual, and so the income from love-offerings was cut down. The good Christian printer who printed THE SWORD OF THE LORD was patient, but we owed him $450 which I could not pay. So I borrowed the money at six per cent interest to pay that, trusting that in a few months' time the money would be in hand to pay off the note.

But in six months' time I had not only been unable to pay off the borrowed money, but we owed the printer $270 more. We owed another printer $200 for printing the booklet, *"What Must I Do to Be Saved?"* which even then was being given away in great quantities. The debts were all on printing bills for the Lord. For myself and for the family we contracted no debts, but paid cash for such groceries and clothes as we bought, and for other expenses, and we sacrificed. But we could not well curtail publication of THE SWORD.

About this time a pastor in the capital city of another state insisted that I come for revival services in "The City-Wide Tabernacle." He believed that the city could be shaken. He urged upon me until I consented to begin on a Monday night or Tuesday night, and to stay through one Sunday and through Friday night of the second week.

When I arrived in his city, however, I was shocked to find that the "City-Wide Tabernacle" was only a small tabernacle seating perhaps 250 people, in a residence district. There had been no money for newspaper advertising, no money for radio programs or announcements. A few mimeographed handbills, five hundred copies, had been distributed within the immediate vicinity of the church. The first night's service saw only fifty people in the tabernacle.

I worked and prayed and God increased the crowd. After a few nights sinners began to get saved. Soon the little tabernacle was full, and God was blessing. On Thursday night of the second week, I said to the pastor, "We will announce that the meeting will close tomorrow night, as planned, and I must catch the night train back to Dallas for our Sunday services."

"But you cannot leave now!" he said. "We have been raising all the money we could to pay on the lumber bill of the tabernacle. The people who come on the week nights have been drained. You must stay over Sunday or we cannot get a good offering for you."

I replied that he should not fret about the offering. I had made no demands and I had set no price on my service. I assured him that I would be content, whatever the offering amounted to, but that I simply must be back to my own pulpit, my radio broadcast, the large tabernacle, our Sunday night crowd, for next Sunday. He was sad. He lamented that there would be a very small offering, but I told him not to worry. Whatever God's people did would content me.

I meant all that from my heart, yet I could not forget the $920 in printing bills that were past due and ought to be paid for Christian literature that had already gone out to serve the Lord. When I retired that night, Satan sat on the footboard of the bed and taunted me. "So you don't care whether you get a good love-offering here or not? Who is going to pay these bills that are due? It seems to me you're not getting anywhere. You work day and night. Your family does not have as nice clothes as other members of your own congregation. You live in a ramshackle rented house with bare floors and secondhand furniture. You give everything you can get your hands on to serve the Lord, and He leaves it for you to carry the burden."

Satan seemed very real to me; but in my heart I said to him, "You old liar, you deceiver! Get on back to Hell! I will take this up with Headquarters."

Then with tears I told the Lord that I had never before fretted about what kind of offerings I would get for any service for the Lord. I said, "Lord, it is too late now for me to start staying awake at night fretting over what kind of remuneration will come to me for preaching. I am not going to do it. If You do not want THE SWORD OF THE LORD, then You let me know and we will kill it; and with some months of sacrifice and labor, we will pay off the debts. But if You want THE SWORD OF

THE LORD, then it is time for You to take over the bills and pay them."

I reminded the Lord, "If You have a copy of THE SWORD OF THE LORD handy, just look at the front page! You'll see that Your name is in big type and mine in small type. Your name is at the top and mine at the bottom. THE SWORD OF THE LORD is Yours. I am just editing it to get out the Gospel, to stir revival fires, and to help people understand the Word of God, to make Christians into soul winners. If You don't want that kind of a paper, then You should say so. If You want that kind of a paper, then You should pay the bills. I'm not going to fret about it. That would be a sin!"

Then I went sweetly to sleep and rested in the Lord.

The next night the pastor took an offering. When the pitiful gifts came in, then he added enough to make it $25 for nearly two weeks' work. That night I got on the train and headed for Dallas. There was not money enough for a berth, so I slept in a chair-car, and slept like a babe in his mother's arms. The next morning, after we passed a principal city, the porter came through the coach calling out, "Dr. Rice! Dr. Rice!" He had a telegram for me. I opened it and found that my two secretaries had wired, "Mr._____ has just sent you a check for $1,000 for your work."

The name was a name that I knew though I had never seen the man, had never written him, nor had any contact with him whatever. God had put it in his heart to send the gift.

I took that telegram and walked through the train. I felt as if I was driving Satan before me. Again I called him a liar, a deceiver, a crook. I told him I would never believe him again! I told Satan that the Lord had taken over THE SWORD OF THE LORD and was going to pay the bills.

Thank God, the Lord has taken over THE SWORD OF THE LORD, and other work of the Sword of the Lord Foundation, and I trust He has taken me over, too, in some sense.

I have gotten other thousand-dollar gifts since then, and God has wonderfully, graciously answered prayer. But my heart sings with joy as I remember that time when I was sorely tested and tempted, but when I took the matter to God in believing prayer, in bold prayer demanding that God take care of His work. Thank God, God answers the prayer of faith!

*   *   *

Assurance of Salvation

Christ Never Fails!

A woman asked me seriously, "After I am saved, after I am born again by trusting Christ as Saviour and have really taken Christ into my heart as Lord and Saviour and have become a new creature, now if I fall into sin will I be lost?"

I answered her thus, "If you earned the salvation and bought it by your good works and deeds and character in the first place, then the first moment that your good deeds and works and character are less than the holy perfection God requires, that moment you lose your self-earned salvation. But if you are depending on the perfect finished work of Christ on the cross and covered with His righteousness imputed to the believing sinner, then you will lose salvation only when Christ fails."

"But He will never fail!" she said.

No, He will never fail. And that is the only safety, the only security, the only guarantee, the only assurance, that any child of God will reach Heaven. We are saved and kept on the merits of Jesus, the perfect Lamb of God. His righteousness covers us. His character is implanted in our character. And God has predestined us to be conformed to His perfect image. His Spirit dwells within us. We are His.

* * *

Flea-Bitten Kitten.

Down in Dallas one day a little bit of a kitten came to our door. He was bony and covered with fleas all around his eyes, and my little daughter Elizabeth said, "Oh, isn't he cute? Isn't he cute, Mother?" And she said, "Oh, listen to him purr. Isn't he cute? Oh, Mother, may I keep him?"

I said, "You don't want a cat like that around here."

But she said, "Mother, let's feed him."

I said, "If you feed that cat, it will be under your feet the rest of the time."

But she begged, and Mrs. Rice could not refuse, so I said, "Well, if you are going to keep it, it ought to have some warm milk."

Elizabeth warmed the milk and put it in a saucer and gave it to the kitten. The kitten got down and lapped up the milk, and left his motor running all the time! It lapped up the milk until its little belly swelled out. A day or two later my wife started across the kitchen preparing the dinner and she stepped on the cat. It let out a meow! She said, "That cat is underfoot all the time! I won't have it in the house."

"Never mind," I said, "you have adopted you a cat."

She would put him out, but he would go around to the front door, and somebody would open the door. As big a family as we have, we can't keep all the doors shut all the time. That cat had adopted us. That cat just stayed there, underfoot or not. He was our cat. He decided so the first saucer of milk he got.

Once I was a poor, flea-bitten, bony sinner, and God gave me salvation and warmed my heart, and He has a cat on His hands, and He cannot get rid of me! God cannot change. If God ever starts to turn me down when I ask Him to restore my joy or cleanse me again from sins I confessed, if the Lord ever starts changing on me I will say, "Lord, look at that verse! What are You going to do about that?" He is without a shadow of turning. "With whom is no variableness, neither shadow of turning" (James 1:17).

*   *   *

"Do Not Pass Me by."

I grew up in West Texas. In that rough cow country I got backslidden. One night I went to a little Presbyterian church. Young friends of mine were being saved, and many others blessed. One night they sang:

> Pass me not, O gentle Saviour,
> Hear my humble cry,
> While on others Thou art calling,
> Do not pass me by.

Some way my heart cried out, and I said, "O Lord, don't leave me out of this blessing! Don't pass me by. Give me the blessing, too!" And the past, my drifting, was all cleared away and I had peace. I walked home over the prairie of West Texas, and looked up. The stars were so near, and God was as near as my breath, and I said, "Lord, I will never grieve You again. I will never go against You, I will never forget to pray and read my Bible from this day on." And I meant it from my heart; or I thought I meant it. I went on for two or three weeks, but the first thing I knew, I had lost my joy. I had lost my blessing. But I had not lost the Lord, and He had not lost me. But I had lost the feeling and joy. I had a heart-searching time, and I went back to the Lord and I said, "Lord, I lied to You. I said I would never do wrong any more. I said I would never drift away, and I thought I meant it. I made a mistake, but if You will give me one more chance, that is all I ask You, and I promise You now I will never grieve You any more."

The Lord in His mercy—He must have smiled when He did it—gave me back the joy, and I started out happy in the Lord. I went along, and as I was busy here and there, my joy was gone. It happened to me as it did to

Samson when he had his head in Delilah's lap, "He wist not that the Lord was departed from him" (Judges 16:20). And I woke up one day as he did, to take a sweet drink, and found bitterness and gall in it. God was not there, as far as my consciousness was concerned. At first I was uneasy, and then I was overwhelmed with a sense of guilt. I had promised the Lord, and now I was afraid He would never believe me any more. I felt that God must have been awfully surprised. After more time of heart-searching and prayer, I finally got faith to say, "Lord, I will try again." But I failed again. Disconsolate, I did not know what to do. But finally it dawned on me that what God wanted was not depending on how well I kept my promise, but depending on how He kept His. What God wanted was not taking more from me so much as giving me more—more believing and not so much working. I found He was not surprised at my sin. He knew my heart better than I did. I did not know anything of the blackness of my heart. Talk about repentance, I did not have any repenting then like I have now. But the dear Lord gave me the joy, and I learned of the unvarying Saviour. He does not vary in forgiveness, in keeping His faithless children.

*　*　*

What Got Him to Town? There was an old colored man, I am told, who drove an old oxcart. Those old oxcarts were made with solid wooden wheels, and they had a wooden axle and it would wear, and the wheels wobbled. But old Sambo was driving this team of oxen, and as he went along, the wheels wobbled this way, and wobbled that way. A white man who loved to tease the old colored man said to him, "Where are you going, Sambo?"

"I'se going to town, Marse George."

"You'll never get there. Look at those wheels. The only time they are ever in the ruts is when they cross them. They wobble this way, and they wobble back that way. You will never get there. And that is just about like you are going to Heaven, too. You will never make it!"

But Sambo said, "Marse George, I ain't depending on these wobbling wheels to get me to town. Old Buck and Jerry are hitched on to this thing, and they are going right on down the road. Buck and Jerry are going to get me to town."

And Somebody is hitched on to John Rice, and I am going right on down the road. The Lord is going to get me to Heaven. The unvarying God who started is going to get me to Heaven. "Whom he called, them he also justified: and whom he justified, them he also glorified"

(Rom. 8:30). Brother, God has this thing in hand. It is the unvarying God, the unfailing God. Salvation is settled because He settled it, and what He settled will never be unsettled.

*   *   *

The Sin of Causing Little Believers to Stumble. When I was about nine years of age I gave my heart to the Lord Jesus and went forward in the First Baptist Church in Gainesville, Texas, to let it be known publicly that Christ was mine. Returning home happily that Sunday noon, I asked my father if I might join the church and be baptized. (He had not been to the services.) He said, "Well, Son, when you are old enough to repent of your sins and be regenerated, you may join the church." He was right in what he said, but he said it in words I did not understand. I only understood that he thought I was too young to be saved, and I did not know what he meant by the words "repent" and "regenerated."

As a result of that discouragement, I thought I must have been mistaken. My father was not only the smartest man in the world and the best, but he was a preacher, so he must know whether or not I was too young to be saved. For three years I went on trying to get saved, but making no outward move. At last I began reading the Bible and found the precious promises in John 3:18, John 3:36 and John 5:24. I found that one who believes or trusts in Christ as his Saviour "hath everlasting life, and shall not come into condemnation." Then I was saved! I did not remember how I had felt; I did not know whether I had met other requirements; but I knew I had, as far as I knew how, believed in Christ, depended upon Him to save me. And now I discovered the Bible said I had received "everlasting life"! Thank God, I never have had any more doubts that I am a saved, born-again child of God!

That illustration from my own childhood shows how serious it is to discourage children who trust in Christ. We dare not neglect to teach them God's way of salvation, to encourage them to come to Christ the best they know how, even if their understanding is imperfect. God is always pleased when a child's heart gropes for Him. And when one comes, ever so hesitantly and ignorantly, Jesus promises him, "Him that cometh to me I will in no wise cast out" (John 6:37).

*   *   *

Will Christ Die Again? A troubled young woman who knew that she had fallen into sin and worldliness and had lost her joy felt that surely she must have lost her salvation. Oh, with many tears she berated herself for her sin. And she felt so guilty that she thought surely God had abandoned her.

"Then I suppose Jesus Christ will have to come back and die again on the cross for you, if you are to be saved again?" I asked. She looked at me puzzled.

"Why, of course not," she said. "The Bible says nothing about Jesus coming back to die again."

"Then do you mean that when Jesus died the first time, He died for all your sins?"

"Yes," she said, "the Bible tells us that He died for the sins of the whole world."

"Did He die for your sins, the sins that you might commit after you were saved?" I asked.

She stopped. A great light began to dawn in her face and then she saw it! When Jesus died on the cross He paid once and for all, for all the sins that ever would be committed. And when she had trusted Christ for salvation, it was salvation from all the sins, past and present and future. Jesus had paid for every one of them. And so gladly she received the truth that her sins were under the blood. Now she needed to have fellowship restored, but she did not need to get saved again. When she got the life, she got the everlasting of "everlasting life" which Jesus promised.

* * *

"I Was Saved. . .When Bud Was!" In a revival service in North Texas, I once dealt at some length with a young woman who said she was not a Christian. Step by step I led her with the Scriptures to admit she was a sinner, to acknowledge that Christ died to save sinners such as she was, then to join me in solemn prayer asking Jesus for forgiveness. Then holding my hand before her I said, "If you will here and now turn to Christ and rely upon him, depending upon him as your own personal Saviour, I want you to take my hand as a testimony and as a sign between you and God and me and this friend beside you."

Very slowly and yet very earnestly the young woman took my hand, then suddenly her face was greatly lighted. Bursting into tears, she said, "I was saved four years ago when Bud was!" I do not know the rest of the incident to which she referred. I know simply that the poor, backslidden girl who had lost all assurance of salvation suddenly found the joy of the Lord flooding her heart, and the Lord Jesus claimed her and sent His Holy Spirit to tell her that she had been accepted in the beloved back there when she had, four years ago, taken Christ as her Saviour. The open profession of faith in Christ brought the assurance again that she was His. She had thrown away her hope, but the Lord Jesus kept His promise. When she claimed Christ, He claimed her in her heart.

*   *   *

The Way to Keep Salvation Is the Same Way One Gets It! A good woman said to me some time ago, "Brother Rice, I am troubled over this matter of 'eternal security.' People say it is 'a damnable doctrine.' Now I want to know: when a child of God falls into sin, is he not lost again?"

My answer proved of great help to her in understanding the Saviour's teaching on this matter, and I felt that God gave me the answer then. Hence I repeat to you what I said to her. "Well, that depends on how you got saved in the first place. If a Christian got saved by his good deeds, his righteousness, his faithfulness, then, of course, he will have to stay saved the same way. If he got saved by his good works, then when his good works fail, he is lost. On the other hand, if one gets saved wholly by God's grace and on the merits of the crucified Saviour who promised to save those who trust in Him, then when Jesus fails, one who trusts in Him is irretrievably lost. If you save yourself, then you must do the keeping. If Christ does the saving, then He must do the keeping."

At once the matter seemed greatly clarified in her mind.

*   *   *

Whose Mistake? One time a man was converted when D. L. Moody preached, and Moody told him, "Watch out or the Devil will hit you about tomorrow morning and tell you that you are not saved. You had better get a Scripture you can hang on to. Take John 3:16."

But the Devil did not wait until the next morning; he got after him that night. He could not sleep. The Devil kept saying, "You are not saved." But he said, "Yes, old Devil, I am. Here is John 3:16: 'For God so loved the world, that he gave his only begotten Son, that whosoever believeth in him should not perish, but have everlasting life.' So I am saved."

But the Devil came along again and said, "You don't know that the translators translated that right. You can't read Greek." The Devil had him in a tight place. "You don't know whether the promises are true or not." So far into the night he said, "I don't know whether it is translated right or not, but I am going to believe it, and when I come to die I am going to say, 'Lord, if I made a mistake it isn't my mistake, it is the translators.' " So he found peace and went to sleep.

*   *   *

You Can Know You Are Saved

Years ago I was preaching in a tent revival campaign in San Antonio, Texas. Two lovely girls sixteen and eighteen years of age came under the tent one night just before the song service began. I gave each of them a songbook and then said to the older girl, "Are you a Christian? Have you been saved?"

She looked at me with an innocent face and said respectfully, "Yes, I think I am a Christian. Of course, I do not know. I don't think you *can* know. But I do the best I know how and I think I can say that I am a Christian. Of course, nobody can know for sure whether or not he is saved."

"Oh, yes, you *can* know," I said. "And you ought to make sure and know that you are saved."

"But I do not think that you *can* know," she said.

"Well," I said, "let us not argue about it. Suppose I find it in the Bible that you can know that you are saved. Would you believe it then?" I asked.

"Yes, of course I will believe it if it is in the Bible. But I do not believe it is there. I do not believe that one can know that he is saved."

I got my Bible and turned to this wonderful passage in I John 5:13, and holding the Bible before her we read it together: "These things have I written unto you that believe on the name of the Son of God; that ye may know that ye have eternal life, and that ye may believe on the name of the Son of God."

"You see," I said, "you *can* know that you are saved. Here in the Bible is a portion of Scripture that was written expressly so you can know that you are saved."

I saw the tears start up in her eyes, and then she looked at me and said very softly and with deep emotion, "Yes! One can know!"

"Now read the rest of the verse carefully," I said. "How does one get to be a child of God so he can know it?"

She read the verse again: "These things have I written unto you *that believe* on the name of the Son of God; that ye may know that ye have eternal life, AND THAT YE MAY BELIEVE ON THE NAME OF THE SON OF GOD."

"I see it now! One who believes in Christ and depends on Christ has a right to know that he has eternal life!" she said. And then we bowed our heads and asked the Lord Jesus to help her trust Him right there. And she did trust Him. She took my hand earnestly as a sign that there and then she would claim Him as Saviour and went away *knowing* that she had everlasting life. And her sixteen-year-old sister likewise trusted Christ and on the basis of this plain Word of God knew that she had everlasting life.

* * *

"I Was There When It Happened"

The fact that you were there when it happened does not automatically guarantee that you will understand fully what happened and that you will always have perfect assurance of salvation.

Let me illustrate. "I was there when it happened," when I was born into the world the first time. Remember that salvation is simply a new birth. If one can know all about his second birth by the simple fact that he was there, then he ought to be able to know about his first birth for the same reason! Now I was born on December 11, 1895, in Cooke County, Texas. How do I know? Do you suppose that on that eventful day I sat up and looked about me and said, "Well! I see by the calendar that it is December 11, just two weeks before Christmas Eve! I'll put this down in my notebook so I will always remember I was born on December 11!"? Do you suppose that I looked at my mother and said, "Your name, please, lady? I want to put it down in my notebook so I will always know who was my mother, who was my father, and the other conditions surrounding my birth"? I did nothing of the kind! When I was born I did not know much of anything except when I got hungry. I learned gradually to know my mother's voice and to know when I was uncomfortable with dirty clothes or with the pricking of an unfastened safety pin. I later learned to focus both eyes and look at one object! Then I learned, I suppose, to smile when people tickled me under the chin. There were long months before I grew a single tooth, and other months before I learned to walk and talk. It is true that "I was there when it happened" at my first birth. But I was very young at the time, I took no note of my surroundings, and I cannot trust my memory about the matter at all!

And yet I know; in fact, it is beyond any doubt at all in my mind, that I was really born on December 11, 1895, that William R. Rice was my father, that Sallie LaPrade Rice was my mother, and Gertrude was my sister, eighteen months older. How do I know? That is easy! I have it on the authority of my mother. It was written down in the family Bible. And recently I saw it written down on a separate piece of paper in my mother's own handwriting. There it was listed by her sweet fingers, "Gertrude Frances, born July 24, 1894. John R., born December 11, 1895. . ." and so on with Ruth and George and baby Porter! I have the written record of one I absolutely trust. And so I know when I was born and who were my mother and my father. And, thank God, I have even better assurance than that about my second birth! I have the written record of God's own Word saying that when I put my trust in Jesus Christ I passed from death to life! I have the written record that "he that believeth on the Son hath everlasting life" (John 3:36). I believed in Him, trusted in Him, depended on Him to forgive me. Now I know He has done it because He never failed to keep His word, and He never will!

* * *

Saved Just Like Mother? A young man in Chicago came forward to accept Christ as Saviour and said, "I want to be saved just as my mother was." He wanted to shout praises to God as his mother down in Kentucky said that she had. But after a half-hour session with the Word of God, under the leadership of a devout Christian, he came to me to say, "Brother Rice, I don't feel as I thought I would, but the Bible says I'm saved!"

Thank God, I can say the same! The Bible says I'm saved! I can say with Paul, "I know whom I have believed, and am persuaded that he is able to keep that which I have committed unto him against that day" (II Tim. 1:12).

Baptism

Scriptures Unanimous on Immersion for Baptism. Everywhere I go, I find many earnest Christians who are amazed to see how they have been misled on the matter of baptism. In a Louisiana town a young woman, a bank clerk, a devout Methodist girl, came to me and said: "Brother Rice, will you give me some of the Scriptures which teach sprinkling for baptism? It is strange, but all the Scriptures I happen to know about baptism seem to teach immersion. Methodists baptize either way, but I do not happen to remember the Scriptures which teach sprinkling."

I was somewhat embarrassed, and I feared she would not believe me if I told her there were no Scriptures teaching sprinkling for baptism. So I said instead, "Suppose we get my big concordance and look up every verse in the Bible which mentions baptizing, baptism, or baptized." So we got the book before us and began. She was amazed that there was no mention of baptism in the Old Testament. We read through every verse referring to baptism, and when I looked up, her face was as white as death.

"Brother Rice," she said, "somebody has misled me. I trusted them, I thought they knew the Bible and had Scripture for everything they did. I have been deceived." Breaking into tears, she ran into her room and lay across her bed sobbing. I was a guest in the home and that night she did not come to supper. But that night she brought extra clothes to the service and at the close, with others, she followed her Lord in baptism. The cry of that poor, misled girl who followed tradition, who had faith in men, is with me today. People have a right to know the truth as to what God's Word teaches about baptism.

* * *

Cold Outside, Warm Inside! I remember so well when I was baptized at the age of twelve. It was in the cattle country in West Texas, near Dundee, Archer County. I had trusted Christ three years before but no one showed me the Scriptures to make it clear so I could have full assurance that my sins were forgiven. I had three struggling, undecided years. At last I had enough courage to be baptized. It was on a cold November day and ten of us were baptized in the "railroad tank" or lake. After we came out of the water we stood at the edge and Christians came by to shake our hands and say, "God bless you." They sang a song that has ever since been precious to me.

O happy day that fixed my choice
  On Thee, my Saviour and my God!
Well may this glowing heart rejoice,
  And tell its raptures all abroad.

'Tis done: the great transaction's done;
  I am my Lord's, and He is mine;
He drew me, and I followed on,
  Charmed to confess the voice divine.

And the chorus rings in my heart again today, "Happy day, happy day, When Jesus washed my sins away!"

Our family went to the baptizing in a two-seated hack, a strong two-seated carriage or buggy. But we had such a big family that I was accustomed to standing up behind. So now when we started to go home, in my wet clothes I climbed up in the back of the hack to stand.

My father said, "No, no, Son. You will catch cold." The wind was sharp on my wet clothes. He wrapped me in a quilt and I sat in the carriage on the road home. But I had not felt the cold, because my heart was so warm! Although that was not the day I was saved, as far as my own joy is concerned, the song, "O Happy Day," fits the day of my baptism much more than the day of my conversion.

Those who claim the Lord in

public baptism as a token of their faith in Christ, find that the Lord Jesus claims them also in joy, assurance, and in blessing on their testimony.

* * *

A Joyous Baptism. At Decatur, Texas, God in mercy used me in a great tent revival campaign. Hundreds were saved. A new church was organized with over three hundred members. Ground was bought, a tabernacle built, and a full-time pastor called within the ten weeks of that blessed revival campaign. As soon as the church was organized we built a baptistry and began night after night to baptize those who came for membership, professing their faith in Christ.

I remember one woman came into the baptistry in deep emotion. Under her breath she said over and over, "Oh, praise the Lord! Bless the Lord, O my soul!" I said to her, "Say it aloud, Sister, if you wish." And she said aloud, "Oh, praise the Lord! I have been wanting to do this nineteen years!" She was baptized in obedience to the Saviour's command and following His own example. Then with happy face she went down the stairs into the dressing room and I heard her say over and over, "Oh, bless the Lord! Praise His name!"

* * *

Saved, but Not Baptized.

When the Westvue Baptist Church moved out of the buildings which we purchased and the big Sword of the Lord Foundation work moved in, one day an old man past eighty, who lived in the same block and back of the big church building which we purchased, came over to inquire if we had any work that an old man could do to make a little money on the side. He had a little income—do not know whether retirement pay or relief or social security; but he wanted some little jobs to make extra money.

My editorial assistant, Miss Viola Walden, and our proofreader, Brother Charles Vradenburgh, talked to the man. We did not know of any job for him, but was he a Christian man? Had he been converted? Did he know Jesus as his own personal Saviour? Had he been born again? No, he had not been saved. No one had talked to him about that, it seemed.

So very sweetly they took the Bible and showed him the plan of salvation. He was a sinner, as all men are, and sin would lead him to Hell unless he got forgiveness. God loved him and Christ died for him. If he would here and now take Christ as his own personal Saviour and rely on

Him and give his heart to Christ and honestly turn from sin to the Saviour, he would be saved.

They led him to trust the Saviour and claim it. How glad he was, this old man past eighty! How long had he lived next door and in the same block with a church? I do not know. It was the best soul-winning church in the county, but in some strange series of circumstances, no one had talked to the man next door about his soul.

He was glad that he had trusted Christ. So on Wednesday night, they took him to the Bellwood Baptist Church (as the Westvue Baptist Church in its new location was called). There he claimed Christ publicly, joined the church as a candidate for baptism that Wednesday night. He was to be baptized on Sunday. But on Friday before he was baptized on Sunday, some of our men saw him in the early morning drop his cane, clutch his heart and stagger and fall to the sidewalk. One of our men called an ambulance and helped put him in the ambulance. He was rushed to the hospital but was dead on arrival.

Oh, the dear Lord knows that he was born again and his entrance into eternal happiness did not depend upon baptism.

The Bible

The Bible, the Word of God—a Certainty

It was in 1921 when my belief, my hope, my conviction that the Bible is the Word of God, supernaturally inspired and infallible, became a certainty. I say a certainty, and I mean just that. I am more sure of the reliability of the Bible than I am of the honesty of any man who ever lived, or the virtue of any woman, or the truth of any philosophy. I have as much evidence for the reliability of the Bible as I have for the Law of Gravity.

I was in the University of Chicago, a graduate student in the School of Education, when I resolved that I would know, once and for all, whether the Bible were true or whether the conflicting claims of the evolutionists, the Bible deniers, must be accepted. I set out to gather all the evidence, to try the Bible in the realms of history, science, prophecy and moral truth. Thank God, I found that the Bible is the only fully accurate Book of history ever written. I found that while human guesses may contradict the Bible, scientifically proven facts never do! That is why evolution is still only a theory or a hypothesis, a guess, a supposition. People who want to believe it and half-baked, poorly trained high school teachers may say that evolution is a proven fact, but no scientifically-minded and reliable scholar will say so.

I found that prophecies of the Bible have proven themselves supernaturally accurate. The four great world empires, Babylon, Media-Persia, Greece and Rome came just exactly as the second and seventh chapters of Daniel foretold them. And the Roman Empire did dissolve into the ten kingdoms represented by the ten toes of the image and the ten horns of the beast. I found that hundreds of details of the first coming of Christ and His life and death were fulfilled to the letter. I found that prophecies about men, about cities, about nations, came to pass exactly. Not one man has ever proven the Bible inaccurate in its prophecies.

Best of all, I have found that God answers prayer just as He promises to do. Millions of dollars He has given me to spend for His work in answer to prayer. He has saved souls; He has blessed with great revivals; He has answered definite prayers in such meticulous detail that the answers could not be happenstance, could not be coincidences, could not be other than supernatural. Thank God, I *know* one can safely believe the Bible.

*   *   *

Keep Your Gun Loaded! When some great temptation comes, it is too late to search for God's warning. Hide it in the heart ahead of time if you would have help when you need it to keep your heart from sin.

A few years ago several of us, as guests of a Christian sportsmen's group, went to the Rocky Mountains to hunt. We wanted a grizzly bear. So we bought an outlaw horse for $25 and used him as a pack horse (with many tribulations because of his rebellion) to pack camp goods up into the high Rockies, just east of Yellowstone Park. The outlaw horse was then shot and used as bait for Mr. Grizzly Bear. Many times we went to visit the bear bait to see if Mr. Grizzly had come to eat his fill of the decaying carcass. I assure you that every time we came the 30-30 rifle loaded and cocked. Should we come face to face with a giant grizzly as big as a horse, the most murderous beast on this continent, it would be too late to load the gun.

O Christian, keep your gun loaded! Then when you meet the Devil going about as a roaring lion seeking whom he may devour, you can defend yourself against him with the sword of the Spirit. Meditate on the Word of God, hide it in your heart, and you will be forewarned and forearmed against temptation.

*   *   *

Use the Word! One cannot be saved without the Word of God. I remember how Henry Hempkins, a junk dealer in Waxahachie, Texas, learned this truth and practiced it. He asked me for a handful of Gospels of John into which I had pasted a decision slip which could be signed and removed when one trusted Christ. He took them in his daily business, and, showing men John 1:12; 3:3-7; 3:14-18; 3:36; 5:24, verses which we had underlined so anybody could find them, he led man after man to trust Christ, sign the decision slip, and set out to live for Jesus Christ. The Word of God is necessary for soul winning!

* * *

"Why Didn't Somebody Tell Me That the Bible Is Like That?" In Dallas, Texas, a good businessman was a member of the church of which I was pastor. I urged upon the people the daily reading of the Word of God until he was ashamed. So reluctantly he set out to read several chapters daily in the Bible and to read it through within a year's time. After a few days he got over in the book of Genesis, to the story of Joseph. How entranced he was with that heart-moving tale, divinely told! He sat up until the wee small hours of the morning reading the rest of the story to see how it ended. The next Sunday he said to me, "Brother Rice, why didn't somebody tell me that the Bible is like that? That is more interesting than any book of history or any novel!"

* * *

The Bible Is Historically Accurate. There are several ways you can know if the Bible is historically accurate. I'm a college graduate. I did graduate work at the University of Chicago, then at the Southwestern Seminary. I have been an editor many years. I have had a good way to find out, and I know the Bible is historically accurate.

This is an interesting fact. In England Dr. William Ramsay, Professor William Ramsey, (I use those terms because they are not what he is usually called, as you will see in a moment) started out to make a study. He said it would be interesting to find out how much truth there was in the book of Acts concerning the Roman Empire in the travels of Paul, as it was related by Luke in the book of Acts and in Paul's epistles.

He spent years studying the monuments, studying the history, studying the inscriptions, studying the old authors and the government records way back yonder in the Roman Empire, and finding the places, and so on. He did such a remarkable work as a scientist and historian that the Queen of England made him a knight, so he is Sir William Ramsay. And Sir William Ramsay wrote a half-dozen books, and came to the amazing conclusion that he had been wrong. Though he didn't say the book of Acts was inspired, he said it is the most perfect historical document of all times; that it is reliable; that it is accurate and true historically.

* * *

The Treasures in the Bible. One very lonely and dreaded Christmastime turned out to be one of the sweetest I ever had. I was about sixteen when for the Christmas holiday all the family went off to visit relatives and left me on the stock farm to milk the cows, feed the horses, and take care of the place. I anticipated a lonely, sad week while others went away to celebrate. But I was a Christian and fortunately I got started reading the Bible. How wonderfully sweet it was! I reveled in it for days and I regard that as one of the happiest and best Christmases I ever spent. No Christian need ever be lonely when he has the Word of God. "Thy words were found, and I did eat them; and thy word was unto me the joy and rejoicing of mine heart" (Jer. 15:16). Christians ought to rejoice in the Bible every day and find there its treasures.

* * *

Light on Every Problem. The Word of God has light on every problem that a Christian will ever face! Learn the Word of God and have the answer to your problems!

As a lad, I wanted to visit with a family where I often went. It was a big family and they had a jolly time. But my father quoted to me the Scripture, "Withdraw thy foot from thy neighbour's house; lest he be weary of thee, and so hate thee" (Prov. 25:17). That bit of divine wisdom helped me then.

My brother and I had some hot words once, and my father quoted the proverb, "A soft answer turneth away wrath. . ." (Prov. 15:1), and I was rebuked and shamed and was taught the better way.

Again one day we needed some farm machinery and I suggested that we borrow from a neighboring rancher. But my father reminded me that the Bible says that "the borrower is servant to the lender" (Prov. 22:7). I did not want to be a servant, and I saw the point at once. There is divine wisdom in the blessed Word of God for every problem a Christian can ever meet. O Christian, take the Word of God as a lamp to your feet and a light to your path!

* * *

Mr. X, the Bronc-Rider. I say, the contemplative Christian has such a strong foundation upon which to base his faith that he finds it easy to believe what the Bible claims, even if he be not scientifically-minded and even if he has not investigated the scientific evidence as I have.

Let me illustrate. I came from the Southwest cattle country. Cattle, horses, saddles, lariats were as commonplace incidents in my life as automobiles, radios, paved streets, typewriters, etc., are to business people.

Now, suppose there is a man we may call Mr. X, of whom I hear much as to his prowess in riding broncs, in use of the lariat, in bull-dogging cattle. Suppose a dozen or a hundred people I know tell me they know this man intimately, that he has the very highest of character, that they have found him truthful in a thousand details of life. Now suppose that I somewhere see this man in a rodeo ride the wildest broncs with a certain grace and ease and ingenuity with which I am well familiar. Suppose I see him throw the lariat so accurately, with such grace and rhythmic timing, that I cannot conceal my admiration. His daring is only equalled by his skill.

Now suppose I talk to this Mr. X and he tells me that he has won the bronc-riding championship at Madison-Square Garden, at Cheyenne, Wyoming, and at the Fat Stock Show at Ft. Worth, Texas. You tell me that I should not consider the man's words on the question? After I have already seen what he can do (and I am an old cowhand myself and a good judge of such matters), and after I have heard him commended as to his veracity by friends who have known him long and well, some of the most reputable people I know, then naturally I would respect what he says.

Now further I talk long with Mr. X and I find that on a thousand matters he proves himself moral, upright, dependable, truthful. You say I am not to believe what he says about matters on which I know he is well-qualified, and my own judgment tells me he might well have done exactly what he said he did.

So I come to the Scripture with a testimony of thousands who knew the Lord Jesus as personal Saviour, who found forgiveness and peace and joy and daily victory through long years. I have the testimony of uncounted thousands of Christians who have found that God's promises were all true. I have the evidence of thousands of lives transformed from sin to holiness of life. Do you wonder that I come to the Bible with an open heart to believe what I find?

* * *

Is He George Brown? Suppose I do not know Mr. George Brown personally. This man says he is

George Brown. He pulls out his wallet and he has George Brown's driver's license. I find he has also a credit card belonging to George Brown. He shows me also a voter's registration certificate of George Brown. Then he takes me with him and we go down to the bank and walk into the president's office and he sits at the president's desk. He gives the cashier instructions, and the cashier says, "Yes, Mr. Brown." He signs an order with the name "George Brown" and it is honored. You see, I have not only the evidence that the man said he was George Brown, president of the bank, but I have the additional fact that he acts like George Brown, wears George Brown's clothes, has George Brown's wallet, takes George Brown's place in the president's office, and is recognized by the workers as President George Brown of the First National Bank.

That is the way it is with the Bible. From beginning to end the Bible makes claims for itself and speaks with authority which assumes and proves that it is the very Word of God.

* * *

When God Spoke. Once I had two young women go through *Young's Analytical Concordance* and mark the times in which we are clearly told that God spoke to somebody telling him what to say

or what to do, and I think there are some eighteen hundred cases listed in the Scripture. The Bible expressly says, not once but literally hundreds of times, that the man writing is writing the very words of God. In any other book in the world except the Bible or in a book quoting the Bible, such talk would be counted purest nonsense. But it is not nonsense in the Bible. The Bible ACTS like the Word of God, which it is.

Christian Living

Unconscious Christianity. It is said that Dr. George W. Truett, long-famous pastor of the First Baptist Church of Dallas, Texas, in the Baylor Hospital in his final illness, was sometimes delirious. Once he asked a nurse, "When I was unconscious, did I say anything that a Christian ought not say?"

"No," she replied. "Sometimes you thought you were preaching, sometimes counseling with Christians, sometimes pleading with sinners. No, you were just like you are when you are conscious."

He answered, "I would be so sad if, when I am delirious, anything comes out of my heart that would dishonor the Lord."

Don't you see that one ought to

be a good Christian subconsciously, whether he is thinking about it or not?

* * *

More Comfortable Than Jesus. The late Dr. H. A. Ironside told me that when Dr. R. A. Torrey first started the Bible conference at Montrose, Pennsylvania, they had few buildings and few comforts. There were yet no comfortable quarters for the speakers, so he and Dr. Torrey slept in a farmhouse on folding canvass cots. In the night he heard Dr. Torrey turning restlessly his big frame on the narrow, temporary bed in the next room.

Dr. Ironside called: "Dr. Torrey, are you comfortable?" He said Dr. Torrey answered, "I am more comfortable than my Saviour ever was!"

Dr. Ironside himself, as a traveling Salvation Army evangelist, had slept on the ground in a city park. Once when I had him to lunch (not expensive but good food), he exclaimed, "Too good for sinners!"

* * *

"The Truth, the Whole Truth!"

I was once forcefully reminded that even sincere, intelligent people do not see things as they are. My dear friend, Rev. P. B. Chenault, was killed when his car was rammed and wrecked by a drunken driver. When the drunken killer was tried I was brought to the stand to identify the car. Mr. Chenault had just concluded a two-weeks' campaign in the church of which I was pastor in Dallas. On the stand the prosecuting attorney asked me, "What kind of car did Mr. Chenault drive?"

"A 1938 two-door Buick Sedan," I replied.

"Did you know the car well?"

"Yes; the car sat in my driveway for two weeks, I often rode in it, I even drove it," I replied.

The district attorney then asked, "What color was the car?"

"It was black," I replied.

"Are you sure?" asked the prosecutor.

"Yes, I am sure; the car is black. I have seen it since the wreck."

I went back to the witness rooms and the case proceeded. That evening I discovered that the deputy sheriff who had seen the wreck, arrested the drunken driver, called the ambulance, and had the car towed in to a garage, had sworm on the stand that the car was green. The district attorney asked that I see the car again and I was summoned as a witness the following day. I went to the garage a block away to see the car and discovered that it was not black, nor green; it was *dark blue!* I had been misled because the car was very dark, and got the impression that it was black. The deputy sheriff, equally sincere, was misled by his remembrance of the green smear of paint left on the car driven by the drunkard. The undercoating of paint on Mr. Chenault's car was dark green and that color was left on the other car. And that glaring impression overruled in his mind the true color which he saw repeatedly with his own eyes.

Both of us swore to tell the truth, the whole truth, and nothing but the truth. Both of us sincerely intended to do so. But neither of us did. So every Christian should be humbly conscious that he cannot trust even his own sight, his own hearing, and his own memory when criticising others. How foolish, then, how wicked, to speak evil of another even when we think we tell the exact truth.

* * *

Power for Self-Control. In Dallas, a construction foreman was saved. He set out to be a good Christian. But he came to tell me, in real distress, that he was having trouble quitting the cigarette habit. "I can do all right, Brother Rice, if I can see you every day," he said, "but when I do not see you every day, I soon get such a hunger for cigarettes, and I can hardly keep away from the habit. What shall I do?"

I told him that if he could live an hour without cigarettes, then he should go hourly and pray and commit himself to the Lord afresh, confess his weakness and ask for help.

He said, "I'll do it! I'm the foreman. I can do as I please. There is a tool house on the job. Every hour on the clock I'll go alone and pray until I lick this thing." And he did.

Oh, I know he can have the power of God for himself, and he learned how to do it. But is it not suggestive that he found that if he could talk to God's man every day, he would some way get courage and strength to overcome this enslaving habit?

* * *

God Was Sufficient. A beloved Christian man came to me with a problem. He had been terribly burned in an automobile accident and had lingered for long, long weeks in the hospital. The shocking accident, the fire, the pain, the long suffering had left their mark. And nightmares came to haunt his bed. The only way he could have a night of rest, he said, was to drink a glass or two of beer before he went to bed. Yet that hurt his conscience. His home was nearly broken. What should he do?

I told him that we would take the matter to God in prayer. We did. I asked the dear Lord to give him sweet rest and to take away the haunting nightmares and let him prove that God was sufficient in this matter. I reassured him, and he went his way. He came back later to tell me that from that hour he had never had another nightmare, his rest was sweet, and he no more was tempted with the beer, and now his home was happy.

*   *   *

"I Have Lost the Joy." I was once in Strawn, Texas, in a revival campaign, and a girl came to me and said, "Brother Rice, I don't know what to do. I'm in trouble."

I said, "What's the matter—are you saved?"

And she said, "I don't know. I thought I was. I lived two years very happily; I thought I had trusted the Saviour. I had joined the church, I was baptized; I was very happy for two years. But now I have lost the joy."

I said, "Why don't you pray?"

"I don't know; I have tried and it doesn't do any good."

I said, "Do you mean business about this thing?"

She said, "I surely do, if I know my heart."

I said, "Do you have a job you could lay down tomorrow, if it took a whole day to get this settled?"

She said, "Yes, I can."

"All right," I said, "get your Bible and go out on one of these hills [in Palo Pinto County, near Strawn, Texas] where there are a lot of stones, big rocks, boulders. Take your Bible along. Get under a live oak tree. Open your Bible and lay it on a rock and read it, and read it. After you have read your favorite Scriptures: the twenty-third Psalm, the fifteenth chapter of Luke, I Corinthians 13, the eighth chapter of Romans—anything you like—after you have read several chapters, stop and lay your face down on your Bible and say, 'O God, I am hungry and I am cold. I am not satisfied. I have lost my first love and I don't know why. But I am not going back until I have the joy again. I am going to stay out here all day, if need be. I am not going home today until I have the peace and joy again.' Will you do that?"

She said, "I will."

The next night I was leading the singing. The choir had already assembled. We started the song service. She came in and around the side of the auditorium to come to the choir. Her face was shining like an angel's. She came by after the service to tell me it was all right. She didn't need to; I could see it!

*   *   *

Christians, Be Thirsty

One of the greatest sins of Christians is that they are not thirsty. They are dried up, yet are not thirsty.

A man told me the other day that because his wife did not drink enough water, she was always ailing. One day a friend said to him, "If you will cooperate with me, I will get your wife well."

This man then saw his friend's wife and said to her, "I have invented what is known as an electro-bar."

"What is it?" she asked.

"It has in it certain radium and chemical properties. If it is put in water and left to stand, then when you drink that water off the electro-bar, it will revitalize you inside and make over your whole body entirely. It will make old folks young again."

"Is that so?" she asked.

"Yes, I sell them for ten dollars each, but if you will use it, I will give you one. You have been going to a doctor and taking medicine, but this will cure you. Will you follow the directions if I give you one of them?"

"Yes, I will," she said.

He went down to the brickyard and got a brick—just an ordinary brick—took it to a steel lathe and had it ground off smooth. After he had it ground to the size and shape he wanted, he then took it to the lady and said, "Now you put this in a certain size vessel, and leave it so many hours, and then drink all the water in that vessel."

She did that every day religiously, and she drank all the water, as instructed. She drank and drank and drank. Then she would fill the vessel up again—of course with the bar in it—and drink the water.

It wasn't long until everything wrong with her got all right. She began to think she was all right. She drank that water until the disease was conquered and everything was all right.

It is one of the saddest things in the world to find Christians who are not even thirsty enough to drink. God has for you an abundance, all of Heaven's floodtides of blessing, but you do not drink. If you are thirsty, He will pour water on you. The trouble is that you are not thirsty. We can have the blessing of God, and springtime in our hearts, and a song in our life all the time. When there is a praise service, you would jump at a chance to testify. A word for sinners would be burning on your lips. You would feel that you must speak for God. You would wake up in the morning with joy because it was a new day in which to serve the Lord. You would have a joyful floodtide, an irrigated life, with your roots down in the abundance of water.

O poor, drouth-stricken Christian, with your leaves all withered and your fruit knotty or no fruit at all, God wants to give you plenty and make you a blessing! "I will pour water upon him that is thirsty, and floods upon the dry ground" (Isa. 44:3).

* * *

Lay Aside Earthly Playthings and Run the Race! I was called for the funeral of a twelve-year-old boy in Fort Worth because I had had the joy of winning him to Christ. He was drowned. The next day after the funeral, the father met me and said, "I want to talk to you, Brother Rice." He said, "You know I have a big tent and awning business and a nice home. I have everything heart could desire along that line. But I went out in the garage and saw Scotty's toys. There were his bat and glove, there was his electric train, and here were all the things he had been making. There were his roller skates and ball that he had left behind. I sat awhile out there, and I said to myself, 'Well, the Lord Jesus has given him something better than that. He doesn't need toys now. Scotty is with Jesus up in Heaven.' And I looked out there at my plant. And, you know, we make the finest tents and awnings and rugs; and the thought came to me, 'Old boy, you will leave *your* toys one day and all these play things. You had better be getting in a grown-up man's business and think more about Heaven and not so much about playthings down here.' "

He said something there! He sure did! When you spend all your time at folly, making money—sure, go ahead! When you spend eight or ten hours a day to fill your belly and cover your back with the best clothes; when you eat like princes and drive a nice car, people think, "He is succeeding, isn't he?" If they knew how lank and poor your soul is they wouldn't say that! The fire at the judgment seat of Christ will burn up all the wood, hay and stubble, and some of you will come naked before the God who made you and the Christ who died for you and saved you! You will regret then that you lived a wretched life. You have made a joke out of this business of Heaven and angels and saints and God who are watching you, longing for you to leave the trash and win souls. All the witnesses look down and are concerned, and you do not take it to heart.

* * *

Soldiers Who Were Christians. Can Christians make good soldiers? Or to put it the other way around, Can a soldier in war be a good Christian? The answer is that he certainly can if his heart is right with God and if he is in obedience to his government in a good cause.

Consider the men of the Bible, the greatest men of God mentioned in His Word who were soldiers. Abraham took three hundred and eighteen men, reared in his own household, and pursued after the five kings and defeated them in the night (Gen. 14:13-16). Moses, Joshua, Gideon, David, Asa— these were great men of God, men of faith, and yet they were all soldiers. And history furnishes some shining examples of great Christians who were soldiers.

Lincoln was a soldier in the Black Hawk War and President of the United States during the Civil War, commander-in-chief of the armies.

Stonewall Jackson was a devout Christian, greatly loved and respected.

Robert E. Lee was one of the greatest Christian gentlemen that America has ever produced, without a flaw in his character. In his case there was no matter of hate nor animosity, but of generous love and daily prayer as he tried to do what seemed to him right. General Lee said, "I have fought against the people of the North because I believe they were trying to wrest from the South dearest rights. But I have never cherished toward them bitter or vindictive feelings, and have never

seen the day when I did not pray for them."

And George Washington, the father of his country, whose brilliant and noble character is admired around the world, was a great soldier, but he was a great Christian soldier. I have no doubt that George Washington, kneeling in the snow to pray at Valley Forge, did more good to free America from the heel of the tyrant than he did in any one battle.

* * *

A Fool for Christ. A man walked down the street with a signboard in front and back. In front it read: "I'm a fool for Christ." In back it read: "Whose fool are you?"

I wonder, can you say, "Lord Jesus, I am going to bear Your reproach. I am going to be a good Christian bearing the reproach of Jesus, and live like a Christian ought to"?

* * *

The Tall Man Who Knelt. The father of his country, General George Washington, was a devout Christian. How nobly he led that little band, poorly fed, poorly clothed, and discouraged men, in the Continental army! And in the long winter in Valley Forge, we are told that George Washington went alone to kneel in the snow and pray for God's blessing on the little army. We may be sure that God did bless the leadership of General Washington and did answer the prayer of good men in giving the colonies freedom from Great Britain.

It is said that a gentlemen from South Carolina visited New York where the Continental Congress was meeting and said to a friend, "I should like to see General Washington. How may I distinguish him in the meeting?" The friend replied, "General Washington will be the tall man who kneels when the Continental Congress stops for prayer."

The Hebrew Congregation in Newport, Rhode Island, wrote to President Washington. He replied that, "Happily the government of the United States gives to bigotry no sanction, to persecution, no assistance. . . ." And he closed his letter with these words, "May the Father of all mercies scatter light and not darkness on our paths, and make us all in our several vocations useful here, and in His own due time and way everlastingly happy." Was not that a noble and Christian sentiment?

* * *

Stay Aside in the Secret Place

One day I was out at Lincoln, Nebraska, and a young woman in full-time Christian service, living a clean life, a lovely Christian woman, a graduate of Northwestern Bible School, said, "May I have just a few minutes of your time?"

I said, "Yes."

She sat down and said, "Well, I don't know whether you'll understand me or not. You know, I love the Lord, and I am trying to serve Him. I have my life on the altar for Christian service. I read my Bible every day, and I pray every day, and I am giving my life, every day, in the Lord's work. But," she went on, "I am not as happy as I once was, and God doesn't seem as near as He did. I don't have my prayers answered as I ought to, and I don't win souls as I ought to. I don't know what the matter is; I'm not rebellious against God. I don't know anything in my life that grieves God; if I did I'd quit it. I don't know whether you'll understand or not—I'm just not satisfied with my life."

I said, "You would be surprised how well I understand! I have been right there in the same place, how many times! Do you know what you need?"

She said, "No, honestly, I don't know."

"You just need to say, 'I'm going to take plenty of time, I am going to stay aside in the secret place with my Bible open before God and I am going to find peace and assurance again.' God is a little jealous of His own work. God doesn't want you to be so concerned about His work that you have no time for Him. God isn't so concerned about your walking in a straight line—you don't go to the movies, and you don't smoke cigarettes, and all that—God isn't half as concerned about what you *don't* as what you *do*. Don't misunderstand; I believe you ought to quit the movies and the cigarettes, but I think God wants you to take time to love Him. And I would just say, 'All right, if a half hour isn't enough, I'll take an hour. And if an hour isn't enough, I'll take two hours in the secret closet. I am going back to Bethel. I am going to return to the God that called me back yonder, and I am going to wait there until joy floods my soul again.' Will you do that?"

She said, with her eyes swimming with tears, "Yes, I will! I think that's the trouble." And she went away to find the peace she had before.

* * *

Which Dog Wins? An Indian was converted, but he had a good deal of struggle to live right. Tapping himself on the breast, he said to the missionary, "Two dogs all the time fighting in here. One is a black dog, a bad dog. One is a white dog, a good dog. They fight all the time."

The missionary explained that one who is born of God has the new nature, but that he also has the fleshly nature to contend with and to overcome. Then he asked the Indian convert, "Which dog wins in the fight?"

"The one I say 'sic 'em' to," was the discerning answer. Thank God, a Christian can live daily in victory over his old self, over his carnal nature. He can confess his sins, can mortify the deeds of the flesh and thus, by walking in the light, can have constant fellowship with God. But he must not ignore the fact of his sinful nature, and he certainly should not deceive himself in thinking that he has no sin or that he does no sin. For all of us do sin.

* * *

Care About Holiness. I have read the story of Adoniram Judson and how he even withdrew from ordinary cultured society to seek Christ, returned the doctor's degree he had well earned by his labors, how rigorously he brought in every penny of money he himself earned outside of his mission work. He cared about holiness.

And George Mueller burned the French novels he had translated and might have sold for much money. He gave up the girl he loved so well, sought out every idle longing or foolish turn of mind.

General Stonewall Jackson walked several miles in the dark one night to correct a chance misstatement. "I said that it was on Tuesday night, but I have learned I was mistaken—it was on Thursday night," he said. How he longed and hungered to tell the truth!

If you read John Wesley's *Journal* you may find that there were many searchings of his heart as he longed and sought for personal holiness.

I mean that Christians ought to seek to do good and be good in their hearts with an intense longing. With fervor of heart we ought to seek goodness, seek purity, seek personal holiness, and beg daily for such an abundant cleansing as will take away every evil thing that grieves the Spirit of God.

*   *   *

Abiding in Christ

Many a time on the coldest winter nights I have had a strange urge to see after my little girls, when they were at home, to make sure they were covered and comfortable and safe. That urge waked me out of the soundest sleep when I had not planned to wake and when there was not a sound or movement to arouse me as far as I knew. Part of the personality does not sleep but can be held in attention on some one matter.

I know that sometimes in the night I have reached my hand out to the pillow beside me and touched my wife's face or shoulder. I was aware that she was there even though I was not awake. This awareness of the subconscious mind that can center itself on some object or purpose even when we sleep, ought to be centered on Christ so that literally we could always, day and night, abide in Christ and be conscious of His presence, eager to please Him, to have His favor and do His will!

Many people can wake without an alarm clock at approximately whatever time they wish to awake. I have known several who never relied upon an alarm clock but would simply definitely set their mind to awaken at a certain time and never miss it far. For months, while in Baylor University, I awoke each morning at 5:20 to begin my heavy duties. Most of the time I got not over six hours of sleep a night and oftentimes I was desperately sleepy. If I got a chance during the day, I could go to sleep almost instantly, but my will to arise at a certain time pulled me from the depths of slumber and sent me about my work.

Oh, how I would to God I could have such a continual will to please Christ and know His presence and blessing and power! It is a wonderful thing what love will do. When Mrs. Rice and I were sweethearts in college

I was conscious of her every moment we were in recitations together, no matter whether I was reciting or concentrating on the lesson. When I entered an oratorical contest and spoke rapidly and from memory a prepared address, I was continually conscious that she heard me. I knew where she sat and knew she was interested in what I did. When I played college football, which is a most strenuous game, exacting the most vigous concentration of mind, will and muscle, again and again I saw from the corner of my eye the flash of an orange-colored blouse and knew she was there. It is not hard to abide in the consciousness of those we love.

I am proving to you, dear reader, that you can abide in Christ. You can be conscious of Him whether you work or play or eat or sleep. You can really "pray without ceasing." You can "rejoice in the Lord *alway*." You can "ABIDE under the shadow of the Almighty" (Ps. 91:1). "The peace of God, which passeth all understanding" can really "KEEP your hearts and minds through Christ Jesus." Christians may have the joy and safety and certainty and power of abiding in Christ.

*   *   *

"The Preparation of the Gospel of Peace" (Eph. 6:15). There are too many barefooted Christians. There are too many would-be soul winners who are not shod with the preparation of the gospel of peace. Once "Uncle William Mullins" said about a certain problem that he faced, "Now this is going to be a battle of wits!" His wife, Mamie, replied, "That is just like you, William, entering into a battle half-armed." There are too many Christians entering into the battle with the Devil, half-armed. The lesson here is that if you want to win souls then get ready.

I well remember about my dear father who is now in Heaven, that the first garments he put on each morning were his socks. He didn't want his feet to get cold. And so one of the first things for a Christian to do every day is to prepare his feet and heart for soul winning. Put the shoes of the Gospel on your feet before you start out for the day!

*   *   *

Prayed Up. I heard the late P. W. Philpott, once pastor of the famous Moody Church, Chicago, tell of a blacksmith he knew who was wonderfully saved, but still had to constantly watch a violent temper. One time a quarrel arose in the church and a meeting of Christian men was called one night to talk and pray about the problem and if possible settle the quarrel. Dr. Philpott and big Bill went to the meeting. A mean and suspicious man made hot charges against the big blacksmith, reviled him, threatened him. Dr. Philpott said, "I was afraid of what might happen. I knew the violent temper big Bill had." But the blacksmith remained calm and kindly, and at long last the little fellow who charged him and blamed him was sorry and apologized, and peace was made.

As they walked home that night Dr. Philpott asked the burley blacksmith, "How did you do it, Bill? I know the trouble you have with your temper, and the man was so mean and unkind, it seemed you almost had a right to be angry. How did you hold your temper and remain so calm and kindly?"

And the big man answered, "I was prayed up! I got ready for the meeting by waiting on God and seeking His face. So I had help when I needed it."

Oh, then, let every Christian beware and "watch and pray, that ye enter not into temptation" (Matt. 26:41).

* * *

"But I Promised. . ."

A young man came to me in Fort Worth and said, "Brother Rice, I am in terrible trouble. I want to talk to you." I told him to wait until after the preaching service, then the radio service running until 1:00 p.m., then wait till after baptizing, then I would talk to him. He followed me through the services that day, and about 1:30 or 2:00 we sat down on that winter day in the sun against the side of the tabernacle.

He said, "I was converted. I know it. I lived a good life for a time. Before I was saved I drank and went with wicked women. After I was saved I got in the wrong crowd and slipped. I fell. Then after a time I prayed and promised God that if He would help me, I would never do this any more. After awhile I got a sense of forgiveness and peace.

"But after about two weeks I slipped again and was as bad as ever. I can't control myself. I tried again and promised God this time, sure enough, I would not do it any more.

"I straightened out, but in a little while I got into some bad company, and again the first thing I knew I was drunk and then out with the wild crowd."

He was in such terrible distress. He said, "I can't enjoy sin. Something happened to my heart that causes me to be miserable. I can't enjoy sin like I used to, yet I don't have strength to resist it. But this is the main trouble. I can't go back to God any more. I have lied to God. I do not believe God will believe me if I tell Him I won't do it any more, and I can't come and pray about it. Now what in the world can I do?"

I said to him, "Your mistake was in telling God you weren't going to do wrong. What you ought to make up your mind to do is this: If I sin a million times—I hope you won't—you see it brings trouble and heartache; you see it is wrong and does not pay—if I sin a million times, I still belong to God. He is mine and I am His. I am bought with a price and I don't belong to myself. I have no right to go my own way. If I do wrong, I will come back and confess it to God. Don't make any promises that you will do better, but tell Him you are His, that He bought you, and He will have to take care of you. Confess your wrong."

He said, "But I promised. . . ."

"I know you promised, but sin is so abounding, you failed. But God said, 'If we confess our sins, he is faithful and just to forgive us our sins, and to cleanse us from all unrighteousness.' "

Why should God be faithful? It looks as if it would be our part to be faithful. But grace indicates that the righteousness is all on God's side. If you find favor with God, get along with God, it is not your faithfulness but it is taking the faithfulness of God, calling on the faithfulness of God, counting on the faithfulness of God. It is taking what He so freely gives. Grace is ours! It is in the bargain when we are saved. It is part of the plan of God. That young man got the victory that day, and what I told him helped my own heart.

* * *

"I Believe You Are Sanctified and Don't Know It!" In Huntingdon, West Virginia, a Holiness preacher attended the services with his people, and was greatly blessed. Oh, he felt so grateful to God that I pressed hard the matter of Christians' cleaning up, quitting the movies, leaving off tobacco; that they start a family altar, discipline their children, set out to winning souls. I was helping Christians clean up their lives and that is what he wanted, too. He called it by another name and described it in other terms, but the results we were getting were what his heart craved.

One night as I approached the high school auditorium where the meetings were held, he drew me aside, put some money into my hand and said, "Brother Rice, I don't have much but I feel led of God to give you this. I have been so blessed by the meeting. Brother Rice, I believe you are sancified and don't know it!"

I received the gift with love and gratitude in my heart for his friendship and his confidence. He was a good Christian and wanted fellowship, as I did, on that basis. I would be willing to help teach him what I believe is the Bible teaching on sanctification, but I was glad he could cooperate with us in winning souls. Actually he wanted the things we wanted, although he would describe them in different terms.

Conscience

Conscience! How often I have seen the Spirit of God work upon the conscience of men. In Sherman, Texas, in a great, open-air revival campaign on the courthouse lawn where many hundreds were saved, I preached one night on "The Scarlet Sin and the Roads That Lead to It." It was sharp and plain. But I found then, as I have many times since, that such preaching is used of God to bring men to repentance.

One man who had lived a life of sin and had never thought much about it heard that sermon and could not sleep. He tossed upon his bed that night. At midnight he arose, dressed, got in his car and drove in a long circuit out to another town, then to the Red River, and finally back home. Then when he drove his car in the garage, weeping he confessed to Christ his sin and begged for mercy and forgiveness. He did not go back to his bed until he had it! How glad I was when that man came to a daytime service under the trees and told us he had trusted Christ last night after the lashings of his conscience brought him to repentance!

* * *

An Honest Confession of Sin, an Honest Judgment of Sin, When You Ask for Forgiveness, Often Means Restitution. In Miami, Florida, during my city-wide campaign with forty Baptist churches in about 1946, a pastor arose in a ministers' meeting and asked the chairman, "When I came to Christ and was saved, did not that mean that all my sins were under the blood, all forgiven?"

The chairman answered yes, that as far as one's salvation is concerned, all sins are under the blood the moment a sinner turns to Christ and trusts in Him.

"But what about debts I made when I was a drunken, unregenerate sinner?" asked the pastor.

"I believe that an honest man must still pay honest debts if he is to please God and have fellowship with God," replied the chairman.

The pastor began to weep and he said, "I think so, too. This morning I have paid two debts that I made in my wicked days without Christ. I have one more such debt to pay and then, thank God, there will be nothing between me and God."

Oh, that pastor was right! Can any man honestly say that he is sorry for a debt unpaid, and still leave the debt unpaid? Can any Christian confess stealing, and hope to have the theft forgiven and cleansed, without restoring that which was stolen? Can one who has wronged a brother, and asked forgiveness of God, get the forgiveness and cleansing he craves without also trying to make right with the offended brother the sin he committed?

* * *

The Pang of Conscience. A young man came forward in one of my meetings, confessing his backsliding, his miserable unhappiness. He told me how he had loved a beautiful and admirable young woman. They were engaged, planned to be married, but they petted each other, were too free, and they went into sin. Now they found that every time they met, each felt some disillusionment, some bitter lashings of conscience, and they felt that now love was defiled and their dreams had faded, being mixed with the awful gall of a consciousness of sin. They now felt they could not marry happily. Oh, when conscience brings sin again and again to mind, it ruins the fair castles of dreams, ruins the idealism of love, and men feel they must get away from the reminders of their sin.

* * *

"What About That $800.00?"

In a Sunday morning revival service in St. Paul, Minnesota, a number were led to trust happily in Christ. After the benediction, a woman with a troubled face came to me and said, "What did you do with my daughter? Where is she?" She was in the inquiry room being instructed by the pastor's wife with a group of other women and girls, I explained. And then I said, "Are you a Christian? Hadn't you better get this matter settled for yourself?"

"I don't know whether I am saved or not. I guess I'm not. I must talk to somebody." And she began to weep. We sat down together, and I asked

her what her trouble was and why it was she could not know whether she
was a Christian or not.

"Well, every time I start to pray," she said, "God says to me, 'What
about that $800.00?' I never can get anywhere with my praying. God
won't talk to me about anything else," she exclaimed.

"Well, what about the $800.00?" I asked.

Then she told me the sad story that she had never told another living
soul. Her husband had died fourteen years before. She had two children.
She knew of no way to make money. So when the children had gone to
school, she set fire to the little home and burned it to the ground. The insurance company paid without question the full $800.00 of insurance.
With that money she had moved to St. Paul, got the children in school,
and got started in a livelihood. The lovely grown daughter who had that
morning accepted Christ never dreamed it, nor did the son. Not a breath
of suspicion had ever been attached to her. Yet God still remembered
that she was a thief, that she was crooked; and every time she started to
pray God said to her, "What are you going to do about that $800.00?"

I told her that she must at once go to the officials of the insurance company and make confession.

"But I have no money; I could not pay it," she said. But I reminded her
that she had beautiful clothes, that both she and her daughter now had
good jobs, and that if she had to pay it just a few dollars a week she could
begin to pay it and at least show good faith.

"But I would land in jail," she said. "I have broken the law, and they
would brand me before the whole world as a thief. I can't do that," she
said.

"But you are a thief, whether anybody knows it or not," I said. "And if
you do not pay this honest debt, you will never have any peace with God.
If you go to jail, then go to jail; and God will there give you peace in your
mind and heart and hear you pray. As it is, God will never hear you pray
as long as this wicked sin is between you and Him."

Again she objected saying, "But I don't even remember the name of
the insurance company. I do not know where its offices are. I could not
pay them if I had the money."

"Just turn the thing around," I said. "If an insurance company owed
you $800.00, and you did not know which insurance company it was,
don't you believe that you could find out who it was?" She agreed that
she would try mighty hard and she thought she could find out under
those circumstances. So I showed her that she ought to try just as

earnestly to find out so that she might confess a known sin and pay an honest debt and clear the way before God so He would hear her prayers which He had refused to hear for fourteen years!

Beloved reader, you may be God's own child, dear as the apple of His eye. You may be as dear to Him as David, a man after His own heart; or as Samson, a judge of Israel; or as Peter, the first apostle. But I warn you solemnly that God hates sin even in the dearest of His children. God demands that you forsake it, that you hate it, that you honestly try to make right the things you have done wrong.

*   *   *

The Hell of a Tormenting Conscience.

I remember reading a newspaper clipping several years ago, how in a western state, Idaho, or Montana, a cattleman and businessman went to a United States marshal's office, and said, "I have come to give myself up—I am wanted for murder." The astonished marshal would not believe him. The man was a well-known citizen, well-known and respected, with a fine family. He was known to be honest and upright in his dealings. He had accumulated property and a good name. Yet he insisted he was a murderer. On his insistence, the official wired back to Vermont, where twenty-three years before, the poor man said, he had been guilty of murder. He had fled away under an assumed name, had gone West, had married, had lived straight and made good. But sure enough, a man had been murdered, and one man of the name given had been suspected, but had never been found. The sur-rendered criminal must be sent back to the East to face the charge of murder and be tried for his life.

"Why did you do it?" asked the United States marshal. "You had made good. You have lived straight. You have a right to freedom. You owe something to your family. Surely you have repented long ago and you have proven your desire to go straight. Why in the world did you come back to confess the crime which could never have been traced to you?"

"I'll tell you why," said the pale-faced, trembling-fingered man. "I never walk down the sidewalks of this town, meeting my many friends, but that if someone jostles unexpectedly against my elbow, my heart leaps with fear and trembling. I expect an officer to say, 'Come with me. You are under arrest for murder.' I have lived in hell these twenty-three years, a hell of a tormenting conscience. In the night if the wind blows the limb of a tree against the side of the house, I wake startled, with my heart in my mouth, half expecting someone to be beating on the front door with the handle of a six-shooter saying, 'Open, in the name of the law!' I've got to face this matter and get it off my conscience."

How many, many times does a preacher hear from souls tormented by accusing consciences! A woman standing in my services once, hesitated to come to Christ, saying, "I can never forget what I have done." Many times sinners believe they have sinned away their opportunity for salvation. Suicide is often but the result of tormenting conscience. I tell you now, that one day your conscience will awake and burn like fire, if you go on in sin.

* * *

Who Can Un-Do? A man lay on the hospital bed who had wasted his life in sin. Now his body was broken and the doctors did all they could. A friend came and hovered around and said, "What can I bring you? Anything I can get you?"

"No, there is nothing you can do."

"Let me bring you a good book to read."

"No, thank you. I don't care."

"Well, then, may I bring you some ice cream?"

"No, no."

"I'll bring a basket of fruit.

What can I do? Is there anything I can do for you? Would you like some flowers?"

"Oh, no, no!" the man said, the man on the hospital bed, an old man. He had gone in sin, his body broken down in sin.

The man said, "What can I do?"

And then the sick man said this: "There is nothing you can do. There is nothing *anybody* can do. Oh, God, if there were only somebody who could *undo*!"

* * *

Tears of Shame. I was in revival services in Chicago in the North Shore Free Church. I lived at Wheaton, twenty-five miles away. One night Mrs. Rice went with me. She gave very clear instructions to the six girls. One was the baby, Joy, two of them we called the little girls and the others were big girls. Mrs. Rice said, "Now you big girls are to be in bed. Remember, I want the house cleaned up—no papers on the floor, the dishes washed. The baby must be in bed at 8:30." They agreed. "And you other girls must be in bed by 9:30."

"Yes, Mother."

We went to the revival campaign and drove back at 11:00 at night. When we came back down Main Street, then down Franklin Street in Wheaton to where we could see our house, every window was ablaze with lights like a hotel! Mrs. Rice said, "Oh, those children are not in bed and it is 11:00 at night!" She said, "You watch! When we drive into the driveway and they hear the wheels on the gravel, they will begin to turn out the lights and go upstairs—the little brats!"

Sure enough! We went into the house and a light flashed off in the dining hall, then in the living room, and the stairwell, and the little girls were frantically climbing into pajamas and trying to get to bed.

Mrs. Rice said, "O girls! Not even the baby is in bed! And the funny papers left on the floor. And it is 11:00 at night, and you promised Mother!. . ."

"O Mother, I forgot," and, "Mother, I didn't know what time it was!"

Now they were ashamed before their mother at her coming and had to have some rebuke. They were sad about their neglect. That doesn't mean Mother didn't love them. That doesn't mean they didn't love Mother.

You, too, are going to be ashamed when you are caught with your job undone and with sin before you. You are going to face God about your sins, you Christian people—tears up in Heaven.

* * *

Made Bitter by Sin—at Fifteen!

Years ago my wife and I went to a hospital to visit a girl only fifteen years old. She came from a good family. In the hospital we talked with this girl, who had an attractive face and form and beautiful red hair. She was bitter, disillusioned, hopeless. As we waited in the hospital room, the nurse brought the fifteen-year-old her little illegitimate baby to nurse. At once she put a towel over her face. She had never seen her baby, had sworn she would never see it, would never look upon it. She hated the baby because the baby was the brand and mark and proof and outcome of her sin.

Does any girl in the world want to turn out like that? Dear girl, if you knew that that was at the end of the road, would you go into sin? Would you dally with temptation in necking and petting and the lewd movie and the indecencies permitted on the dance floor? Would you? If you knew it would end with an illegitimate baby, a broken heart, a ruined name, and the wreck of your hopes for a happy marriage and a happy home, would you go on and trifle with sex sin? In Jesus' name, I beg you, consider how it will end before you go on in such sin. Remember that the Bible says, "Her end is bitter as wormwood, sharp as a twoedged sword" (Prov. 5:4).

* * *

What Happened to Pilate?

Pilate was procurator in Judaea for

about ten years. Then because of severity in treatment of his subjects, he was dismissed and went to Rome to face charges.

There are many traditions about him. One is that he committed suicide. Another is that he retired to Switzerland, near Lake Geneva, and that Mount Pilatus there was named for him. The tradition tells that on a moonlit night some have seen two hands rise from Lake Geneva and wash and wash themselves—the hands of Pilate trying to wash away the guilt of sending Jesus to the cross, knowing He was innocent.

Pilate washed his hands, disclaiming any responsibility for the crucifixion. But we know he did not thus free his soul from sin. If he died unsaved, it may be that in Hell he lifts his guilty hands in an agony too late for cleansing from the blood of Christ.

In Shakespeare's "Macbeth," the Macbeth who, with his wife, murdered the king, was hounded by his conscience. With blood on his hands he said,

"Will all great Neptune's ocean wash this blood
Clean from my hand? No; this my hand will rather
The multitudinous seas incarnadine,
Making the green one red."

And Lady Macbeth, who helped murder the king, cries out, "Out, damned spot! out, I say!" And again she says, "Here's the smell of the blood still: all the perfumes of Arabia will not sweeten this little hand. Oh, oh, oh!"

Let Pilate remind us that there is no cleansing from the awful guilt of sin but by the blood of Christ. And no avoiding the haunting of conscience and eternal retribution but by trusting Christ!

~~~~~~~

Curse of Booze

"I Am Free!" Fred Hawkins of Springfield, Missouri, drove me through Southern Missouri and showed me place after place where he once drank with the boys. He tried again and again to break away from the habit but could not. Then one day he asked the Lord for a new heart and got it. God set him free. Choked with gratitude and with tears, he said to me, "Thank God, I don't want it anymore. I don't need it! I am free."

* * *

Biggest Fool in Dallas! I drove into a filling station in Dallas one day to buy some gas. I said to the young attendant, "Hello, there. How are you today?"

He said, "If you want to know, I am the biggest fool in Dallas."

I asked him what was the matter.

He said, "I got paid yesterday and went out and got drunk. Oh, I pulled off a big one! I got on a real bender. When I got up this morning my paycheck was all gone and I have only a few pennies in my pocket. I am supposed to pay my rent today and I don't have any money. I have a guilty conscience and a dark brown taste in my mouth. I am the biggest fool this world ever saw," and he said it with a cuss word. I said, "Just take out the cuss word and I will say Amen to that."

It is a bad business having "fun" when it doesn't end up funny. It is a bad business when your amusements break hearts and lead one into sin and give bitter years later. Why not set out to have the kind of fun a Christian can have, clean, and joyful and fun that does not end in heartbreak. Christians ought to be happy.

* * *

God Changed a Drunkard.
Years ago in Decatur, Texas, I held a revival campaign. My father, in a Chevrolet car, hooked on to the block and tackle and pulled up the eight-hundred-pound tent center poles. Some men helped me drive the stakes; we put up the big tent and held a revival.

On one corner of the same block was a garage. In that garage lived a drunkard with his family. Though it was during prohibition days, yet he was a drunkard. One day as I went into the back of that garage, I saw some bed springs, not a mattress, just the springs with a couple of quilts on them. That was the sleeping place of the two boys of the family. The only wall or partition was a sheet which was hung on a string. This cut off that greasy, dirty part of the floor of the garage from the public workshop. That was the only home for that family of four. Each of the children had only one pair of faded, dirty, dingy blue overalls. His wife had no change of clothing. They were in the barest scrapings of poverty.

The man, this drunken man, was a good mechanic. He sold lots of gasoline through his fuel pumps. But he never stayed sober long enough to make a good living. Nearly everything he had went for liquor.

Once during the revival campaign that man stood against the corner of the garage and heard me preach. I prayed for God to reach his heart. The next night he again stood there and listened. The third night Dad persuaded him to come over and stand by the corner of the tent. He had no clothes but overalls, so he would not come into the tent. That night at the invitation, my father, with his arms around him, led him to Christ. He was wonderfully saved.

Isn't it wonderful what God can do for a drunkard? Isn't it wonderful what He can do for a sinner?

Then the man buckled down to work. I went by to see him. When people found he was sober, they began to bring their cars to him, for he was a genuine mechanic. He could fix anything. He had plenty of work.

One day a truck backed up to that old garage and a Singer sewing machine was unloaded. The woman began making clothes. A few days later she came to me and said, "Brother Rice, we've rented a three-room house! It has a sink, running water and electric lights, and gas to cook with. We are moving there tomorrow."

The next day the moving truck loaded the little trinkets. A pickup truck could haul all they had. They put in the sewing machine, the bed springs, a few old quilts, and a broken-down chair or two, took them over to the house, and they started housekeeping.

Yes, poverty, trouble, broken homes, pale-faced widows and little children without shoes in the winter are a natural picture of what inevitably comes when people go on in drink. Broken homes, broken hearts are the results of drink. The roses leave the bride's cheeks. With a broken heart she holds on as long as she can. Cold houses, ill-clad children, curses and beating, no money with which to buy food, are her lot. After

awhile she gives up. Then other women come in. A man who drinks has no sense, no loyalty, no character. Everything is gone. Oh, the curse of God is on liquor.

* * *

Whose Sin Was Greater? How often it is that our self-righteousness is only a cloak for more wicked sins than those we condemn in others! A woman called me across a certain city once to talk to her husband who had the habit of drink. The husband prayed with me with contrite confessions, with many, many tears, pleaded with God to give him grace. But his wife with eyes snapping and bitter words accused her husband, "I don't believe he even tries! He has promised me he would never drink again. He has promised his children the same. But just as soon as he gets his pay check, if some of his cronies want him to go to the tavern he takes one drink and then he is off on a big drunk again. I don't believe he loves us as he says he does. I don't believe he loves God as he says he does. If he did, he wouldn't get drunk."

I told the wife, "Your husband is sick. His will is broken down. He needs your love, your pity, your help, and not your scolding. He has one temptation and you have another. He has a temptation to take a glass of beer with the boys, and you have a temptation to lose your temper and nag and scold until he has no peace, until life is a burden, until home is a hell on earth. Then to drown his sorrow he is tempted all the more to drink. Your sin is at least as great as his."

Not long afterwards it was discovered that he had an incurable brain tumor. On trying to operate, the surgeon found he was beyond help. How many scathing words had struck like arrows in the heart of this poor, sick man trying to hold on to his job, trying to walk straight, yet the victim of temptation he could not master, especially in view of his infirmity.

* * *

Cursed by Booze. In a tabernacle revival campaign at Petersburg, Illinois, years ago I preached on "The Double Curse of Booze," and I challenged people to follow carefully what happened to the families and homes of bartenders and liquor sellers. I stated my conviction, that in every case the curse of God would in some way be manifested on those who are under this woe pronounced in the Bible. A liquor dealer was enraged at my sermon and cursed and blasphemed up and down the streets saying that his business was legitimate, he was licensed to sell liquor, that if people drank too much and if people were cursed by

booze, it was not his fault.

I closed the revival and returned home. In two weeks, I think it was, a pastor wrote me that the same liquor dealer went down to his bar one morning and as he put his key in the lock to open the door he fell over dead. Trouble followed his children, too.

I am saying there is a woe, a curse, pronounced of God on those who sell liquor. "Woe unto him that giveth his neighbour drink, that puttest thy bottle to him, and makest him drunken also. . ." (Hab. 2:15).

* * *

"Old Bill" and "New Bill." In Evansville, Indiana, some years ago, there was a man converted, an old drunken bum. Everybody knew Old Bill. I don't remember his last name because he wasn't called by his last name. He was Old Bill the drunkard. He would beg to get enough money to get drunk. He picked up cigarette butts off the street; asked for handouts at the back doors. Sometimes he would paint a few mail boxes to get a little money.

One day while drunk, he and one of his buddies got into a fight, and his buddy knocked his eye out. Later this guy they called Old Bill was converted, and when he got saved, he got saved all over. (You know about the little dog named

Rover. When he died, he died all over!) In fact, he had become such a remarkable Christian and won so many souls for God that people quit calling him Old Bill. They named him New Bill.

New Bill was wonderfully saved! But let me ask you a question. How many eyes do you think he had after he got converted? Just one eye. Well, didn't God forgive him for that time he got drunk when he got his eye knocked out? Yes, God forgave him, *but he still reaped what he sowed!*

* * *

Drink Moderately? On October 15, 1958, in the General Convention of the Episcopal Church meeting at Miami Beach, Florida, a commission on alcoholism headed by Delaware's Bishop J. Brook Moseley of Wilmington said, "There is no scriptural command requiring total abstinence for the God-fearing man. A Christian who drinks moderately with due regard for the feelings and needs of his brothers and with a conscientious care for the claims of God can drink with thanksgiving to Him for these blessings."

With seventy million Americans drinking regularly, and with alcohol the greatest single factor in crime and divorce and accidents, we have come to a sorry state in America when church leaders encourage Christians to "drink moderately," and to "drink with thanksgiving to Him for these blessings."

May I suggest that it will probably be a long time before it becomes a custom to start off a cocktail party with a prayer of thanksgiving to God, as reverent people thank Him at a meal.

* * *

The Woe of Poverty Caused by Drink. *"For the drunkard and the glutton shall come to poverty: and drowsiness shall clothe a man with rags."*—Prov. 23:21.

What is the curse on the drunkard? Poverty. I need not prove that. How many of you here ever knew somebody who was poor because of liquor?

In the second grade at school I had my first love affair! I fell in love with Miss Mabel Blossom, my second grade teacher! One day Miss Mabel said to the class, "All you children but Sammy will have to stay in today. Sammy, you have been a good boy. You may go home on time. Get your lunch bucket, your cap and coat, and go on home. Good-by, Sammy. I am going to keep the rest of the class in."

Sammy left. When the door was closed, Miss Mabel got off her rostrum, walked down near us, stood there with tears in her eyes as she said, "Children, some of you haven't been very nice to Sammy.

You don't like to play with him. You have nice lunch baskets, while he brings his lunch—if he has anything at all—in a lard pail. Your Mother fixes your hair nice. You little girls have nice starched dresses; you little boys have white blouses and clean pants, but little Sammy only wears dirty old patched overalls." She said, "Children, I want to tell you something. Sammy is not to blame. His father is a drunkard, and Sammy's mother does the best she can. They don't have money a lot of the time. Sammy can't bring any lunch some days. So don't you be mean to Sammy. He can't help it if his father drinks."

I have never gotten away from that. Here is a little boy who didn't have lunches like the rest of us. Our family was very poor, but we always had clothes enough, and they were always clean. We came with our hair combed and looked nice. We were well cared for. But Sammy, with a drinking father, couldn't have nice clothes; he didn't have enough to eat, and he went barefoot in the wintertime. I was impressed then with the thing I have wept over I guess a thousand times since—the poverty of wives and little children who suffer because of a husband and daddy who is a drunkard.

* * *

A Personal Experience of the Curse of Drink. "Why is it you are so against liquor?" someone asks. I am against it because it tells me in the Bible to be against it. But it comes closer home than that. I have seen it ruin lots of people. But it comes closer home than that. Let me tell you about it.

Once I was called back to Dundee, the little cowtown in West Texas where I grew up. A young fellow who had three sons and a beautiful wife, a Christian wife (no Christian ought to marry anybody who is not saved, but this woman did) went out on a weekend trip and took with him some bottles of liquor and some homebrew. Yonder on the riverbank he and others with him drank and drank. Then he got sick. Liquor often makes people sick. He drank until he was violently sick. The men who were with him brought him back home and called the doctor at Wichita Falls. Intestinal paralysis had been caused by liquor. They rushed him to the hospital for an operation, but he died on the operating table.

I went back there among that family whom I loved. The next afternoon the funeral was held. That young wife nearly died that afternoon. The doctor had to give her a stimulant to keep her heart beating. She was left a widow, with three little fatherless boys to support. All she had was just a little two-room house. With her husband gone, she had no way to make a living. She loved him, but he drank himself to death while he was still young.

That night friends stayed around, so we looked up some bedding for the kinsfolk and others who stayed all night. The young wife said, "There is a mattress out in the garage." It was the same mattress that had been used on this drunken party on the river, when a bunch of men took a big keg of beer, lots of homebrew and whiskey, drank, gambled and played poker by the firelight, and when her husband got drunk to his death.

My brother Joe and I unrolled that old mattress. In it was a pint of government liquor and three or four bottles of homebrew. We took them out under the stars on the prairies of West Texas and by an old mesquite stump my brother and I stood. Taking one bottle at a time, I held it up before me and God and said, "God, there is a curse on it," then broke the first bottle. I took the second bottle and said, "God helping me, I'll fight it; I'll expose it everywhere I go," then I broke that one. After I had broken them all, we stopped and had prayer, then went back to the house.

That widow was my baby sister!

With a holy hate, I hate the dirty liquor business. I am trying to keep people from the heartbreak of it.

Death

Fear of Death After Death. I
remember a pioneer officer of the law in New Mexico in wild frontier times. He had risked his life again and again. He had gone out to track down and arrest and bring in many a murderer, many an outlaw. And he said to a preacher, "I am not afraid to die! You know I am not afraid to die. I have risked my life many and many a time. I am not afraid to die—but, O God, what comes after death! That is what I am afraid of!" So Jesus connected the two together (physical death and spiritual death) when He said, "The rich man also died, and was buried; And in hell he lift up his eyes, being in torments" (Luke 16:22,23).

* * *

"How Much Did He Leave?" It
is folly, it is wicked obsession with things instead of eternity and God and righteousness and forgiveness and goodness, that lead men on to Hell. One of these days that grasping hand will grow stiff and cold, and all the coins in it will slip

between those palsied fingers!

Six honorary pallbearers sat at a grave side while the closing ceremonies of the funeral were completed. One whispered to the other about the rich man who died, "How much did he leave?"

The other whispered back, "He left it all!" He took none of it with him!

* * *

The Failure of Deathbed Religion. Years ago in the South a wicked old man lay dying. The family called the preacher. Maybe Father would turn to Christ on his deathbed. But when the preacher stood by the bedside and talked about Jesus, an eerie light came into the eyes of the old man, and in delirium he cried out, "They are in there again! Get out of my apple trees you boys or I'll call the law!" He was thinking of his orchards, and could not think about his immortal soul.

* * *

At the Bottom of the Hill Was Death. Ten miles from Elmira, New York, a man got in his car and started down an icy hill toward the highway. At the foot of the hill ran the Erie Railroad. He did not see the approaching train until he was already headed down the icy hill. He tried desperately to stop but could not. The car slid onto the

railroad track and the man was instantly killed. How foolish he was not to have looked for the train before he started down the hill!

In that tragedy there is a double lesson. The man lost his life because he did not look ahead to see how his trip down the hill would end. But the same man the preceding Sunday heard me preach. I pleaded with him personally to take the Saviour but he would not. Although he was a middle-aged man, he decided to risk it longer on Satan's side and turn down the Saviour. He lost his life by starting in his car down the hill without looking ahead. But he lost his poor soul forever because he turned down Jesus and neglected his opportunity without looking ahead to see where it would end!

Dear sinner, look before you leap! Find out how sin ends before you go on in it!

* * *

All Must Die. I preached in Chattanooga at the big Highland Park Baptist Church to some 3,400 or 3,500 people on "Missing God's Last Plane for Heaven." I took for my text Jeremiah 8:20, "The harvest is past, the summer is ended, and we are not saved." I said everybody there was going to die. I said, "Three thousand four hundred people will die, we will say, in 70 years. That will mean that every nine days somebody who hears me tonight will die. Oh, it may go ten days or maybe eight days, but it will average that now for the next seventy years somebody of this congregation will die every nine days." That night they announced ten funerals going to be in that church that week. I am just saying death comes; so don't you think people ought to weep for loved ones going to die? Some of you wait until it is too late to weep. Some of you wait until they are already gone, then you can't warn them. If there were any good thing you could do, you can't do it after they are gone so you had better weep now while you can.

* * *

The Time of Departure

My father, like Paul and Peter and Jacob, said he would know when death was coming and he did.

About 1928 I was in revival services at Vinton, Louisiana, when a telegram came saying that my father had a serious stroke, was not expected to live, that I must rush home if I wanted to see him before he died. That night, as the wheels clicked on the rails under my head in a Pullman berth, I gave up my father. When I arrived at the old home at Decatur, Texas, I found all the family walking on tiptoe, talking through tears and in whispers, but my dad making fun of all their fears! He could not breathe lying down so was propped with pillows in a big chair.

"Son, I am not going to die now," he said. "I will know when my time arrives; God will tell me, and He has not told me yet."

Strangely enough, Dad slowly, steadily improved, got to where he could walk with a cane, then drive his car, and with some care, attend to business.

Two years later, I was in revival services at Duke, Oklahoma, and without telling anyone, he planned to come visit me and the revival. He went by a store building under construction for him. To the contractor he said, "Now are we both agreed on the prices? the time of completion? the terms? I may not be here when it is done and the understanding must be clear."

Mr. Lambert, the contractor, said, "Why, Mr. Rice, aren't you feeling well? You look stronger than before."

"Yes, I am well, but I will not be here long. My wife is gone, my children are grown, my work is done. The Lord has told me I am to go soon."

He drove away in the car to Oklahoma. He drove by to see Cousin Georgia and told her, "I won't be here long, Georgia, and I wanted to see you and your boys." When she protested that he seemed so strong and well, he answered, "Yes, I feel fine, but I just know." He came to Duke to attend my revival services in a big temporary tabernacle. In two days he won four men, heads of families, to Christ. Then he came in at 5:00 o'clock to the rented house where I stayed with my family and said, "Son, I'd better lie down; I do not feel well." A little later he said (I think he thought of our own concern and future peace), "Son, I think you should call the doctor."

I had already called the doctor—at that minute he was coming up the walk. But Dad was gone in a few minutes, one hour from the time he walked in. Death to him was no terror, but a friend, welcomed gladly, and announced in his heart by sweet revelation from God's Holy Spirit.

* * *

The Tragedy of Johnstown.

Johnstown, Pennsylvania, is a city seventy-five miles east of Pittsburgh on the Conemaugh River. In 1889 the little town, in a deep valley walled in by mountains, had over 8,000 population. Above the town was a dam on the South Fork, twelve miles above the city, built thirty-seven years before to provide a storage reservoir for the Pennsylvania Canal. But on May 1, 1889, the dam broke. The thousands of people in Johnstown had been warned, the dam was about to give way. A man on horseback rode down the valley warning, shouting to people to leave the valley and to hurry! They laughed at him. The dam had held for thirty-seven years. But it broke. A flood of water twenty feet high rushed down upon the town at twenty miles an hour and within one hour almost completely destroyed Johnstown and did destroy seven other towns in the valley. Between two thousand and three thousand people died, all of them warned, but died because they sat there and would not believe the warning, would not flee to safety. What a tragic illustration of the folly of careless delay! Death comes on apace. Your sins will find you out if you do not flee to Jesus for mercy.

* * *

Preach for Immediate Decision.

Some years ago in Dallas, Texas, in the Galilean Baptist Church, Rev. P. B. Chenault was preaching in a series of meetings. The last night came. He preached on "Today and Tomorrow." He had two texts. One was in Hebrews

3:7, "Wherefore (as the Holy Ghost saith, TO DAY if ye will hear his voice. . .)." The other text was Proverbs 27:1: "Boast not thyself of to morrow; for thou knowest not what a day may bring forth." The fervent, godly preacher made his final appeal. He laid upon all of our hearts that TODAY was the only day that someone present might ever have; that today was the day of salvation. He urged the folly of neglecting and postponing any duty and especially of neglecting salvation since none of us could boast of tomorrow and none of us could know what a day might bring forth. The service came to a close. After an earnest session of prayer and affectionate good-byes Brother Chenault with his wife and baby drove away into the night, toward another engagement in Illinois.

Mrs. Rice and I retired, but at 2:30 in the morning I was awakened by the insistent ringing of the telephone. Dear P. B. Chenault had had his speeding car wrecked by a drunken driver and he, with crushed head, had gone to meet the Saviour he loved. Oh, how it pressed upon my heart that we should be faithful in preaching for immediate decision. No man knows what will be tomorrow. I think the dear Saviour must have laid upon P. B. Chenault's heart the need for preaching that

sermon, his last night on earth.

* * *

The Singing of Angels. Years ago my stepmother's father, a Christian man about fourscore years of age, went home to be with God. In the days preceding his death, he called his daughters to help him sing over again with halting and weak voice the songs he sang long ago. He said he heard the angels singing. He thought they were in the room with him and were ready to carry him home to God! Were those simply the imaginations of a delirious man? Had his mind grown feeble? Was be beside himself? No! No! Multiplied thousands of saints have come down to death's door and have told their loved ones that they heard the voices of angels or that they saw angels in the room.

* * *

The Final Rest. As my mother lay dying she asked us to sing,
"**How firm a foundation, ye saints of the Lord,
Is laid for your faith in His excellent Word!**"

My counsin played it on the little reed organ and we sang it to the old Southern tune. My mother clapped her thin, frail hands and rejoicing made us promise to meet her in Heaven. I can remember she then looked up and said, "I can see Jesus and my baby now." The things of the earth began to fade away and she saw Heaven. Then her eyes softly closed, and with her hands folded on her breast, my mother went to be with the Lord. Oh, Heaven, Heaven! My mother is in her mansion! My mother lived in a little unpainted house papered with newspapers and with an old plain floor scrubbed with lye water until it was white. On the floor there was a homemade rag rug. It was very neat and clean, it seems to me in memory. My mother never lived in a house with electric lights but four months in her life! She carried water from a well all her life except for a few weeks. Now my mother is in a mansion in Glory! Oh, Heaven, where none will ever grow old, where we will never be sick or tired, where there will be no disappointments.

There'll never be crape on the doorknob,
  No funeral train in the sky,
No graves on the hillsides in Glory,
  For there we shall nevermore die.

My mother is in Heaven! She is in that place where the roses never fade, where people are never old or sick or tired or poor; where there is never a parting nor a sad good-bye. I am going to meet her and then there will be no more saying good-bye to my family and going up and down the earth as if I were the offscouring of the world, hated and slandered by some people wherever I go. I am going to Heaven; I already have a ticket; I have a reservation; I have the promise of God. My sins are already forgiven. I am going to Heaven.

* * *

No Time for Christ.

My evangelist brother, William H. Rice, had revival services in the north woods of Michigan, and many, by God's grace, were saved. I have before me my brother's letter telling an incident of sudden destruction on one who had been often reproved and hardened his heart. He said:

"One incident occurred, John, that stirred the entire community and which none of us will forget very soon. A family named F____ lived near the church. Mrs. F____ and their grown son were saved, but Mr. F____ was not. Several had tried to talk to him but he would not listen. He had one of the finest farms in the county and had no time for Christ. He was rather bitter about it. One Saturday, Pastor Clare Dafoe tried to deal with him. He climbed into the haymow where he was storing hay and helped him with his work. When they were finished and started to go down, Mr. Dafoe, who is a real soul winner, began talking with him about the Lord. The man sat on the floor with his legs dangling through the opening of the door and told Clare he very definitely had no time for Christ. . . . The next Monday morning Mr. F___ was again working in the haymow when he slipped and fell to the ground below, landing on the right side of his face. He died in a few hours and was buried the following Thursday.

"The news spread like a forest fire and made many think seriously about the foolishness of rejecting Christ. Four were saved that Monday night when I spoke on the text, 'It is appointed unto men once to die.' Others were saved during the meetings as a direct result of Mr. F___'s death."

* * *

How the Cow Was Led. I heard a man tell about a strange sight he had seen one time. He saw a wagon coming leading a cow behind it. The team just walked right up and trotted briskly and the cow led right along behind the wagon so strangely. He thought, "That sure is strange." Do you know what was queer about it? A cow's legs are shorter, so she doesn't walk as fast as a horse.

Then another thing: cows are like some people I know—they have ideas of their own. They don't want to be led. Has anybody ever tried to lead a cow, with a team, behind a wagon?

He said, "That is queer. She sure does lead well." When he got a

little closer he said, "I don't see a rope. They must have a chain or some kind of a wire on her halter." He got closer, and it wasn't even that. There was nothing on her at all. When he got closer and looked in the wagon, he saw a newborn baby calf.

Listen, God has to take the calves sometimes to get you old cows. Did you know that? God has ways.

When Lazarus died, Jesus said, "This. . .is. . .for the glory of God" (John 11:4). Sometimes God takes one child and breaks your heart.

* * *

Decide Today. In September of 1965, song leader Bill Harvey was with me in an areawide campaign near Laurel, Delaware, in the big Del-Marva camp meeting tabernacle. The crowds increased, the power of God fell, and many were saved. On Tuesday night of the last week of the campaign, in the audience was a truck driver. I did not know him. He heard the Gospel preached in earnestness, in fervor, in tears. He heard the sweet singing of the Gospel. He doubtless felt the power of God which others felt. He saw people come to claim Christ as Saviour and receive assurance that sins were forgiven. He went away lost that Tuesday night. On Friday night he shot himself.

During our Sunday afternoon service, they were conducting his funeral. Oh, I do not know what awful extremity, what shattering tensions came upon him! Was it an unfaithful wife? Was it a lost job? Was it the awful depression after some orgy of sin? I do not know what led him to the despair that put a gun to his head and a bullet to his brain! I only know that on Tuesday night, God spoke to him and said, "To day," but he surely must have said, "No, not today, but some other time." The Holy Ghost said, "To day if ye will hear his voice, harden not your hearts" (Heb. 4:7), but he did harden his heart. He went away lost, and in three days he went out to meet God, I suppose and fear, unprepared.

* * *

All Must Die

I preached one night in Roosevelt, Oklahoma. A young man about twenty years old heard me. The next afternoon at one-forty he was instantly killed by a train. He never lived to say a word, or to pray, or to repent. Oh, if I had realized death was so near for him, wouldn't I have wept over him more, wouldn't I have pressed the invitation more?

In Kaw City, Oklahoma, we spoke to a Kaw Indian boy, a young fellow of twenty, and asked him to give his heart to Christ. We begged him to come to the meeting, the pastor and I, and he promised he would come. But that afternoon he got drunk, and before morning he was cut in two by a train. I saw the poor, maimed body in an undertaker's parlor. Oh, if I had known that was the last day that boy would live, don't you think I might have wept more, pled more, and made sure he came? I didn't do as much as I might have done. Death! Oh, death is coming! Somebody here may die tonight!

In a union revival campaign in Binghamton, New York, I preached one night on "The Coming Electrocution of Bruno Hauptmann," who had just been condemned to die in the electric chair for the murder of the Lindbergh baby. I said, "Thirty days, and by the process of law, Hauptmann will go out to meet God and pay for his sins. Thirty days and Hauptmann will prove that 'God is not mocked,' will prove that 'whatsoever a man soweth, that shall he also reap,' will prove that 'the wages of sin is death.' But, hear me, somebody who is in this building tonight will die before Bruno Hauptmann. Somebody hearing me now will die and go to meet God before Bruno Hauptmann dies in thirty days."

That night it was bitter zero weather. The meetings were being held in the great Binghamton Theater. A man who heard me make that statement stayed to help shut the doors of the theater. Then he got in his car to drive home. The car went all over the slippery, icy street. One of his boys said, "Daddy, what's the matter?" "Oh, my head, my head!" His son pushed him over in the seat, got under the wheel and drove home. The man was taken to the hospital at midnight. At four o'clock in the morning he died.

I don't know when, but I know that somebody here in a few months, in a few weeks, in a few days, maybe even in a few hours, will die and meet God. I say, death is on your trail!

* * *

He Waited too Late! I conducted a tent revival campaign at Decatur, Texas, about 1929. Hundreds were saved. A few months after that campaign closed, I lived in Dallas, and my sister, then a resident of Decatur, called me long distance. She said,

"John, something has happened that I think you ought to know. Do you remember Mr. Blank (that was not his name) who attended the tent campaign night after night but was never saved?"

I replied that I did not remember him by the name she gave.

"He came in overalls and jumpers and sat outside the tent and laughed, night after night. I spoke to him many times about his soul. Don't you remember how he made a joke of it?" she said.

Then I recalled the man as she continued to tell me the story of his tragic death. He had gone to the Rogers Hospital for an appendicitis operation. Although he was

seventy years old he seemed to be unmoved at the prospect of a serious operation and possible death. After some days in the hospital he was brought to his home. Soon his case became serious, then desperate. The doctor did all that could be done and then plainly said to him one day,

"Have you made your will? If there is anything you need to do, old fellow, you had better get it done. I have done all I can for you, and things look mighty serious."

It was summertime and windows and doors were open. That man lay on his bed and cried out to God so that he was heard for a block up and down the street in either direction. He screamed and pleaded, cursed and prayed! He said, "O God, don't let me die like this! I am not fit to die. I need more time to repent! O God, it isn't fair to take me this way without any time to get ready!" The sweat of terror was on his face as that poor, old, wicked, Christ-rejecting sinner screamed out at God in the few minutes before he died.

His dying cries revealed that all along he had thought he would one day be saved. But, alas, he waited too late! Someway, in his dying hour, he could not believe that God would forgive him, he could not repent, he felt he had no time to get ready! *Men cannot escape dropping off, unprepared, into a Hell of eternal torment, if they persist in neglecting so great salvation offered through Jesus Christ!*

God

The Hallowed Name of God.
Years ago, when I was a young preacher, and not so many cars were on the road, I drove out far to a revival appointment. A hitchhiker beside the road waved to me, and I stopped and let him in the car. As he talked he rather casually used the name of God in vain. I turned to him immediately and said that he must never do that again, that I could not have anyone riding in my car and take the name of God in vain. He talked on, and after some time, apparently forgetting, again he took the name of God in vain. I stopped the car immediately and said, "Get out!" He started to argue the matter, and I

simply reached under the front seat and got the crank which we kept for cars then and said, "Get out of the car and then we can talk about it!"

A little angry, but thoroughly convinced, he got out of the car, and I told him plainly that no one could ride in my car and take the name of Christ in vain, that I was a Christian, I loved the Lord Jesus, and that it was shameful and wicked for anybody to speak slightingly that dear name that is above every name.

Oh, yes, you may be sure I would have put him out of the car by force if need be!

When we come to pray, oh, may our hearts long exceedingly that every knee shall bow to Him and every tongue shall confess Him as Lord, and that the sweet name of God and the name of Christ be everywhere hallowed and revered.

* * *

All Else May Change.
I went back to a little place where I lived when I was four years old. It was a little country place called Vilot community in Cooke County, Texas. My father was pastor of the church that met in a little building down at the crossroads. The blacksmith shop was on the other corner. I remember where the washpot was, and where the cowpen was when I would go and

sit on the fence with a tin cup in my hand, and my dad would milk the cup full of foaming milk for me and I would drink it down. A young cow Dad was milking one day ran around sideways and knocked me over. My dad thought it was so funny. I remember the old cellar when I went down to see the goose and the eggs she had down there, and the old gander came down and got me by the palm of my hand with his bill and led me out! I was yelling bloody murder!

But, I say, after I was a grown man I went back to that old place. The old house had burned and a new one had been built in its place. I went out to the old cellar outside, and it was all fallen in. I went out to the old cowpen, and it was all changed and gone now. I went over the little hill to see the little tank where my father used to drive the team to slake their thirst, and it was all filled up with dirt now and all gone.

Other things change, but God is the unchanging God. Many verses in the Bible say so. In Malachi, the third chapter, the Lord says, "For I am the Lord, I change not; therefore ye sons of Jacob are not consumed" (Mal. 3:6). The only reason they were not burned up and sent on to Hell is because God says, 'I do not change. When I promise, I keep My word.'

* * *

God's Infinite Mercy. I was saved when I was not more than nine years old. Though I was saved so young, I remember a long series of incidents through which God spoke to my heart and convicted me of my sins. I remember the Sunday school lesson when we learned about the baby Jesus' being born in a stable because there was no room for Him in the inn. I was not more than four years old at the time I kept that little pictured Sunday school card and felt guilty in my heart that human beings like me had no room for Jesus!

When I was not more than five I was deeply moved by a song my mother sang, "Turned Away From the Beautiful Gate." I seem to have known that it was by their own sinful rebellion and rejection of Christ that men missed Heaven. I remember some unrest of soul about it. About the same time my mother, after I had told her a lie, talked to me with tears of how God hated a lie, and what a sin it was. The occasion was burned on my memory, and I know that I felt I deserved the just condemnation of God. Surely that was God speaking to me through His Holy Spirit! When my mother lay on her deathbed she talked so of the Saviour as she had us all promise to meet her in Heaven that I felt myself under the spell of her dying smile and testimony until the time I trusted

Christ as my Saviour.

After mother's death I remember the tears and the exhortations of my Sunday school teacher. I remember the godly pastor who told the story of the prodigal son, told how he himself had once been a prodigal, how he ran away from home and came to want and trouble and how he was forgiven on his return. How strange, but it seems that God must have been calling from the first day I knew anything about good and bad, from the first time I ever had a sense of moral responsibility to God!

Oh, the infinite mercy of God's Spirit who strives with men lest we should go to Hell! What condescension! What long continued mercy! Nearly every person in the world who was ever saved can testify that long before he heeded God's call he was dealt with by the Holy Spirit of God who strove with his soul, warning him, urging him to be saved.

* * *

Perfectly Protected

January 1, 1940, I was led of God to leave the pastorate of a beloved church in Dallas, Texas, to enter full-time, nationwide evangelism. I remember with what heartsearching, with what holy dedication I gave myself to God. I pledged myself, at any cost, to help bring back citywide revival campaigns, mass evangelism, in America. I believe that God accepted the little I had to offer, but which I offered with such love and prayer. I believe also that Satan hated my decision and would have gladly killed me.

About that time I was speaking in Chicago, in the Grand Opera House in services at noon, broadcast each day. God saved a good many souls and reached hundreds of thousands of people in those grand early days of the Christian Business Men's Committee of Chicago. One day I drove north on LaSalle Street. As I crossed Division Street, a light and power truck with a large pump mounted in front of the radiator, like a battering ram or deadly weapon, ran around a horse-drawn milk wagon and plunged into the side of my car. It seemed like an engine of destruction aimed by Satan to take away my life. That heavy pump crashed into the left front door of the car and crushed the door in until it rested against my side. The car was spun around on the icy street. It was very badly damaged. But, thank God, the impact which crushed the door in until it rested against my side, left not a scratch, not a blue mark, not a bruise! I was perfectly protected. I felt then and feel now that the angel of God said, "Thus far and no further!" God would not allow Satan to kill His servant.

Another time a beloved friend and his wife, and Mrs. Rice and I took three days off to visit Carlsbad Cavern in New Mexico. As I drove from Dallas to Stamford, Texas, I bought a large beautiful watermelon at Weatherford, Texas; we would eat that watermelon beside the road the next day.

But the next day there were showers of rain from time to time. When at last we decided we would eat the melon, the roadside was muddy. So we four took the melon to the tracks of the Texas Pacific Railroad which ran beside the highway, and there we cut it. We ate all we could hold of its red heart and sat talking of God's goodness. Suddenly I was impelled to look up. Bearing down upon us was a train roaring along perhaps eighty miles an hour. There was no whistle, no warning. I leaped to my feet and pulled my friend to his feet. Startled, he pulled his wife away. My wife sat on the culvert nearby. The train roared by within inches. A half second more and three of us would have been instantly killed. All of us felt then that God had delivered us from a malevolent Devil who hated us. He hated my friend's fight on the liquor traffic. He hated my fight for the return of old-time revivals, my pressure against modernism and sin. But God delivered us. With all my heart I praised God then and praise Him now "who redeemeth thy life from destruction."

*   *   *

A Cry From the Dark. Some years ago our fifth daughter, Joanna, came home in the evening from a school or church engagement of some kind and, to avoid coming in over the freshly painted front porch she entered by a side entrance in the dark. The side door opens on a landing of the basement stairs. Alas, that evening, to take a dryer into the basement, we had removed the upper stairs. And in the dark Joanna stepped off the landing and fell some five feet into the basement blackness.

How my heart was jolted with deepest concern when I heard her cry for Daddy. We rushed to turn on the light and to help her out of the basement. Soon the doctor sewed up the cut in her knee and I comforted her again and again. I was reminded again by the tender concern of my own heart of God's compassion for us, His children. Joanna called for help, and we came at once to help her.

God's Blessing

Money Can't Buy Happiness.
Some years ago after a blessed citywide revival campaign in Buffalo, New York, the pastors asked me to return for a week of services in the interest of Buffalo Bible Institute. They had procured a mansion, a very expensive property on half a city block, in an expensive section of Buffalo. The three-story mansion had bedrooms large enough for classrooms. The flooring was hardwood parquet. The bathroom by each bedroom had silver-mounted hardware. The interior doors were of three-inch thick solid mahogany, imported from Honduras. There was a private elevator. The dean lived in what had been the servants' quarters and said that his home was like a seven-room mansion. The walls of this beautiful building were covered with tapestry instead of wallpaper.

I understand that the big home itself cost a quarter of a million dollars, besides the cost of the half of a city block in downtown Buffalo. So I asked one of the committee who had helped to obtain the new property, "Where in the world did you get $300,000 or so to buy such a property as this?"

"It did not cost us $300,000," he said, "but only a tenth of that amount!"

I wondered how this came about. And he told me that the rich man's wife, for whom he built the beautiful home, had died. When she had been afflicted with heart trouble, he had put in the expensive private elevator; but one day she died. Then his only daughter ran off and married against her father's will. The hungry-hearted man, left alone, found his wealth no better than dust and ashes. He told his agents to dispose of the property, to sell it at any necessary price at once and get the matter off his hands. He never wanted to see the place again!

Oh, there are no pleasures in the revenues of the wicked, but trouble! And men who do not know Christ can never find themselves satisfied with the husks of this world, no matter what money can buy.

* * *

"You Figure It Out for Yourself!" Dear Brother Reveal of the Evansville, Indiana, Rescue Mission was praying in a public service the first week in March 1940, praising God for the blessings of the last twenty-three years. It was the anniversary week and he was overwhelmed at the record of God's blessings, many thousands saved, tens of thousands fed and given beds. Brother Reveal was a great man of prayer and really got things from God. He said in his prayer, "Lord, You have been with us twenty-three years; 8,400 nights we have been open and never closed a night, Lord!" Then he mentioned the souls saved, people fed, the buildings God had provided, the record of the years, and said, "Lord, how wonderful it will be if You will just let us run another twenty-three years for You, stay open another 8,400 nights and days; that will make —"; but when he began to try to figure out how many souls saved that would make, how much work would be done if it were all doubled, he floundered, and finally told the Lord, "You figure it out for Yourself!" and closed his prayer! Well, I laughed in my heart, but how it has blessed me since to remember that only God Himself can figure out the full fruits of our feeble ministry and the blessed rewards He will give! His doing and His giving are so "exceeding abundantly above all that *we* ask or think" that we must let *Him* figure it out for Himself.

* * *

The Goodness of God Brings Salvation. In Fort Worth, Texas, years ago, a young man came to see me in my office. Would I perform the marriage ceremony for him and his sweetheart? I inquired in some detail: Who was the girl? Were they both Christians? Was there anything to hinder a godly marriage?

He was not a Christian, he said, but the girl was a wonderful Christian. He told me, "She is one of the best Sunday school teachers in the First Baptist Church. She is one of the best Christians I know." But he was not a Christian. I solemnly pressed upon him: Was not God good to give him the love of a good woman? Did he not love her partly because she was good, because she loved the Lord? Wasn't that the kind of wife he wanted?

Yes, it was.

Well, then, wouldn't it be wicked for him to go on unsaved, take a woman like that and make her unhappy? Ought he not be a Christian and have Christ in the home and make it a godly home?

At once his heart was filled with the idea that since God was so good to give him the love of such a wonderful young woman, he ought to be a Christian and they ought to have a Christian home. He was wonderfully saved. And they married; but strangely in three months he was taken fatally sick and died. Oh, but how good it was that because of God's goodness to him, he turned and sought the Lord!

* * *

Rich Beyond Expression.

Sometime ago I was thinking about the limited and restricted life of a young farmer I met. He had little education. He was in a provincial community and would probably never be heard of beyond the small community in which he lived. His house was small and plain. His life included hard work and a boresome routine of chores. But then I reflected; he had a wife who was young and beautiful. She was not only radiant in face and beautiful in form, but she was modest, natural, unspoiled. She delighted in her home, her children. Her house was spic and span. She loved her busband with a constant outpouring of service, admiration and delight. Her greatest desire in the world was to make her husband happy.

I looked on the poor young fellow with wife and children and thought, "How blessed he is!" The richest man in the world could not have a more beautiful wife nor rejoice in a love more pure and unselfish and sweet! No king on a throne could have healthier, happier, more beautiful children, nor better taught and better mannered. That young farmer was not poor. He was rich beyond expression. God had flooded his life with "loving-kindness and tender mercies."

* * *

A Righteous Man With a Little.

There were only two or three rooms in that little home in McComb, Mississippi. I met there a good old Methodist couple. We sat in the swing on the porch and talked about the Lord. And when the godly old man, eighty years old, talked about Jesus, he filled up and began to weep and praise God aloud. Then he clutched his heart and said, "This old heart won't take much." I suggested we pray, and he said, "Yes, let's go in here where we always pray." He wanted to kneel down by the same chair. He said, "God's in here." So we knelt down there by the chair where he regularly knelt to pray, and God was there.

That dear old couple didn't need wall-to-wall carpeting. They were happy. They had vines around the front porch, and there was a heavenly sweetness, unseen by the world, around that little unpainted cottage. And how simple were the meals, but the food tasted mighty sweet and good with God sitting at the table and the angels around about them, and where love for each other and love for Christian brethren and love for God warmed their hearts on the coldest winter day. Yes, "A little that a righteous man hath is better than the riches of many wicked" (Ps. 37:16).

* * *

"I Will Serve Him 'Til I Die!"

A man from Rock Island, Illinois, came to visit me as I conducted revival services in Gary, Indiana. We sat in my hotel room. Some two years before, the dear man had heard me preach in Jackson, Michigan. He recently had been widowed and was left in loneliness. The depression and hard times had robbed him of his cherished job. He heard me preach on "Ye Have Not Because Ye Ask Not." He said that that was the first time he had ever heard that it was all right to ask God for a job.

As he sat in my hotel room with his hands upon his knees and with tears trickling down his cheeks, he told me his story. He had prayed and the next day he had gotten a job in the big manufacturing plant where he wanted to work, in the very department he chose and under a foreman whom he greatly admired. Then he had been transferred to Rock Island, Illinois, for a better job. While there he found a little church where he was happy and where he heard the Gospel. He prayed for God to give him some work to do, and God led him to teach an adult class. The church then elected him as assistant pastor. Then he prayed again and God sent an evangelist and a great revival with many, many souls saved. He told me how his whole life was transformed and how his empty heart was filled with blessings. He said, "After all He has done for me, Brother Rice. . ." and he broke into sobs, then continued, ". . .after all He has done for me I will serve Him—I will serve Him 'til I die!"

* * *

Joy From Answered Prayer.

Years ago I was in a citywide revival campaign in Clarksburg, West Virginia. The fundamental, Bible-believing churches that sponsored the campaign were small. The faith and wisdom of those who prepared the campaign were small. We started in the great City Auditorium following the reproach of a disgraceful, so-called revival by cultists, with bribed witnesses to fake healings, etc. A thousand dollars was borrowed for the down payment on the rental on the auditorium. Oh, how we struggled to get out advertising and to build up the crowd. Little by little the crowds increased. There were nights of prayer. There was pleading before God. There was burden indescribable to reach a city calloused and indifferent, and to stir cold Christians and to reach the unsaved. Yes, and a burden, too, to meet the expenses so we could pay back borrowed money, pay the musicians, and come out with victory and a good name.

At last the windows of Heaven

seemed to open. The floodtide came. Wonderful conversions of drunkards! Oh, the deep-settled conviction, the tears, the repentance, and the glad decisions! The crowds came. Soon all bills were paid, and many were saved.

On the closing night, I left my wife and secretary to meet me at the entrance. I walked down across the viaduct to get the car, which, because of the great crowds, had been parked far away from the auditorium. As I walked along in the moonlight my heart overflowed with joy. Before I knew it I said aloud, "Praise the Lord!" It was the joy of answered prayer. Again I said it, louder still, "Oh, praise the Lord!" And then louder still until I caught myself and thought, "I may get arrested! Somebody may think I am drunk!"

Oh, God has a way to happiness: praying in the will of God, getting our prayers answered and then rejoicing about it! A life of joyful answered prayer is the proper lot for every child of God.

* * *

Call for God's Comfort. I
remember a man who had been saved from a life of drunkenness, whose broken home had been restored, who had gone back again to a respected life and a good job, after sin had pulled him down to ruin. Trying to express how happy

and comforted he was, all of his days he said, "Why, I am happier now when I am sad than I used to be when I was glad!"

Healing

Divine Healer Confined to Bed. In some cities these spiritists have what they call "churches." Sometimes these wicked deceivers pretend to be Christians and to teach Christianity. In Dallas, Texas, I once announced to preach in the Galilean Baptist Church on the theme of the devil-possessed fortuneteller and, in a newspaper announcement, promised to show what the Bible had to say about spiritist seances and fortunetelling. A man came to see me and said, "I don't think you ought to run down other churches. My wife is the pastor of the First Spiritualist Church here in Dallas. She sent me to see you." Then he gave me her card. It read about as follows: "MADAME ZELMA, pastor of the First Spiritualist Church, divine healer. Foretells the future, helps in problems of love and business."

I said, "Why did your wife not come to see me personally, if she is pastor of the church?"

He replied, "She is confined to her bed with inflammatory rheumatism and could not come."

She claimed all kinds of miraculous powers, she claimed to be a "divine healer," yet she was confined to her bed with inflammatory rheumatism!

* * *

Seek God First, Before the Physicians. Years ago I was troubled with tonsillitis. Every winter I had a wretched time with sore throat and fever. One can feel so much like dying with tonsillitis, and not be very sick! The family doctor insisted that I should have my tonsils removed, and at last, reluctantly, I consented. A certain day was set for the operation. That morning in my devotional reading I read II Chronicles 16. How startled I was to read in verses 12 and 13, "And Asa in the thirty and ninth year of his reign was diseased in his feet, until his disease was exceeding great: yet in his disease he sought not to the Lord, but to the physicians. And Asa slept with his fathers, and died in the one and fortieth year of his reign." I was not ready to 'sleep with my fathers' so decided I should seek God first, before the physicians.

Immediately I told my wife that I had sinned in settling any matter about my health without a season of prayer. I postponed the tonsillectomy, I went to the Lord in earnest prayer for my throat. Soon thereafter I had occasion to talk to a doctor who was an earnest Christian. He said to me that if I would take his counsel, I would never need to have my tonsils removed. He gave me a diet list; I left off fried foods, fats and sweets and began to use more fruit juices and eat more green vegetables, and I have never had tonsillitis from that day to this!

* * *

Brother J. A. Middleton Is Wonderfully Healed

Near the first of March, Brother J. A. Middleton, an earnest Christian man, and treasurer of the Fundamentalist Baptist Tabernacle in Dallas, was taken seriously and dangerously ill. He was unable to work and was confined to his bed with such agonizing pain that the doctors felt compelled to give him unusually large opiates. Much of the time he was delirious and for long periods he had no recollection of what transpired about him. The pain was so bad that doctors said something must be done at once.

After all medicines had failed he was taken to St. Paul Hospital in Dallas. His physician frankly said, "I do not know what is the trouble." Four other good doctors were called in. Their answer was the same. They did not know where the seat of the trouble was that was causing such violent illness and pain, but all agreed that something must be done at once. They decided that the tonsils should be removed. If that did not settle the difficulty, the optic nerve must be clipped. If that did not stop the pain, they would do something else.

The tonsils were removed. Still the illness was not cured. Recovering from the tonsil operation, Mr. Middleton was brought home, and he was still taking regular injections in the arm, was still under the care of the physician.

On a Sunday night, in March, I was called to Brother Middleton's home to pray for him. He was in such pain that he buried his face in the pillow and rolled from side to side, trying to keep control of himself. I had been praying for him for weeks, while I was in the Oklahoma City revival and after I returned. Many members of the church had been praying. But now all the treatments by the doctors had failed, five of them, the best they had known to consult. Brother Middleton had spent two weeks in the hospital.

It seemed time to get the matter settled with God. So there in Brother Middleton's home we agreed that we would do exactly what the Bible said, "pray over him, anointing him with oil in the name of the Lord," according to James 5:14. Mrs. Middleton, Mrs. Rice and I got down on our knees and confessed our sins to each other and to God. We wanted to fulfill every detail of what God commanded. Remember that James 5:14-16 says:

"Is any sick among you? let him call for the elders of the church; and let them pray over him, anointing him with oil in the name of the Lord: And the prayer of faith shall save the sick, and the Lord shall raise him up; and if he have committed sins, they shall be forgiven him. Confess your faults one to another, and pray one for another, that ye may be healed. The effectual fervent prayer of a righteous man availeth much."

After confessing our sins and quoting God's promise, I put my hands upon Brother Middleton's head and prayed that if it would please and honor Him, He would heal Brother Middleton either without any known medicine, without doctors, or with doctors and medicines—just as He chose—but so that everybody would know that God did it, not the doctors. Then Mrs. Middleton prayed, then Mrs. Rice, then Brother Middleton. We promised God that if He would heal we would give Him the glory and that we would tell about the anointing with oil as well as the prayer of faith which actually gets the healing.

While we were on our knees, God gave us some faith that he had heard our prayers.

After our prayers, Mrs. Middleton said, "I don't want Mr. Middleton to go back to the doctor tomorrow. If he is willing, we will just trust the Lord and Him alone." Brother Middleton answered, "That is just what we will do." After a time of quiet conversation, Mrs. Rice and I went to our home late that Sunday night.

Before we left that night Brother Middleton's pain was a great deal lighter. By the next morning he was better. The next day he did not go back to the doctor. Wednesday came and again he did not keep his appointment with the doctor. The doctor phoned to know why, urging him to come back the next Saturday.

Saturday Brother Middleton went to see the doctor but refused to have an injection in his arm and he had the doctor dismiss his case so he would be free to go back to work.

Brother Middleton had lost twenty-five pounds but he rapidly regained his strength. The following Friday he went back to work. After losing exactly thirty days' work, after a $115.00 doctor bill, after a $150.00 hospital and nurse's bill, losing his tonsils and after almost unbearable pain, God healed Brother Middleton in answer to prayer and following the anointing with oil. I say praise the Lord for answered prayer and for proof that God is just the same, and that the Bible is still up to date!

* * *

Preach or Die! Nearly two years ago Dr. Lee Roberson at Chattanooga had throat trouble. Doctors found a growth on the vocal chords. There was an operation. Then he needed another operation and there came a time when Dr. Roberson could only talk for a little bit and a little above a whisper, I think. And the doctor, sadly, after the second operation, said to him,

"Dr. Roberson, you will never preach again!"

I talked to Dr. Roberson on the telephone and he said, "I would rather die than not preach again."

But God put on my heart this matter so urgently, and I wrote to Dr. Roberson: "Dr. Roberson, I am asking God, like the Christians at Jerusalem, 'grant. . .that with all boldness they may speak thy word,

By stretching forth thine hand to heal; and that signs and wonders may be done by the name of thy holy child Jesus.' " I said, "Dr. Roberson, I need some signs and wonders!" I can't go on preaching unless I have some evidence that God, the God of Abraham and Isaac and Jacob, the God of Peter and Paul, the God of New Testament Christianity is the same today and that He wants to manifest Himself today to His people. So many, many joined, of course, and not my prayers alone but the prayers of many were answered and in August a year ago or two Dr. Roberson announced sermons in his church and since then has been preaching regularly with great power and blessing. And when Dr. Roberson preached he said, "If I never preach again, this is a miracle." But he does preach again and again.

Oh, Christians, in Jesus' name, let us plead with God to stretch forth His hand to heal and "that signs and wonders may be done by the name of thy holy child Jesus" (Acts 4:29,30).

* * *

"Momma, Where Are My Pants?"

When I was a lad of fifteen in the West Texas cattle country, my father fell sick. He had been solemnly warned by a specialist that he must leave all his business cares and rest for months. But since he had a large family to support and debts to pay, he felt that he could not take a vacation. And so he strained himself to the breaking point and collapsed. He lingered for days in a coma, growing steadily weaker. One afternoon the two doctors attending the case warned my stepmother that Dad would not live through the night. The long overstrained heart would stop beating. The light would flicker out that night!

No one had ever argued in my hearing as to whether healing was for New Testament times only, and not for today. No one had ever suggested that that was a dispensational matter, and that God had changed His way of dealing today. I had trusted Christ as my Saviour. I knew that God answered prayer. So that night, after wandering, disconsolate, with no one else to whom I could take my burden, I went out in the horse lot to the stables to pray.

As I passed the buggy shed I heard a voice. Listening, I heard my older sister sobbing in prayer that God would spare our father! I went on in the darkened stable and knelt in a stall, and there I pleaded, unashamed, that God would spare my father and raise him up.

Comforted in heart, I returned to the house, and before I went to bed I heard another voice talking. I listened; it was my stepmother kneeling by the side of the bed where my father lay unconscious. She was crying and asking God to spare her husband. What would all of us have done, a household of a wife and six children, without our father!

I very simply left the matter in God's hand and went to sleep.

My father lived through the night. The next morning at seven, as we were gathered around his bed, he opened his eyes and looked about, rational and in full control of his faculties as he had not been for days. He said to my stepmother, "Momma, where are my pants?"

Laughing and half crying, she said, "You're sick. You don't need your pants. You stay in bed and get well!"

"No, I want my pants. I have some business to attend to in town. Get me my clothes!"

So my stepmother got Dad his clothes, then hurriedly phoned for the doctors. By the time the doctors could catch a team of horses, hitch them to the buggy and drive to our house, my dad had walked two or three blocks to the store, had attended to some matter, and slowly returned. The doctors met him in front of the house and scolded him for being up.

My father said, "No, I am not sick. I will go to bed and rest awhile, but I am not sick any more." He went back to bed until afternoon, and each day for a week or two he would spend some time in bed while he slowly recovered his strength. But God had healed my father. I believe that He did it in a moment. I know He did it when the doctors said it was impossible. I know that God healed him in answer to simple, believing prayer.

* * *

Healed From the Poison of a Spider. In 1926 I was on a daily radio broadcast in Fort Worth. People wrote me about their troubles. A woman bitten by a spider was about to die. The flesh had rotted from the bone and the doctor despaired of her life. The mother wrote and asked me to pray. I did pray and then came the wonderful report that the day I prayed the woman suddenly sat up in bed, said she wanted to dress. She did dress and help her mother prepare the dinner! They looked and found the hole, where before they could see the bone, now beginning to heal. She had no more trouble.

* * *

No Chance to Live, but She Did! In 1931 I was in a tabernacle revival campaign in North Fort

Worth, Texas. One night a young woman asked me to pray for an unsaved young woman friend who was in St. Joseph's hospital near death. She had quarrelled with her husband that day, and then took four bichloride of mercury tablets in a glass of water, and now was expected to die. It had happened that day; she had been rushed to the hospital. We prayed that night; the next morning I was in that Catholic hospital to see her. (In Catholic hospitals it is often much easier to deal with the sick for Christ than in others). First I showed her that she needed a Saviour, and told her I would be willing to pray for her body if first she would trust Christ as her own Saviour. Soon she claimed Him, though desperately sick. Then I read to her God's Word about praying for the sick. When she confessed her sin and promised to do right about her home if God would heal her, we prayed, and I left.

Outside the room I asked the nurse about her chances, and she said the doctor said there was no chance at all. I reminded her that God could do more than men dreamed, and she replied, "But you do not understand; even if the poison did not kill her, the lining of the stomach is destroyed and she could never digest food; she cannot get well."

I went away remembering the red rash over the sick woman's face, her heavy breathing, her humble turning to God, and I continued to pray. The next morning I saw her again, and the nurse said the doctors had decided there was one chance in a thousand. Loved ones had come from Oklahoma to see her before she died. The next time I called, the doctors thought there might be one chance in ten. A day or two later they said there was an even chance that she would live. I went out of town for revival services, and when I returned, found that she was well, had gone home with her father and mother who had come to see her die! I understand that her home was reestablished happily. God does answer prayer!

* * *

The Prayer of Faith Saved the Sick

About 1931 in Fort Worth, Texas, a Mrs. Kelly called me by telephone, asked me if I would go to see a woman, Mrs. Jewel Duncan, and pray for her, anointing her with oil in the name of the Lord. I have her signed statement somewhere. I said that if it were the woman's own request and if she were a Christian I would. I was reluctant about it because I knew the fanaticism that sometimes accompanies praying for the sick. I do not recall that I had ever anointed anyone with oil before, but there it was in the Bible, and I could not explain it away as many do in unbelief. So I agreed.

When I arrived at the home, a sign on the door said, "Do not knock." The nurse was gone, so I stepped inside. In the bedroom lay Mrs. Duncan. I already knew that she was dying with tuberculosis. She had spent two years in the state sanatorium for T.B. patients, and then was sent home to die. Already arrangements had been made to give away the two little boys. Humanly speaking, there was no hope. She resisted the idea of having a preacher pray for her until the last, because she said that was not the way Baptists believed. But the fact that I was a Baptist preacher and that doctors gave no hope at all, led her earnestly to seek the Lord and ask for me, whom she had heard, I think, on the radio, to come to her home to pray for her.

She could barely whisper. I talked quietly about God's power, His willingness to answer prayer whenever it would honor His name, His blessed promises. Then I asked her several questions. 1. Did she know she was saved? 2. Was she willing to confess to God any sins He would bring to mind? 3. If God would heal her would she give her life to Him in consecration, and tell openly what He had done in healing her? To all these she answered in the affirmative. By this time the nurse had come in, and got for me a bottle of olive oil. I put oil upon the sick woman's forehead in the name of the Lord, reminded her that it represented the Holy Spirit who lived in her body and who must heal her if she were to be healed. Then I quietly prayed, sitting by the bed. I felt peace in my heart and went away.

I was called out of town for two revival campaigns. A few months later I spoke in Fort Worth, and after the service among those who came to greet me was Mrs. Kelly. She brought forward a fine looking woman and said, "You know this lady, don't you?" I did not and said so. Then Mrs. Kelly told me it was Mrs. Duncan, for whom I had prayed about six months before. She was the picture of health. She told me she had felt immediately strengthened after I prayed for her, anointing her with oil in the name of the Lord. Within two weeks after that she was up and going about. Now she had been doing all her own housework, her children had been brought back home, she never had another indication of the tuberculosis which after a fight of years' duration had brought her to the door of death. She wept for joy as she told me how strong and well she was.

Four years later I preached in Commerce, Texas; this woman was in the audience and came weeping as soon as I entered the building, to tell me God had wonderfully kept her well. Later she wrote me a lovely letter of testimony, which I still have. God simply kept His Word that "the prayer of faith shall save the sick and the Lord shall raise him up" (James 5:14,15).

*   *   *

Spiritual Music Helps in Holy Decisions. Years ago this evangelist preached in a revival campaign in a town forty miles southwest of Fort Worth, Texas. B. B. McKinney, long music editor of Southern Baptist S. S. Board, blessed and anointed songwriter, led the singing for the services. He and I were guests in the same home. But in the midst of the revival, when great crowds attended and many were being saved, I was stricken with tonsillitis. My fever mounted high, my throat was sore, it seemed impossible to preach. I prayed much and was able to preach that night, but the next day my fever rose high again and my inflamed throat made it seem impossible for me to go on with the revival services. Brother McKinney and the pastor and I prayed together. Then I said to my beloved brother:

"Brother Mac, if you will sing for me I'll trust the Lord and I believe He will give me faith to get well. Sing Paul Rader's chorus, 'Only Believe.' "

McKinney sang it sweetly, and with the blessing of God upon it.

"Sing it again!" I said.

Again he sang,

Only believe, only believe;
All things are possible, only believe;
Only believe, only believe;
All things are possible, only believe.

My heart reached out in faith for God. I said to Brother Mac, "Sing it again, please!" And he sang it again.

Over and over in our room together that good man of God sang the chorus and I prayed. After some long time the blessed Spirit of God gave me assurance that our prayer was heard. And sure enough, before the day was gone my fever was gone also. I went to the pulpit, preached with ease and with great power that night and many were saved, and thank God I was not hindered more during that campaign by my tonsillitis.

This is only an illustration that God's Holy Spirit has an affinity for sweet music and that we ought to use this holy means of grace and means of blessing to stir hearts, to help people to trust in Christ, to help Christians to lay all on the altar.

*   *   *

Diphtheria Healed

In 1926 I began a daily radio broadcast in Fort Worth, Texas. The radio was young then, and in little crystal sets all over the country people eagerly listened for every word that could come out of the magic box, through a horn-like loudspeaker, or more usually through the little earphones on a wired plug. How people listened to the preaching of the Gospel on those crystal sets! My, the flood of letters we received!

Soon people began to write asking for prayer for their sickness. In God's mercy I was led to pray for these distressed sick people, and in many, many cases, God answered prayer. Some of the recoveries were almost instantaneous; a good number were remarkable. I was led to grow greatly in grace and more and more to emphasize the fact that God answers prayer.

One day our oldest daughter, Grace, then five years old, had fever and a sore throat. We gave her medicine. After some three days the fever mounted to 105°. We rushed her to the family doctor. After Dr. Reeves examined her carefully he said, "John, I'm afraid it is diphtheria. But we will not guess about it. We will send germs from her throat to the laboratory in this building."

He swabbed the child's throat with a cotton swab and smeared mucus on a glass slide, then rushed the glass slide to the medical laboratory. In a few minutes the telephone rang; diphtheria germs were present in abundance. The child had diphtheria and the throat was nearly closed.

The child and her little sister were given toxin and antitoxin injections. The county health officer was notified to quarantine our home. We took our little girl home and put her to bed. Then I said to my wife, "I have prayed for others; now I am going to pray for my own. I will kneel by this bed and pray until I have perfect peace that God has heard me. Will you pray with me?"

She gladly joined in our covenant to pray until God gave assurance that He had undertaken in the matter. So I prayed, then she prayed. Then I prayed, and she prayed. We alternated for some time. Finally I said, "I have peace in my heart. I feel that God has heard our prayer. I am willing to leave the matter in His hands and thank Him." Mrs. Rice also had sweet assurance that God had heard our prayer.

That afternoon little Grace's fever went down, down, and then disappeared. She had a good night's rest. The next morning she insisted on getting up, but I told her no, that she must stay in bed. She asked, "Daddy, am I still sick?"

With choked voice I answered, "No, Dear, I think you are well! But we do not want to be presumptuous. We will call the doctor. You must stay in bed until he gives you permission to get up."

"Well, may I sit up in bed, then, and play with my dollies?" she asked. I gave her permission.

The county health nurse came to check. She found no fever, the throat almost normal, no soreness, no pain! She said, "This child does not have diphtheria!"

I replied, "I know she does not have it now, but she did have yesterday afternoon!"

I cherish in my heart and thank God for many memories of answered prayer, many healings of the body. God has healed me and healed my loved ones and healed others many times. So like David I can say, "Bless the Lord, O my soul. . .who healeth all thy diseases."

Heaven

Sinners in Heaven?

That longing to lay down the sword, to have the fight all ended, to earn victory at last, I have expected to be fulfilled in Heaven.

Suppose one fine day I wake up in Heaven and all my loved ones are there. As I settle down to enjoy my wonderful mansion in Heaven there comes a ring on the door bell and I find the Angel Gabriel waiting for me.

"John, get your Bible. The Lord wants to send you out on an evangelistic tour," he tells me.

"Well," I say hesitantly, "I thought I would get to rest with my family now. I thought the fight was all over. But, bless God, Jesus died for me and I will preach for Him a million years if He wants me to." So I take my Bible and get ready to leave with the Angel Gabriel.

Meantime he explains, "Well, all the sinners, you know, are up in Heaven. God was too good to send any sinners to Hell so they are all here and they need preaching mighty bad."

As I go out the front door with the Angel Gabriel, with my Bible under my arm, ready for an evangelistic tour, Gabriel turns and warns me sharply, "Don't ever leave your door unlocked! Remember, every thief, every bum, every crook and burglar that ever lived on earth is in Heaven now. Lock your door!"

Rather startled, I turn and lock the door and Gabriel continues, "And that reminds me, don't you have some lovely daughters?"

"Boy, you ought to see my six girls with their long, lovely hair!" I say.

"Well, don't let them out at night unescorted. They must be warned to keep themselves very carefully. Remember that Heaven is now a city of criminals. God was too good to send any sinner to Hell, and so all those wicked Sodomites who would have raped the angels are now in the streets of Heaven, and every lustful man who ever betrayed and seduced an innocent girl is here, so take good care of your girls!"

By this time my eyes are misty and I am feeling the keenest disappointment. This is not the kind of Heaven I was looking forward to! But bravely, taking my Bible, I start down the street. Here we are interrupted by a funeral procession; for if there are sinners in Heaven, there will be death. We find policemen on every corner because with all the unregenerate sinners who hate God and would not turn to Christ, of course Heaven would be filled with crime unless carefully policed. As we go down the street we pass a great jail, for where sinners are, there must be jails. Soon I hear the cry of a newsboy, *"All About the War! Hitler's War in Heaven, Towns Wiped Out and Now in Flames. Thousands Homeless, Millions Under Arms, Other Millions Dead."* Oh, yes, of course, if God were too good to send sinners to Hell, then Hitler would be in Heaven and with him would be war and murder and misery.

God in Heaven, is that possible? No! Thank God, that is not a true picture. I am sorry that sinners reject Christ and sorry that they must go to Hell, but with all my soul I thank God that one day there will be a place where every wicked, Christ-rejecting sinner will be shut out, and those that love God can at long last have peace, sweet peace!

* * *

How to Spell Heaven! I was having a book published by Moody Press some years ago, *The Soul-Winner's Fire.* Good Dr. Norman said, "Brother Rice, we don't put a capital H in Heaven." I said, "Do you spell Chicago with a capital C?" "Yes." "Do you spell New York with capitals N.Y.?" "Yes." "Do you spell Dallas with a capital D?" "Yes." "Well, let's spell Heaven with a capital H. It is a real place." And so it was done!

* * *

A Nest for the Bird. My father performed a marriage ceremony for a deaf couple, so he had to write notes, and they wrote back the answers. He wrote a note to this young man, "Now you have the bird; what about the nest?" The deaf man wrote back, "I have the bird now, but I have already built the nest." He had already built a home, bought all the furniture and now was taking his bride home to the nest he had already prepared!

Well, the Lord Jesus is not taking me to a barren, unfurnished room up in Heaven, but "in my Father's house are many mansions. . .I go to prepare a place for you" (John 14:2), Jesus said.

* * *

No Goodbyes in Heaven

Years ago I had a letter from Evangelist Mel Trotter, the founder and director of the famous rescue mission in Grand Rapids now called by his name. He wanted me, he said, to come and preach in that great rescue mission where so many thousands had been saved. Well, it was not long thereafter when I went to Grand Rapids to preach in the Mel Trotter Mission, at the invitation of the mission, the Maranatha Fellowship of Christian Business Men, and the Christian Endeavors of the city. I preached in the mission for two weeks, and on Easter Sunday we had two great services in the big city auditorium. But Mel Trotter was not there. Already he had gone to be with the Lord.

I walked reverently into the office where Mel Trotter had planned and prayed and studied and directed the activities of this mission and from which he had gone out to hold great revival campaigns over America, to organize other rescue missions, and to win tens of thousands of souls. And on the wall of the office that had belonged to Mel Trotter, now in Heaven, I saw a motto with these words, as I recall them: "Christians Never Say Goodbye for the Last Time."

And that is truth, blessed truth! I often have revival campaigns where my heart is knit to the heart of some brother and I long to have further fellowship, but the time comes soon to part. Or new converts cling to me, as to a spiritual father, and I love them and brood over them and weep over them and pray for them! But God calls, and I must go up and down the land to win other precious souls.

Some time ago as J. Stratton Shufelt and I closed a great union revival campaign in Huntington, West Virginia, with a "New Converts' Night" on Monday, our hearts were all glad with the blessing of God. They had given us gifts in token of their love. When the service closed they sang, "Goodbye, and we'll be praying for you." Our eyes were all misty. And for an hour and more, they gathered around and thanked God for blessings received during the campaign. Our voices were not quite steady, and tears, half glad and half sad, welled up from our hearts as we shook hands, gave parting counsel and rushed away to the train. *Goodbye! GOODBYE!* It is a word I have to say again and again and again and again! *Goodbye* is a word for this world and fits all the fleeting, changing patterns of our lives; but, praise the Lord, it will not be all goodbyes in Heaven! When Jesus comes, there will be a grand reunion, and the saints of God will rejoice in the fellowship of all the redeemed.

* * *

Let the Lord Furnish the Robe!

It is said that once a king was accustomed to giving each month a great dinner for his lords and ladies. But the poor people who could not dress for the occasion were allowed to come too. The king furnished them with clean white garments so they would be unashamed in the presence of the rich and mighty of the realm.

It is said that one of the lords, with beautiful garments all prepared, in some way soiled and ruined them. He dared not appear in the soiled garment before the king. Then he remembered: "The king provides garments for the poor!" So he entered the palace with the poor people and was furnished a white garment, and ate at the banquet table. The king furnished the robe!

That is the way it is to be in Heaven. All who are to come there must have on the white robe of Christ's righteousness, imputed to sinners. God reckoned Jesus a sinner and let Him die as a sinner. Now God has a right to reckon me righteous and good, since Jesus died in my place and paid my debt. And I have on the robe, thank God!

Hell

Judas, the Traitor Goat.

In the stockyards at Fort Worth, Texas, years ago a packing company had a goat named Judas. He deserved his name, for when he was turned in with each new flock of frightened sheep, he confidently led them through a passage into the slaughterhouse. The unsuspecting sheep followed the goat. Always the goat was spared and sent back to lead others to their doom. But those sheep, blindly following their new friend, Judas, hoping again to find the pasture or meadow, are not so pitiful as sinners who go on to Hell right merrily, feeling confident that with holy water put upon their head they cannot be lost, or with the catechism and confirmation over, they surely are saved, or with confession made to the priest and penance done, the church will surely see to their salvation! Sad, sad it is for religious people to wake up in Hell because they would not come to Christ and did not personally trust Him for salvation.

* * *

No Present on the Christmas Tree. When I was a small boy in West Texas, the entire community would have a Christmas tree at one of the churches. There nearly everybody would bring his presents for children, for parents, for sweetheart, for friends. Those were exciting days. We could hardly wait until the program of songs and "recitations" and speeches was over and "Santa Claus" would begin to read the names on presents taken from the tree one by one and handed out by his helpers to boys and girls. What anticipation! What thrills! I sat many a time hoping against hope. Could that air gun be mine? Was that the ball and bat and glove that I had wanted so long? A thousand hopes and fears made the suspense almost unbearable, and we waited breathlessly each for his name to be called. The packages, mysteriously wrapped, might be

almost anything glamorous and fine!

But my father was poor and we never spent much for Christmas. Year after year I saw the finest presents handed out to others and I waited while hope ebbed slowly away. If the last present was given and my name was not called, then the mock Santa Claus would reach under the tree and get some little bag made of netting, holding hard candy and perhaps an orange, and these would be handed out to any children who had gotten no presents, and sometimes to all alike.

It is a faint picture, I know—for how can one picture the despair of a lost soul? And yet it reminds me of how a poor, doomed sinner must feel when the book of life, God's last witness, is brought out against him and his despairing eyes search those holy pages; and finally with such sadness as none of us can ever know, unless we go to Hell, he must say, "Oh, God! It is not there! My name is not in the book of life!"

* * *

Where Are There No Tracts? A young man about to go out into a night of sin found a tract placed with his hat and gloves, a tract which urged him to turn to Christ. Irritated, he said, "Where in the world can I go that I will not have somebody always giving me a tract! On the street car today someone handed me a tract. Mother leaves tracts on my table. Now here is one in the hall. Where can I go that no one will bother me with a tract?"

His mother sadly replied, "When you go to Hell, nobody will give you a tract there."

*   *   *

A Visit to Hell

I imagine that if the Lord should allow me to go to Hell to interview those who had a chance to be saved, I might there find King Agrippa. Well, he would have no crown, no robe, and no titles. Now he would be only a poor, doomed soul. I imagine that I might say to him in Hell, "Agrippa, what a shock to see you here in Hell!"

And Agrippa might answer, "Yes, just think! I heard Paul the apostle preach! He stood before me with the chains rattling on his wrists as he motioned. His voice trembled with concern as he spoke to me! I remember how his eyes burned and how he forgot all about his chains, all about his own danger, and pleaded with me to be saved. Oh, just think! I heard Paul the apostle preach and still I was never saved, and I came to Hell!"

I imagine that I would meet in Hell Felix, a contemporary of King Agrippa. You remember that Paul stood before Felix, as the scene is described in the twenty-fourth chapter of Acts. Acts 24:24,25 tells us that Felix "sent for Paul, and heard him concerning the faith in Christ. And as he reasoned of righteousness, temperance, and judgment to come, Felix trembled, and answered, Go thy way for this time; when I have a convenient season, I will call for thee."

But when was Felix ever saved? We do not know that he ever was. He trembled as Paul preached of righteousness and temperance and judgment. He said, "When I have a convenient season, I will call for thee." But the convenient season never came. Acts 24:26 tells us that Felix really hoped Paul would give him some money to be freed from prison. But poor Felix, convicted Felix, Felix who was almost persuaded, yet died, we suppose, and went to Hell. Poor Felix, to hear Paul the apostle preach and to tremble before him and promise to hear him again, and yet never be saved! Almost persuaded, I say, is still altogether lost. Millions are in Hell who expected to go to Heaven.

But down in Hell I should meet another man. I imagine I hear him say as he tears his hair in Hell, as he looks wild-eyed about him to his companions in torment: "I tell you I saw Him raise the dead! I saw Him when He cleansed the lepers and sent them away to show themselves to the priest! I ate beside Him. I slept on the pallet beside Him. I heard Him talk to Nicodemus about being born again. You don't believe it? I did! I tell you I did! I was with Jesus. I was one of His twelve chosen apostles. I heard every sermon. I saw almost every miracle, and yet I turned Him down and came to Hell!"

That would be Judas Iscariot. Oh, how his heart must have burned as he heard the teachings of Jesus and saw the miracles of Jesus and looked into those mild, loving eyes and heard the tender tones of that voice! And yet he was never saved! Judas must have been often "almost persuaded," and yet he was forever lost!

* * *

Hell, a Madhouse. Once I was entertained at a ranch home in West Texas. The hospitality was of that cordial and sincere warmth that is proverbial among ranch people. Yet in the case of this Christian man and wife, there was a reserved soberness that hinted at some secret sorrow. Their pastor, when I inquired, told me the story.

They had a son, I believe the youngest boy, now grown, and they loved him as you love your baby boy. He was their pride and joy. In the midst of a summer harvest, he lost his mind. With unfailing love they tended him day by day like a baby. His poor, unbalanced mind conceived a hate for his mother. He fancied that all the family had conspired against him to take his life. They guarded him, waited on him. After the mother had worn herself gray in a few short months caring for him, the poor, demented lad seized a knife one day and would have killed her!

It was the family physician who pressed on them their inescapable duty. "You cannot make the boy happy here. You cannot give him back his mind. You cannot even give him the proper care. There is only one place for him and that is a padded cell, watched by trained keepers, given every attention, until death shall ease his sufferings. There is no hope that he will ever be better." Turning to the father the physician said, "You had better do it now before you let the boy kill his mother."

With broken hearts they saw the wisdom of the doctor's advice and followed it. The arrangements were made, and the sheriff kindly took the insane boy to a madhouse. The father and mother did not love him less. They did not send him there because they hated him. They were inconsolable in their loss. They simply did the only right thing which was made necessary by hopeless insanity. The boy is no more miserable, for anywhere with him would be a madhouse. It was the only way the home could be made safe and have some measure of peace.

God is like that father; He has no choice. If He would do right, He must provide for the safety of His own in Heaven. Incurably wicked sinners who rejected every offer of mercy, trampled under foot the blood of Christ, scorned the Holy Spirit and hardened their hearts; sinners who will not let God change their hearts must be put in the madhouse of Hell, made by their own sin. A loving God gave His Son to keep people out of Hell. If men will not be saved, they must be lost. Those who will not go to Heaven must go to Hell. Sinner, do not blame God if you go to Hell!

*   *   *

Saviour, Yet Judge. It is said that years ago in a Southern city—I think, Houston—down a street a run-away horse clattered with a buggy wildly careening behind it. A young man had lost control and was about to be dashed to his death. A young lawyer jumped from the sidewalk, seized the bridle and held on to the plunging horse until he brought him to a stop. The young man gratefully thanked his benefactor.

Years went on; that young man went into crime. One day he was hailed into court on a charge of murder. He was convicted and the judge who was about to pass sentence was the same young lawyer who had saved his life but who had now become a judge. The young man said to him, "Judge, don't you remember me? You couldn't condemn me to die!" But the judge honestly and sadly answered, "Then I was your saviour; now I am your judge. I can only do what is right."

And there will come a time when the forbearing and long-suffering of Jesus will be turned into wrath on all who would not heed His mercy. There will come a time when those gentle eyes which wept so much over sinners will be piercing and sharp in condemnation. And He will say to them on His left hand, "Depart from me, ye cursed, into everlasting fire, prepared for the devil and his angels" (Matt. 25:41). Yes, Jesus will be the Judge. All the judgment is given to the Son. And every knee must bow to Him and every tongue must confess to Him both in Heaven, on earth and in Hell!

*   *   *

The Sword of Damocles. God is particularly angry with those who knowingly, persistently reject the Saviour. In plain words we have it in John 3:36, "He that believeth on the Son hath everlasting life: and he that believeth not the Son shall not see life; but the wrath of God abideth on him." Oh, the anger of God hangs like a suspended sword of judgment over every Christ-rejecting sinner!

Do you remember the story of the sword of Damocles? Damocles wanted to be king. He felt it would be wonderful to sit on the throne. When his wish was granted, he felt some strange unease. In looking up he saw a great sword suspended by a hair, over his head.

Oh, Christ-rejecting sinner, a sword of judgment, the holy wrath of God, hangs over your head and one day, if you do not flee to Jesus for mercy, it will fall upon you. God is angry with the wicked.

Holy Spirit

He Got What He Asked for! I know that Paul was praying to be filled with the Holy Spirit in Acts 9:9 because that is what he got. Let me illustrate it by the following simple story.

Once in Dallas, Texas, I sat in my study on the second floor of the Galilean Baptist Church. Across the street men were painting a house. Under the hackberry trees that grew outside my window I could see the lawn and the first story of the house. The upper story was hidden by the leafy branches. But I saw a man come around from the back of the house and stand by the front porch and lift his face and his hands as if he were in prayer. He looked up, though I could not see that which he saw. He spoke, but I could not hear his words.

Suddenly from above I saw a ladder descend. He seized it with his hands, laid it on his shoulders and turning, walked around the house and out of sight. The man asked an unseen person for something; I could not hear him, but I know what he said. To the man on top of the front porch he said, "Hand me down the ladder, Bill!" I know that is what he said because he took the ladder and went on his way satisfied. He got that which he requested.

Just so, I am sure that Paul, during those three days and nights when he fasted and prayed, was pleading for the power of the Holy Spirit. He had been convicted under the mighty preaching of Spirit-filled Stephen. He had seen

Stephen stoned to death, but with a face like an angel's, and Stephen's message had pricked his heart ever since. Paul wanted to be like Stephen—filled with the Holy Ghost! And he waited on God until he got the blessing he sought. Then straightway he arose and was baptized and began to preach Christ (Acts 9:17,18)!

* * *

The Holy Spirit Opens a Door. There are a thousand doors to be opened by the Holy Spirit, if we rely upon Him. Once I stepped out of a hotel room in Lima, Ohio, and felt led to speak to the maid who was making up the room next door. As she came into the hall to her cart I said, "Are you a Christian?"

She looked at me strangely, dropped her hands to her side, and said, "No, I am not, but I have been wanting to be for a long time." It was so simple and sweet to win her to the Lord. What if I had not listened to the Spirit's leading?

* * *

Hindering the Spirit of God. In a little town in Southwest Texas, I was in revival services at the First Baptist Church. A young married woman came greatly distressed. She said she feared she was not saved. She had no joy, no happiness, no assurance.

Her husband was astonished. "I know Bessie is a Christian!" he said.

Her father-in-law said, "Why, Bessie is about the best Christian I know. I know she is saved."

But she had no comfort, no assurance.

Then God revealed a secret to her. As I preached earnestly upon soul winning one day, she saw her trouble. When she had lived in the country and attended a country church, she went happily and boldly among her friends and neighbors, winning souls. And God had given her a number of precious souls. But when she moved into the little town, she felt self-conscious and inferior. Surely these town people would laugh at her if she tried to win souls. So when the Spirit of God spoke to her heart she would argue that she was too ignorant, that she dared not be conspicuous. She said, "After awhile the Spirit didn't speak to me any more. After awhile I felt no more impression and leading about soul winning or other duties. It seemed that God had forsaken me."

But when her resistence to the Spirit of God was removed and she confessed and humbled herself and was willing to listen to the Spirit of God and begin again to follow His leading in soul winning, all the joy and the consciousness of God's presence and help came back.

* * *

Filled With the Spirit

In 1936 I drove, with my family, through New York City. We saw many of the interesting sights. We went down to the Battery and saw the Statue of Liberty. We saw the aquarium. We saw Fifth Avenue. We saw Brooklyn Bridge. We went over the George Washington Bridge. We went through the Holland Tunnel. We saw Riverside Drive, Riverside Church, Grant's Tomb, the Little Church Around the Corner, the lower east side—we saw all those things. Then we drove down Wall Street. As I sat looking down that little narrow canyon of a street only two or three blocks long, I choked up, and tears filled my eyes. I said to my children, "There is the financial center of the world." But that was not what I was thinking about. There was the stock market. There were J. P. Morgan's headquarters. The financial center of the world was down that little short block and that little narrow street, but that was not what I was thinking about. I remembered that D. L. Moody came once to seek some gifts for one of his schools. As he visited from office to office, he said, "Oh, my heart was not in the begging for money. I was thirsty for something else!" Down there in that little narrow street the Spirit of God came on him in power, and he was overwhelmed. Somebody with him said, "Are you sick, Mr. Moody? Shall I call a doctor?"

"No! No! Leave me alone! Leave me alone!"

"Well, what shall I do?"

"Don't do anything. Leave me alone!"

"Well, how can I help?"

"Get me in a room, and get everybody out and leave me by myself!"

They put him in a room and he said there the waves of God's power seemed to overwhelm him and overflow him and run over him. Finally Moody said, "Lord, You will have to stop or I will die! I've got all I can hold! God, it is about to kill me!" Later he said, "I would rather lose everything in the world than to lose what I got then!" When he went to preach he said he used the same outlines, he used the same Scripture; the preaching wasn't any different. But where there had been seven or eight saved, now there were hundreds! The difference was in the power! Do you know D. L. Moody's secret? It was not personality. It certainly was not education. He said "ain't." He mispronounced many of his words. He had gone to about the fifth grade in school. What was the secret of his power? He was filled with the Holy Ghost. That was it! That is the Bible term, "filled with the Holy Ghost."

Oh, how God's power came on Charles G. Finney! Soon after he was converted, he would go to meetings and take time off to pray all night, and the power of God would come on him. One time he walked into a mill, and a girl there saw him. She suddenly began to tremble and could not do her work. Then she began to sob and fell down on her knees and began to cry. Other workers felt the power of God so that they could not go on with their work. The unconverted mill owner said, "Everybody stop the machinery. Better have the power of God on us than to have the mill running. Mr. Finney, preach to us." He did, and many were saved. Why? Because the power of God was on him. That is it; the miracle-working power of the Holy Spirit. That is what we need.

That is what R. A. Torrey had. That is what made great soul winners. The power of God is what we need. You cannot explain Billy Sunday with education. You cannot explain Billy Sunday with brains. His sermons were good sermons. Most of them he did not write himself but hired a man to work with him getting material. Then this man helped write out the sermons and Billy Sunday memorized most of them. But even at that, they were not profound. It was not Billy Sunday's brains. It was not education. He had a good personality, but it was not personality. The truth of the matter is, there came a time that when Billy Sunday preached he did not have the crowds, he did not have the power, he did not have people saved. I knew him in those days. What I am saying is that the secret of the great revivals always has been one thing, a supernatural enduement of the power of God on His people. God's people had the power of the Holy Spirit. They were filled with the Holy Ghost. That is the point. I say, that is God's secret for revival.

*　　*　　*

Billy Sunday, Filled With the Spirit. In my book, *The Power of Pentecost,* I have one chapter on "How Great Men of God Were Filled With the Holy Ghost." I found how Moody had told of his enduement with power, and I found the testimony of Torrey and of Chapman and Charles G. Finney. But Billy Sunday was only a high school graduate, and he wrote no books. However, one day while reading Rodeheaver's book, *My Twenty Years With Billy Sunday,* I found what I wanted. Billy Sunday, no matter where he preached or how many times he preached in a campaign, always opened his Bible at one place, to Isaiah 61:1. Then he would put his manuscript and notes on top of the open Bible and preach away. "The Spirit of the Lord God is upon me; because the Lord hath anointed me to preach good tidings unto the meek; he hath sent me to bind up the broken-hearted, to proclaim liberty to the captives, and the opening of the prison to them that are bound."

If some shallow-minded hearer thought that he was moved by the charming stories, the startling colloquial style, or the unpredictable sensationalism of Billy Sunday, Billy himself knew better. He knew "the Spirit of the Lord God is upon me; because the Lord hath anointed me to preach. . . ."

* * *

Bill and Little Bud. Dr. Jack Hyles of Hammond, Indiana, tells how in a strange, cold, formal church where he was asked not to give a public invitation, he preached on the prodigal son. Always, he said, he was accustomed to calling the prodigal boy John and the elder brother Bill, as he told the moving story. But when he came to tell the prodigal's name, he strangely could not think of "John"— instead, he said, "We will call him Bill." Then when he came to the elder brother, he had already used the accustomed "Bill," so he stumbled momentarily, and said, "We'll call him 'Little Bud.' "

Near the close of that blessed story of the prodigal's return, a strange thing happened. A young man suddenly arose, left his seat, went to the back of the church down another aisle, went to an elderly woman, and sobbing they came to the front of the church together. Then relatives from all over the church came to weep, and pray, and to hug the prodigal!

"How did you know?" asked the pastor. "How did you know?"

"How did I know what?" asked Dr. Hyles.

"How did you know that boy has been gone a year, and no one knew where he was till he came in the church today? How did you know his name was Bill? How did you know his brother is called 'Little Bud'? How did you know?"

The answer was that the blessed Spirit of God knew! Oh, to be always led by the Spirit who has the power, who knows all hearts, who holds all the keys.

* * *

Do You Have What He Had? A Spirit-filled soul winner ministered in Philadelphia some years ago and on the golf course two beloved men of God walked with him and talked together of spiritual things. He had preached on the fullness of the Spirit just as I do. He also had preached to the unsaved and God had graciously moved the hearts of sinners to turn to Christ as He had moved Christians to forsake their lukewarmness and earnestly set out to win souls. One of these beloved brethren said to him, "I do not believe in all you have said about the Holy Spirit but I surely believe in what you have!" Do you have what the great soul winners have?

* * *

Keep on Waiting. I wonder if you are thirsty enough for God's power to keep on waiting until He fills you.

In 1941 a young couple were deeply in love. The young man was called to the Army, but the young woman who loved him promised to wait for him. He was soon sent overseas. The war raged on and on. The weeks became weary months, the months became dragging years! Her letters became cooler, less frequent. Then she wrote him that "it was all a mistake." She sent him back the ring. She was not willing to wait longer and had fallen in love with another man. When the soldier returned, the girl he loved, the girl who had promised to wait, was another man's wife!

Are you willing to wait on God until He fills you with the Holy Spirit?

* * *

"No Substitutions, Please." In a restaurant I saw these words on the menu, "No substitutions, please." With pork chops one would have apple sauce, cole slaw, mashed potatoes and coffee. With roast veal one would have sage dressing, green peas and combination salad, with coffee. If one ordered a certain entree, he took what came with it, with no substitutions. And about this matter of the fullness of the Holy Spirit, God says, "No substitutions, please!" You say that you want to be filled with the Spirit. All right, God says that the fullness of the Spirit brings an enduement of power from on high so that you will be a witness, a soul-winning witness. Do not ask for substitutions! Do not ask God for the fullness of the Spirit and expect sanctification, or tongues, or a selfish enjoyment of an "experience."

* * *

Prayer in the Spirit. In Ephesians 6:18 we are commanded, "Praying always with all prayer and supplication in the Spirit. . . ." So when we pray, we should let the Spirit of God join us in prayer and guide us in prayer, then we can learn to pray in the will of God.

I was once in the home of a pastor in Kansas. They were so glad to have me. We had supper and after awhile at bedtime the family gathered around and the good father read the Bible, then we got down to pray. Everybody in the family knelt down. Then the father prayed, then the mother, and the young people, then I prayed. A five-year-old boy prayed the most wonderful prayer. The father knelt down and with the little one in his arms—that five-year-old boy—he said, "Now, you pray." And the father gave a sentence and the little boy repeated it; another, and the little boy repeated it. The prayer went something like this: "God bless Daddy and Mother, and help me to be a good boy, and help me to understand the Bible,

and help me to grow into a good man," and so on. The father gave him every word.

That is the way the blessed Holy Spirit does. When I kneel to pray or bow my heart in prayer, the blessed Holy Spirit puts His arm around me and puts words in my mouth and in my heart and helps me to pray. And He helps you to pray. Blessed Comforter and Teacher and Guide and Companion, the One who protects us and intercedes for us and prays with groanings that cannot be uttered.

*   *   *

"Mister, Did He Really Get the Owl?"

A businessman advertised for an office boy. A number of applicants appeared, and he sat down with the boys and told them a story something like this:

"Boys, I am going to tell you a story. When I am through, you can ask me any questions that you like. Then I will try to pick out one of you for my office boy.

"Once a farmer had been greatly troubled by the loss of his chickens. Each night some wild creature got in the open door of his henhouse, killed a chicken, and carried it away. The farmer resolved to catch the intruder. So, loading his shotgun and lighting his lantern, he waited in the night for the first squawk of a chicken in fear. When the noise began, with lantern and gun he rushed to the chicken house. But he had trouble. First, the light in the lantern went out in the wind. He held it inside his coat, and finally lighted it, after many trials. His dog was barking furiously. Rushing toward the commotion at the chicken house, the farmer stumbled over the pig and sprawled headlong on the ground! Retrieving his lantern, he put his head in the door of the chicken house and held the lantern aloft. A frightened rooster squawked and leaped first to the farmer's bare head and then out into the night. But in the light of the lantern the farmer saw the nocturnal prowler. A large wood owl held one of his hens with claw and beak. Setting down the lantern, the farmer blazed away with his shotgun. He accidentally pulled both triggers and both barrels of the gun went off at once. The recoil of the gun knocked him over backwards. The heavy load of shot killed three hens and blew a hole in the side of the chicken house. The farmer's dog barked excitedly and neighbors from all sides began to arrive to see what had happened.

"That is the end of the story. Now, boys, are there any questions you want to ask?"

One boy asked, "Were the chickens white leghorn chickens?"

Another boy asked, "What was the name of the farmer's dog which was barking?"

Other boys asked about the neighbors, about what time of night it was, about the farmer's name. And as they asked questions, one little fellow got more and more concerned. Finally he piped up with this question, "Say, Mister! Did he hit the owl? That is what he started to do; Mister, did he really get the owl?"

Strangely and sadly, people read the marvelous second chapter of Acts and have their minds all absorbed with speaking in tongues, with the origin of the church, with a supposed new dispensation, with some theory of sanctification, or some other matter of relatively minor importance; never noticing, many times, whether the disciples got that for which they were waiting on God—the power of the Holy Spirit to help them carry out the Great Commission! And it is said that the businessman hired the office boy who could keep his mind on the main business at hand and look for the principal result. How sad it is that God's people are divided on a lot of secondary matters and so have missed the great principal point that God has for us in the events at Pentecost!

* * *

A Definite Enduement of Holy Spirit Power Essential of Soul-Winning Preaching. Evangelistic preaching must be preaching with a definite enduement of Holy Spirit power. Let me tell you now, magnetism won't do it; personality never saved a soul; psychology never saved a soul. All the shenanigans, tricks, and wire-pulling will never save a soul.

I read an article by a man who was lamenting that in these days we can't have revivals, that there is a great falling away. He said: "You know we had so many preachers here: we had chalk talks, motion pictures, special music, all those, and yet we didn't get but about fifty people saved." They didn't have a musical saw at Pentecost, but 3,000 people were saved. John the Baptist didn't wear a cowboy suit and bring a long lariat into the pulpit. That is not what won them. Elijah didn't set out to Mount Carmel with a boy prodigy who could play an accordion. It takes more than these incidentals, more than cowbells, and tricks, and solos. *It takes the fire of Almighty God!* Nobody is going to win souls and have a revival, unless he has an anointing from God.

* * *

A Soul Winner's Joy. In Toronto, after I had preached one night to a tremendous crowd and some fifteen adults had come weeping to trust Christ as Saviour and had gone into the inquiry room for further instruction, I stepped out of the pulpit as the great crowd filling the building filed out so that hundreds of others could come in for a second service. A man stepped up to me to ask, "Brother Rice, have you been baptized with the Holy Ghost?"

I told him that by God's loving mercy I had some measure of the breath of Heaven upon me, the fullness of the Spirit. I told him it would be folly and presumption for me to suppose that human education or any human talent or human industry had resulted in tens of thousands who had come to Christ under my ministry.

"I didn't mean that," he said. "I mean have you talked in tongues?"

I replied that I had talked in the English tongue, the tongue that people could understand, and that God had blessed it, and that I had not sought nor had I ever had any jabber in some language I did not know and which would do no one any good, nor did I understand that we were commanded to seek such.

"Oh, but you don't know how happy you would be if you just turned everything loose and said things you didn't understand or know anything about," he said.

And with deep emotion I answered him. "If God will just give me enough sinners coming down the aisles, turning to Christ, and if I can see enough drunkards made sober, enough harlots made pure, enough infidels made into believers, enough sinners made into saints of God, that is all the happiness and joy I ask for!"

* * *

Listen to the Spirit of God. I was on the platform in a revival at Sherman, Texas. The song service was just beginning. A great crowd had assembled. I felt led to leave the platform and as I walked down the aisle, the Spirit of God said, "That's the man." I stopped, put my hand on the man's shoulder and asked, "Are you a Christian?" He began to sob as he answered, "No, I am not. No, I'm not. But I ought to be." And in a moment he got saved.

In that same revival I walked down the aisle one night and asked a man as I passed by, "Are you a Christian?"

"No, I am not."

I said, "Then you ought to be ashamed of yourself. Living in a land where you have heard the Gospel and you are not a Christian," and I walked on.

Two years later I went back to Sherman. That man came to me in the service and said, "Do you remember when you got me, Brother Rice?"

I said, "No; tell me about it."

"Remember when you walked down an aisle and put your hand on a fellow's shoulder and asked him, 'Are you a Christian?' I was not. Then you said, 'Then you ought to be ashamed of yourself,' and you left me. I went home mad, but conscience-stricken. I couldn't get away from those words, so I settled the matter. I have already joined the church and have already been baptized."

It is not hard to win souls. If you will listen to the Spirit of God and do what He says, there are plenty of people you can win. Go after them! Go after them! Go after them!

The Home

Did He Raise His Boy Right?

As a pastor of a country church years ago, I preached on the subject of a Christian home. One man, a member of the church, came to me with a good deal of indignation and said, "Pastor, you must go home with me." At his insistence I finally excused myself from others with whom I had agreed to visit, and went to his home. There he said to me, "Pastor, I do not believe what you preached this morning. It simply isn't so!"

I answered back, "What is there I preached that isn't so?"

"It is simply not true that if you train a boy right he will not leave the right way after he is grown. I know I did raise my boy right!"

After a good deal of inquiry, he finally sadly admitted to me that his boy was in the Texas Penitentiary at Huntsville. I said to him, "Now that you have made an issue of it and have denied the statement of God's Word on this question, answer me this: Did you raise your boy right?"

He insisted that he did, but I pressed the matter, "Did you ever have family worship in your home?"

"No," he said. They had been busy people, working on the farm and never had time for such things like some city people did.

"Did you try to win your boy to Christ when he was small and you had influence over him?" I asked.

"No," he said, "I never did believe in begging little children into the church and overpersuading them."

I showed him what the Bible taught about it. "Suffer the little children to come unto me, and forbid them not: for of such is the kingdom of God" (Mark 10:14). I showed him the command in the Bible, "And thou shalt teach them diligently unto thy children, and shalt talk of them when thou sittest in thine house, and when thou walkest by the way, and when thou liest down, and when thou risest up" (Deut. 6:7).

Then I asked him, "Did you whip your boy and make him obey when he was at home?"

He answered, "See here, Preacher; you cannot treat all children alike. My boy was a nervous, high-strung boy, and he couldn't be punished like others could. It would just make him worse instead of better."

And then I honestly and faithfully told this father that he himself had sinned and that his boy was in the penitentiary because he had not followed the plain commands of God's Word about chastening his son and training him in the way he should go.

* * *

Influence Your Child for Christ. I remember in a revival campaign a lovely, bright, ten-year-old girl who was unconverted. I spoke to her mother about it. The bright child was in the fifth grade. But the mother said, "I want her to make up her mind for herself. She thinks everything I do is wonderful. She would do anything to please me, so I do not want to overinfluence her about this."

I asked her, "If she were a thief, would you not do anything to see that she learned to be honest? If she wanted to drink whiskey, would you let her make up her own mind about that? If she decided to be a harlot, a prostitute, would you leave it to her to make up her own mind? Why does God give a mother influence over a child if not to use it to get the child to Heaven? You must answer to God for your daughter."

The next service the mother and daughter both came weeping, the girl trusting Christ at her mother's insistence.

*   *   *

What Intimate, Sweet Relation of a Child and His Father

My mother died before I was six years old, so for some years my father had to be both father and mother to me. Nearly five years later my father married again—to a lovely young woman—and it was not her fault that she could not suddenly replace the mother so long mourned.

I remember times when I was sick with whooping cough and measles and typhoid fever. Traditionally, a woman's hands are thought to be tenderer than the heavy hands of a man: it was not so with my father. How delicate and gentle were his cool hands upon my forehead when I was sick! And I remember that, pushing aside the well-meant ministrations of the good woman who kept house for us four motherless children, my father personally went into the kitchen to prepare a little soup or poach an egg or toast a biscuit. And how gentle and understanding he was when I was sick at my stomach! And he held my head and then washed my face and patted my pillow.

In a big family there were often times when there was company, and some of us children would need to wait for the second table, of course. And we would argue for the privilege, then, of eating out of Dad's plate— and it need not be washed! I remember a holy reverence for my father and how I would kiss him good-night until I was fifteen years old, and then I grew ashamed to express the affection that I felt.

And I remember the time when we were very poor, and Christmas came on. There were six of us children at home. The times were hard, hard—and Dad had heavy debts to pay. He told us plainly that we would have to be content without Christmas presents. He felt we simply could not spend any extra money. We would love one another and have Christmas in our hearts, but he could not afford any presents.

We could not imagine that our father would not some way provide; so, despite his warnings, all of us hung up our stockings on Christmas Eve— hung them around the mantel! And after we were all in bed, my father went down to the home of the owner of the general store, had him get up in the night and go to the store so my father could buy on credit the oranges and apples and candy and little trinkets that would make a happy Christmas, he thought, for his children!

Well, my father and every earthly father has limitations in his ability and resources, but my Heavenly Father has none. But as this intimate sweet picture of a Heavenly Father is the proper approach to prayer, oh, then, let us come boldly, happily, to pray and say, "Our Father which art in heaven. . . ."

* * *

Daddy and the Baby. I remember once when I came in from revival services—and of course that meant taking the lead in the family devotions. At the table the baby always sat by me, and now Joy was the baby. She said, "Daddy, will you please cut up my meat?" And Mrs. Rice said, "Honey, Daddy has been gone so long, and he is tired! Now let Daddy eat in peace; I'll cut up your meat."

But Joy said, "No, Mother, Daddy will cut it up. He likes to!" And I did like to; so I cut up her meat.

She was about eight years old. At bedtime it was Daddy's place, of course, to come and kneel with her by her little bed, in the room next to ours, and have part in the goodnight prayer. She said, "Now, Daddy, shall I pray, 'Now I lay me. . .' or shall I pray, 'Our Father which art in heaven. . .' or shall I just make up my own prayer?" Well, I suggested that we would first pray together, "Our Father. . . ," and then we would each make up our own prayer. And so we did.

She had a right to pray that prayer, for she had already been converted; she was a child of God and she knew it.

Oh, how wonderful that the most ignorant and the most untaught and timid new convert has a perfect right to come straight into the throne room of his own Heavenly Father and ask for what he wants and what he needs.

* * *

Always Have Thanks at Meals. We ought to take time to thank God. You don't know how much that means. It somehow makes a concept of life that is proper. When I was pastor at First Baptist Church in Shamrock, Texas, Grace, my oldest daughter, was just a little thing about four or five years old. Mother said, "Lunch is ready. Come to the table." I came to the table, but Grace had to go wash her face. She had the idea of washing your face without getting it wet, which is pretty difficult! She would dip the tips of three fingers in the water and shake the water off and get a little spot on her cheek and go around and around. It takes a good while to wash your face that way!

Finally Mrs. Rice said, "Let's go ahead and return thanks. She'll get here when she can."

So we had thanks. After a while Grace got to the table. So I said, "Honey, do you want some potatoes, nice potatoes?"

"Daddy, we didn't pray."

"Yes, we did, Honey, before you got here. Would you like some potatoes?"

"Daddy, we didn't pray."

"Yes, we did, Honey, before you got here. Would you like some potatoes?"

"Daddy. . . ." And her lips began to quiver. "Daddy, we didn't pray."

I said to Mrs. Rice, "She ought not to eat without praying, and we will never leave the children out from this time on."

You had better thank God every time you eat. You had better teach your children to thank God for everything good they get.

* * *

"Chasten Thy Son While There Is Hope." The Scripture says in Proverbs 19:18, "Chasten thy son while there is hope, and let not thy soul spare for his crying." Chasten thy son while there is hope. When? While he is young. Begin in time. How soon should you whip a little child? I don't know.

I wonder, Dr. Lee (Dr. R. G. Lee was in the audience), did you know B. B. Crimm? You surely did. He was a Texas cowboy evangelist. I don't say this is authoritative; I am giving one good man's opinion, but B. B. Crimm said, "Personally I don't think you ought to whip girl babies as early as boy babies. I don't think you ought to whip a girl until she is three weeks old! A boy you can begin on as soon as he is born!"

* * *

The Day I Got to Be a Grown Man. I wanted my first baby to be a boy, then grow up to be a quarterback at Baylor University, then a preacher, an evangelist. So I ordered a boy! But they were all out of boys and sent me a girl! Then I ordered another boy, but they were still out of boys and sent me another girl! I kept on ordering boys until I had a house full of girls. I used to be partial to boys, but I know when I am licked! I am now partial to girls! When the first baby was born, I sent telegrams to all the kinfolk. When the other girls were born, I sent a post card when I got around to it!

But when the first baby was born I thought, "That beautiful little thing!" You will forgive me—I still think so. There never was a baby as pretty. When they laid that little 6¾-pound baby in my arms, suddenly I think I became a grown man. I began to feel, "O God, a little body to feed and clothe!" I guess if I had known what I know now—all the nylon stockings, all the piano lessons, all the college tuition, all the church weddings—I would have fainted instead! But I said, "A little body to feed and clothe! A little mind to train for God and Heaven, and an immortal soul for Heaven or Hell!" I thought, "O God, help me to walk straight!" I think I got to be a grown man the day they put that baby girl in my arms.

* * *

The Father in the Home. A man in the home is a picture of God the Father. Little children come along and have hero worship. I thank God for something wonderful that was built into my character by my old Southern father, and for the hero worship I had for him. My dad was the smartest man in the world, I thought. After I was grown, and was a football tackle, and a broncobuster, and was in the United States Army, and all that, my dad could handle me. The truth is, he had a bluff on me. That is all. My dad was somebody, a real man. And I believed in my dad with that hero worship that is proper and natural for little children toward their father.

Jesus said when you pray say, "Our Father which art in heaven." The best picture little children ever have of God is their own father, if he be a godly man. Oh, men, you had better watch! God intended for you to take that responsibility.

* * *

Family Worship and Prayer. In my home we felt that the best time for family worship and prayer was following breakfast. At night some were out late and could not take part regularly. The little girls were sleepy. All needed the help the blessed service brought, before the tasks and trials of the day. Before breakfast it interfered with serving hot food. So after breakfast, as the last one finished there was long, until the last girl left home, the cry, "Girls, get your Bibles!" In a moment they were open at the chapter that came next after yesterday's reading! We read consecutively, a chapter a day, through a book. First I read two verses, and around the table each one read two verses. That was repeated till the chapter was finished. Some extra long chapters were cut in two. Sometimes two or more short Psalms were read. Then we had comments, questions, or a chorus, or memorized a verse. Always I led in prayer, then each one prayed in order, around the table. When I was away from

home, as I was much of the time, Mrs. Rice carried on. How sweet, how blessed was that time of prayer and Scripture together! I know it has made its imprint on the tender hearts of my six daughters who are now all married. They will never get away from its reality and influence.

* * *

"Daddy, Cut That Off." I remember some years ago, Dr. Joe Macaulay came to see me at Wheaton. He was then pastor of the Wheaton Bible Church. He came to talk to me about holding revival services in the Wheaton Bible Church. We sat out on the back steps. The young people were playing croquet on the lawn. Joy, my baby girl, was then three years old. She was nearby, and she found a crooked piece of cardboard. I sat on the porch steps, whittling and talking to Dr. Macaulay about this revival. The other folks left us alone. It was a pretty important time. I did not have much time at home, and the good pastor had come to see me. We were planning and praying and talking about the revival, and what we would do about it. My little baby came up with this little bit of a cardboard. She had figured out that one end of it was not square. She held it out there like she wanted it. She held it out to my hands and interrupted our conversation. She said, "Dad-

dy, cut that off." I stopped, took my pocket knife and cut it off so as to make the thing square like she wanted it.

She said, "Thank you, Daddy," and went on about her work. I turned to Brother Macaulay and said, "Any time I want anything, if the Lord God of Heaven and earth is having a conference with all of the archangels, I am going to butt in and say, 'My Father, will You do this for me?' And He will do it!'" I have a right to come to my Father. I am born of God, a child of God, inheritor of all the blessings from God.

* * *

The Joy of Children. In God's mercy, I have been given six daughters. I loved them passionately when they were little children. If possible, I love them more now. Not one of them but that I sometimes bathed and usually fed when I was at home, corrected them, entertained them, taught them. The baby's high chair was always by me at the table. I carefully drilled them so that the first consecutive sentence each could say would be, "I love Daddy." One of them always, when I carried her, held on to my ear which is big enough for a good handhold! Another always held on to my tie. Now the youngest is twenty-two. A few years ago I said to Mrs. Rice, "I have been accustomed for twenty years to having a little girl in my arms, holding to my ear or to my tie, or spitting down my back, or spilling milk on me at the table. I need a baby!"

That hunger is now partly fulfilled by grandchildren. But I can speak on good authority when I say that any man who has had the tiny hand of a baby gripped around his finger, a little face looking up into Daddy's and asking questions and believing every answer was gospel truth, little feet running to meet Daddy when he came home at night, and little arms around his neck and warm wet lips kissing his face in greeting, has worn the crown of a king! Oh, the crowning glory and the lovingkindness and tender mercy that God gives every man to whom He gives faithful and sweet children!

* * *

Blessed for His Father's Sake

After my father died, my brother Bill lived for a time in West Texas with my sister who taught school there. He decided to go back to Decatur to college. He had no money. He rode his gray mare. The miles were long. He had no money to buy food. He would expect to sleep somewhere in a haystack at night. Maybe somewhere he could get a handout. As he rode along he became rather bitter. He had tried to live right. He had tried to listen to his father's instructions. It did not seem to have paid off. What would he do?

He rode on without the noonday meal. As evening approached the sky grew dark with clouds. It was going to rain. He stopped at a house beside the road and called. A man came to the door. My brother said, "It is going to rain. Could I sleep in your barn tonight?"

The man said yes if he would not smoke, would not use matches, he could sleep in the barn. Then the man said, "What is your name?" And he answered, "My name is Bill Rice. I am going to Decatur to college."

The man said, "Rice? Rice? Are you any kin to the late Senator Will Rice from Decatur?"

"Yes," Bill said. "I am his son." The man immediately called his wife. "Set the supper back on the table. Here is the son of Will Rice! I want you to meet him." He unsaddled the mare and fed her. They washed on the back porch and Bill sat down to a good supper. A bed was made for him on the front porch in the dry. Before they slept this godly man prayed and thanked God they got to meet the son of Will Rice.

The next morning he woke Bill up early. Breakfast was ready. He would want to get on his way. Before they left he told Bill a story.

Years before in hard times he had been about to lose his farm. He couldn't raise any money. The mortgage was about to be foreclosed. And my father had gone to the bank and arranged for a loan. The farm was saved. Then my father had taken time to tell the man he needed more help than money. He needed Jesus Christ. The man and his wife were saved. They had raised godly children and they had all gotten farms nearby. Now how glad he was to do something for the son of Will Rice who had helped him so greatly years before!

Oh, I say, children are often blessed for the sake of their fathers!

* * *

The Results of Stripes. Every good parent grieves when he must punish a child painfully. The old saying, "This hurts me more than it does you," has been joked about a great deal, but it is a tearful and sad fact known by multitudes of fathers and mothers who honestly punish their children as the Bible commands. To do what the Bible commands is not easy, but it is certainly profitable and happy in its fruits.

I never will forget the first time I whipped one of my children until blue marks appeared on her fat little body. She had been stubborn and rebellious and I had to spank her several times for the same thing before I got results. Eventually I did the job so thoroughly that she surrendered and obeyed me, though my own heart was torn and grieved beyond expression. I could not keep back the tears later when I saw the tiny stripes or marks left by my spanking. Since that time she has left black and blue marks a hundred times on her body in her play, but no other marks ever did her so much good!

* * *

The Image of God. I remember with joy the reverence I had for my own father and my unbounded trust in him. I felt he was about the bravest man who had ever lived. I asked him the most unheard-of questions, and I took, without a grain of doubt, his answers as being absolute truth. When my father sometimes said, "I do not know, Son," I had a feeling that if he would think awhile on the matter or give it a little attention he soon *would* know. If my father said a thing was right, I felt it was right; if he said it was wrong, then certainly for me it was wrong. I thank God that I have had few occasions even yet to believe my father was essentially wrong, now that he has been in Heaven a number of years. In his affection, in his providing, in his punishment of our sins, in his kindness, in his counsel, my father was to his eight children the best earthly image we ever saw of God.

* * *

Children Are Often Blessed of God for Their Father's Sake

How often we find statements like this in the Bible: God blessed Rehoboam for David his father's (his ancestor's) sake. When Jehoram went wrong, God would not take the kingdom of Judah from him for David's sake.

Oh, a son may be blessed for his father's sake!

I grew up in the cattle country of West Texas. The village school had sometimes only two and sometimes three teachers for all the grades, from first grade through high school. So we had no high school graduation. We went as long as there was something to be learned. And then I got books and studied and took a teacher's examination, got a second grade teacher's certificate, then I studied more and went back to the county seat and took examinations and got a first-class teacher's certificate.

When I first went to Archer City, Texas, the county seat, to take my teacher's examination, when the morning session was done I found waiting for me Judge Walker, a prominent, good man. He must take me to his home. His horse and buggy were waiting. I felt embarrassed, but nothing would do but that I should go for the noon meal at his home. I went. And the judge insisted I must make this my home these two or three days I was to be in Archer City. I protested but the family would not take no for an answer.

It was a lovely home. The table linen was so white and the silver gleamed, and the manners in the household were beautiful. I was not accustomed to such luxury. And the judge must personally drive me to and from the courthouse for every session! Nothing was too good for me.

I was grateful, but I wondered. I did not know till later why the judge had taken me to his heart and so wonderfully cared for the rather naive and poor country boy.

But I learned the secret. Once my father had been in Wichita Falls and there he saw on the street a tramp, a bum, with unkempt beard and shaggy hair and dirty clothes. My father recognized him. He said, "Bruce Walker, what are you doing here!" And Bruce told a sad tale. He had gone to Wichita Falls for a brief time. He had gotten drunk and spent his money. And then his clothes were so soiled he could not get a job. He slept in alleys. He got a handout where he could. He was ashamed to go back home, not wanting his distinguished father and his cultured sister to see him as a poor bum.

My father took him to a barber shop where he had a bath and a shave and a haircut. He took him to a clothing store and bought new clothes for him. He took him to the railroad station and got a ticket for him and put him on the train to go back to his father in Archer City.

The months went by, and Judge Walker had a chance to do for my father's son a little bit in appreciation for what my father had done for his poor, prodigal boy.

Oh, children get many blessings from God because of their godly fathers!

*   *   *

The Oldest Institution. The home is the oldest of all human institutions. Before there was any government, God started a Christian home. Before there was a school, God started a home. That isn't all. Before man ever sinned and got out of the presence of God, God made Adam and Eve together. And God performed the first marriage ceremony. And God made a woman out of a man's rib and He brought her to Adam.

Adam said, "Wow! Lady, you are the prettiest girl I ever saw." (She was. I know!)

I think she said, "Big boy, I'd rather have you than anybody else in the world." (There wasn't anybody else!)

They loved each other. They slept on beds of rose petals. Roses didn't have any thorns then. Animals were all friends then. And if there were mosquitoes, they just joined the symphony orchestra. They did not go around with hypodermic needles puncturing anybody. God, in the Garden of Eden, started man with a home. Home is precious.

*   *   *

"If I Had Only Heard Him Pray One Time!" In a sad funeral at Dallas, Texas, when the brief service came to a close and the undertaker shut the family and me, the preacher, in the small alcove with the open casket for a few moments that they might say their last goodby to their loved one, a young man, twenty years old, cried unconsolably over his dead father's body. "Oh, Brother Rice," he said, "if I had only heard him pray one time! He said he was a Christian. I guess he was—I don't know. But, oh, if I had only heard him pray!" I joined in the sadness that young man felt. How desolate he would likely feel if he had no better evidence of his father's salvation, than that he had one time, somewhere, made some kind of a profession, but had never had thanks at the table, had never prayed with nor for his children. "I never heard him pray!" What a sad thing to say over his father's casket!

* * *

The Prayers of a Country Mother

We do not know how many of the blessings God showers upon us because of the godly lives and the believing prayers of our fathers and mothers and of others who pray!

In early 1921 I was a teacher in Wayland Baptist College at Plainview, Texas. On a week end I visited my mother's baby sister, Aunt Essie McLaughlin in Amarillo. She was beautiful, gifted and good. We sang together and talked of many things.

As I opened an old book in her home a letter fell out. "Do you want to read that letter?" she asked.

As I began to read it she asked, "Do you know who it is from?"

"It looks like Mamma's handwriting," I answered. "I have seen some of her love letters to Dad." Sure enough, it was.

My mother had been dead twenty years. But the letter had been written when I was barely five, when we lived in Southwest Texas, below San Antonio. It was a voice from the dead come to comfort my heart and to bring me a message from God.

"It is very hot down here now," my mother wrote to her sister. "We have had no rain in months and the crops are not good. Willie is not very well [Willie was my father]." Then she began to speak of her children. "You should see Baby Porter now. He has his first little teeth and is so sweet. And Gertrude is a great help. She minds the baby and dries the dishes [Gertrude is my older sister, Mrs. R. C. Nutting, now of Murfreesboro, Tennessee]. Ruth is the quietest little thing," she continued. "She is never ruffled but is always in a good humor. But George is into devilment from morning till night. [George, my younger brother, went Home to be with the Lord not long ago. He was a high school principal, a fine Christian, though a mischievous child. And Ruth is a gifted teacher.] And let me tell you what my little preacher boy did. . . ," my mother wrote on.

I stopped reading, suddenly startled. My mother had already named

Baby Porter, George, Ruth and Gertrude. I was the only child left.

"Did she call me her preacher boy, Aunt Essie?" I asked.

"Of course she did. She never called you anything else!"

I was deeply stirred. Later when I went to Decatur, Texas, and saw my father, I told him what I had read and asked him to explain it to me.

"When you were born," my father said, "we were both so glad to have a boy to be a preacher. God had given us a lovely girl. But we wanted a boy to be a preacher. So the day you were born, your mother and I gave you to God and asked Him to make you a preacher."

"But, Dad, why didn't you tell me? I feel like I have wasted so much time!"

He replied, "I wanted God to tell you."

God soon did. Soon it became clear that I would never have any peace or ever meet the destiny God had for me except as I should preach the Gospel. And He knows how gladly I gave myself to this holy business of preaching the Gospel.

*　　*　　*

"I Don't Believe You Will Listen to Me." I had a letter some time ago from New York State and a man said, "Our daughter, fifteen years old, is breaking our heart. I am really her stepfather but I love her. At fifteen she suddenly wants her own way. She sasses her mother. Sometimes she doesn't come in until one o'clock in the morning. What are we going to do?"

I wrote back, "I don't think now you will listen to me. You let her go to the Devil until she is fifteen, and now when she is about to turn out to be a street walker, you write me, but I don't believe you will listen to me. But I have to tell you what is right. The next time that girl speaks harshly to her mother, the first time there is a hint of disobedience, the first time she does not come in by the deadline you set, you take her across your lap, put one knee over her legs, one hand on the back of her head, and you use a belt or razor strop or ping-pong paddle, and you whip her until she cries and begs for mercy, and tell her if there is a next time it will be twice as long and twice as hard." I said to the mother, "You say 'Amen, that is right' to your husband. And don't you take the side of the girl."

I got another letter later and the stepfather said, "A strange thing happened. She did sass her mother, and I did take her down and whip her good. Her mother stood by and cried and cried but she said, 'That is right. We have to get this settled.' That girl is now the kindest, nicest, obedient child."

* * *

My Father's Bible

My father died in 1930. Among his effects, an old, old Bible came to me. Looking through it one day, I chanced upon the first chapter of Luke, and read how Zacharias, dumb until the child should be born because he had doubted, was asked what they should name the child. Friends insisted on calling him Zacharias after his father, but Elisabeth insisted, "Not so; but he shall be called John." Then we are told, "And they made signs to his father, how he would have him called. And he asked for a writing table, and wrote, saying, His name is John. And they marvelled all" (Luke 1:62,63). And there in my father's old Bible, heavily underlined in ink, were these words, *"His name is John."*

Then suddenly I knew; no one needed to tell me. My father had wanted a boy to be a preacher. He had earnestly prayed. When God gave the child, he wanted him named John, which means "a man sent from God." So he heavily underlined these words, "His name is John."

My father was not converted until he was past thirty. He was born shortly before the Civil War; he grew up in pioneer days; he had little schooling. He was already married when he was saved. He struggled to get one year in the academy at Baylor University, and much of one year in the Southern Baptist Theological Seminary. But he was never able to get much education. Although he preached with blessing, he was always harrassed by family cares; he felt continually pressed to enter other work to make a living. As a preacher, I am sure he felt that he was never all that he longed to be and dreamed of being.

After God laid His hand upon me, I came back to Decatur, Texas, and brought a big tent. My father hitched his Chevrolet car on to the block and tackle, and so from a gin pole we lifted the big eight-hundred-pound center poles and put up the big tent. My father had grown somewhat cold in the Lord's work, though he still lived a good life. He was still a noble Christian example. He had gotten occupied with the lodges and rarely preached, rarely even attended church services. But in that revival service he came out to hear his boy preach. He brought a cane-bottom chair and leaned back against a tent pole. Soon I saw his eyes filled with tears, and he openly wept as he listened to his boy preach the Gospel. Soon at the invitation time he left his seat and went up among the men of the city where he was greatly respected, the men who had sent him to the state legislature, and one by one he brought men weeping down those aisles to Christ and to claim Him openly. How many precious souls my father won in personal contact in that ten weeks of blessed Holy Ghost revival!

I knew some way that my father, in it all, was rejoicing that he had a son who would try to fulfill the dreams and plans and calling which God had begun with him.

*   *   *

"I'm Sorry, Daddy!"

One day as I lay sick on my bed, one of my little girls needed a whipping. I was sick, but a whipping means a lot more when it is delivered by Daddy. Father, you cannot shirk your duty. It was a sad occasion for all of us. She had been warned and warned again, and when she persisted in her wrong-doing she had to be whipped. The Scripture was clear on my duty. "He that spareth his rod hateth his son: but he that loveth him chasteneth him betimes" (Prov. 13:24). Again we are told, "The blueness of a wound cleanseth away evil: so do stripes the inward parts of the belly" (Prov. 20:30), and, "Chasten thy son while there is hope, and let not thy soul spare for his crying" (Prov. 19:18). That is old-fashioned, but it is the Word of God, and well I know I have no hope of success in rearing my family except I do it by God's Word. Sin must be punished. Not in a temper, but sadly and resolutely I did what God commanded. When she brought me my belt and the first painful blows began to fall, my child said, "I'm sorry, Daddy, I'm sorry! I'm sorry!" I stopped for a little and reminded her that she had had much time to be sorry before but she was not sorry until punishment came. Then I talked some more and then whipped some more. She cried and my heart bled. Then she promised to do better and went back to her work.

I lay back on my bed and cried out to God. I well know that it takes far more than a whipping to make good women out of my girls. It takes prayer and the leadership of the Holy Spirit and careful training. We must aim for definite results, results of character and love for right. I prayed that God would give me wisdom about it and that He would not let the stripes and the tears and the pleading and the teaching be in vain!

Then suddenly my heart turned to God for myself. I, too, have cried out to God many a time, "I'm sorry! I'm sorry, Lord! I'm so sorry!" I am always sorry when my sin finds me out, when grief catches up with me. But God knows that many a time I seem careless and indifferent about the things that displease Him until I feel His wrath!

Weeping, I began to pray, "O God, whatever this sickness is for, do not take it away until You accomplish Your purpose." I thought, "What a tragedy if these days of pain, fever and sickness, with the work delayed and sorrow to many, should go by and yet I not be a better man, not be a better preacher." I know that often I have begged God to heal me immediately when I have been sick, and sometimes He has. I have never been sick very much, nor very long, but now I see the importance of the chastening rod of God.

*   *   *

Joshua 24:15. I can imagine I met Joshua one day and I said, "Hello, Joshua, how are you?"

He said, "Oh, hello, John." (First name basis, Joshua and I.)

"How old are you now Joshua?"

"I am 100, going on 115."

"Look! You say you and your family are going to serve the Lord?"

"Yes, sir."

"Well, now, wait a minute! You have children. You must have some boys 60 or 70 years old; you have children, grandchildren, great-grandchildren."

"Oh, yes."

"Well, how are you going to see that that crowd serves the Lord?"

I imagine Joshua said, "John, I am man enough to see after my family. As for me and my house, we will serve the Lord."

God said about Abraham, "For I know him, that he will command his children and his household after him, and they shall keep the way of the Lord" (Gen. 18:19).

Abraham just stomped his foot and they all jumped.

"As for me and my house, we will serve the Lord." A good start on a Christian home.

Infidelity, Modernism, Evolution

Dr. Ham Made His Stand! In a hotel room in Dallas, Texas, Dr. Mordecai Ham and I talked. And that great evangelist told me of the discussion he had had with a prominent Baptist preacher. "What does it matter whether the inspiration of the Bible is verbal inspiration, or not?" said the denominational leader, "just so we have in some sense the Word of God, that is enough for me." Then Dr. Ham told me that he replied, "It may be enough for you, but it would not be enough if you were an evangelist trying to keep multitudes out of Hell, trying to make drunkards sober and harlots pure, and making infidels into believers. I must have a miraculous Bible that is absolutely reliable, on which one can risk his soul, to be a successful evangelist." And Dr. Ham told me that he continued, "Some of you pastors with well organized formal churches could go on with your work without any miracles, without any hardened sinners saved, and if God should die you wouldn't know it for a year!"

Of course that is an extravagant statement, but there is truth in it. The defense of the faith must depend primarily on the soul winners. Those who do not obey the plain command for Christians to go out to get the Gospel to every creature are not so likely to obey the command to defend the faith. There is no way to separate soul winning from the great principles of the historical Christian faith and the great duties commanded in the Bible.

*   *   *

Evolution of a Jeep. I read the other day a story, a very interesting one. The man didn't know he was giving me an illustration of the folly of evolution.

American military personnel flew in a great flying boxcar into Pakistan. Out of it rolled a jeep.

One native would-be scientific man explained to his boy that that little thing would grow and sprout wings and be like the big machine. Here is the plane. It has wheels. And out of it came the jeep. So the jeep will grow up to be an airplane too! But it won't. That boy will be disappointed. The local 'scientist' was mistaken. Don't jump to conclusions by a little bit of superficial likeness. That isn't very sensible. No, the truth is, man made both the plane and the jeep. Both had rubber tires. Both had engines. Both of them go. People ride in both of them. But the one did not come automatically and naturally out of the other. They didn't develop themselves. Men created them. They did not naturally make themselves. The argument for likeness is not a sensible argument. Similarity is simply an argument that the Creator used certain great principles in making man and animals.

*   *   *

Doubts Are Defeated by the First Step. An infidel who had long denied the truth of the Bible and insisted that the rational mind could not accept many of the doctrines of the Bible, was converted in a great revival campaign, as Dr. Bob Jones tells the story. The assault of this Spirit-filled evangelist was on the man's will and conscience and was not primarily a cold matching of wits on the intellectual plane. The unbeliever, deeply convicted of his sins, surrendered to Christ and then told the evangelist, "When I took the first step out into the aisle to confess Christ as my Saviour, every doubt I ever had fled away!" The infidel may have been sincere about his doubts, but they were nevertheless the result of a wrong heart attitude. He would not previously come to Christ in his heart, and that left his mind darkened to the truth.

*   *   *

God Did It! Dr. L. R. Scarborough, once president of the Southwestern Theological Seminary at Fort Worth, many years ago told the story of his six-year-old son who returned from Sunday school and expressed his unbelief in the story of Jonah and the whale. "I don't believe what the Sunday school teacher said, Daddy. I don't believe a whale could swallow a man, and the man stay alive three days and nights and then come out of the whale and preach."

Dr. Scarborough said that to his six-year-old skeptic he answered, "Well, if there is a God who could make a man and who could make a whale and prepare the whale to swallow a man, couldn't He keep the man alive in the whale for three days?"

"Oh, well!" said the six-year-old boy, with the wisdom that modernistic preachers have never yet learned, "if you are going to put God in it, I can believe it, too!"

*   *   *

"No Atheists in Foxholes." It is said that on Bataan Peninsula in the Philippine Islands, before our forces there were compelled to surrender, a sergeant and a colonel were together when Japanese planes came over, and together they plunged into a small trench just deep enough to keep them below ground level if they lay flat, so that machine-gun bullets would miss them. Such holes were called "foxholes." When bullets and bomb fragments had shattered all around them and the planes were gone the colonel said, "Sergeant, I noticed that you were praying back there. I thought you didn't believe in God."

The sergeant replied, "Sir, I heard you praying too. There are not any atheists in foxholes."

It would be a blessed result in terrible war if all over the world men repent of their folly and their senseless indifference toward God, and by their troubles were led to call on God!

*   *   *

Evolution's Best Proof. I will tell you the best evidence I ever heard for evolution. A man went hunting out in the mountains of New Mexico and he came upon a panther, a mountain lion. This lady was on the warpath and came after him. He took up his gun to shoot, but the gun jammed. So he turned and ran for his life, the mountain lion after him.

Down the mountain he went to a deserted vinegar factory in the valley. He anxiously wondered what to do? The mountain lion was right behind him. There was a big hogshead there and he jumped in that and turned it down over him. The mountain lion got on top of it, snarling and clawing. He looked out of the bung hole and saw the lioness swishing her tail back and forth across that hole. He pulled her tail in through the bung hole and tied a knot in it. When he did, she let out a squall and away she went, that big barrel bouncing behind her. (I wasn't there, but this is what I heard. This is the best proof for evolution I ever heard.)

The next year the same man went back hunting again and he saw that same mountain lion, and she still had the hogshead on her tail. By this time she had mountain lion kittens, and each one of them had a little keg on his tail!

That is the best evidence I ever heard for evolution! (This is what I heard and you can take it for what it is worth. No evolutionist has any evidence but guesses and hearsay.) People who do not want to believe the Bible can believe that, if they will not listen to something sensible.

*   *   *

An Ignorant Infidel. Christians should not be afraid of modernists.

I remember how startled I was to read Tom Paine's *Age of Reason* and to find that the book, as first published, was written without the author's seeing or referring to either a Bible or Testament! Without any investigation of the Bible, Paine culled from other infidels what he could of argument against the Book he had never read but hated! Later he found it necessary to write a second part, and he says: "Under these disadvantages, I began the former part of the *Age of Reason*; I had, besides, neither Bible nor Testament to refer to, though I was writing against both; nor could I procure any: notwithstanding which, I have produced a work that no Bible believer, though writing at his ease, and with a library of Church books about him, can refute." (!!!)

And this second part of the book, written after he got out of jail in Luxembourg and with the Bible before him, abounds in mistakes and evidences of ignorance! You may be sure that unbelief always, in infidels, in the church or out, comes from bad hearts, without a solid foundation of fact.

* * *

"Bob, Make It Good!" A drinking man went to hear Bob Ingersoll, that infidel, speak in Chicago. When Ingersoll said, "You don't have to be born again! Jesus was just a good man, not the Saviour! There is no everlasting Hell," etc., this old drinker said to Ingersoll, "Bob, be sure and make it good, now. A lot of us are depending on you!" They were depending on something like that, some infidel's teaching, because they knew if the Bible was true, they would go to Hell, as the wicked, Christ-rejectors they were, and as they deserved to do.

* * *

Only a Guess. Evolution is no more than a theory. You might call it a guess, a supposition, a working theory. It is not a proven fact. For example, in Darwin's *Origin of the Species* some three hundred times, Dr. William Jennings Bryan noted that Darwin said, "We may well suppose," or "We infer." Three hundred suppositions and guesses are not enough upon which to base a doctrine that denies the Bible.

* * *

The Ignorant Infidel. I grew up in the ranch country near a little cowtown of three hundred people in West Texas. The only infidel I knew in my boyhood was a wicked, profane, drunken blacksmith. I think he had never been beyond the fourth grade. And this poor, ignorant, drunken, cursing, blaspheming, dirty-minded, dirty-talking, profane man with a criminal record was an infidel. Now his infidelity did not come because of his education. He had little education. It did not come because of a high, humble, seeking mind, because he had a dirty mind and an immoral background and filthy talk. It did not come from high standards. No, his infidelity came from a dirty, wicked heart that was against God and the Bible.

* * *

Infidel in a Christian Country. Tom Paine had written useful tracts for liberty to stir the people for the Revolutionary War, but since he was an infidel, when he returned to America from France where he had been imprisoned, he was poorly received, was given no place in the new government, retired to the little farm given him where he spent his last days in filth and drunkenness. The early leaders of America were not for atheism. They were for the Bible and for God.

The Designer. Do you think all this is accidental about the earth? Here is a watch. I say, "There must be a watchmaker then." But you say, "Oh, no! That is just evolution. It came through natural processes from inherent forces, and it developed of itself"! Well, but there is a dial on it. Someone must have known that there were so many hours in a day and in a night. And the hands go from one hour to another. The small hand goes from twelve to one. In one hour it goes the full circle—sixty minutes to the hour. Somebody must have planned it. "No," you say, "I think that is accidental. It was first a chip of wood, then a checker, then afterwhile a compass, then a steamguage, then it was a watch—hocus pocus, presto chango, it just invented itself." That is crazy. But it is no crazier than the fellow who says, "Here is a man. God did not make him. He is just an accident. Nobody planned him." I say that is credulous, ignorant, profane resistance to facts.

* * *

It Does Not Cost Much to Be a Disciple of Infidels. Consider the moral standards of infidels. Remember that Tom Paine was a patriot, writing tracts to help forward the cause of the American Revolution and the founding of the American Republic. He ranked near Washington and Jefferson in influence at one time. But his infidelity, his disbelief in the Bible and in Christ, set no great standards for him to live by. He died a poor, dirty, drunken wretch. It does not cost much to become a disciple of infidels.

A great doctor told how he was in Rush Medical School long years ago, before it became a part of the University of Chicago, when Robert Ingersoll, famous infidel, gave one of his lectures on "The Mistakes of Moses." Ingersoll said that there was no Hell. He scoffed at eternal retribution. He said that the Bible was a lie. And that great physician told how that night the other medical students went by droves to the bawdy houses. If there were no Hell, no judgment, if the Bible were not true, and if they were really descended from beasts, they might act like beasts. It does not cost much to be a disciple of infidels.

* * *

"Hypocrite!" I heard Gipsy Smith, preaching in a citywide campaign in Dallas, Texas, turn to the platform and say, "I have heard that some one among you does not believe in the virgin birth and the inspiration of all the Bible. Hypocrite!" his voice rose to a shout. "Get out of the pulpit."

Jesus

The Thirst of the Dying. I
remember that when I was a boy,
old Grandfather Cavender used to
tell about the Civil War. He told
how, following the battle—or even
in the midst of it—between the two
opposing armies, the wounded
would lie bleeding and dying, shot
down in a charge or a retreat. And
he told me that the most horrible
suffering of the wounded was a
thirst for water. The cry, "Water!
water! water!" would go out from
fevered lips until sometimes their
comrades, tormented by their
anguish, would carry them a can-
teen of water, at the risk of life
itself. As the blood ebbs away from
the body, the whole body cries out
for water. Often water alone would
guarantee the recovery of the
wounded and sometimes only
water could ease their torment as
they died. I have thought many
times of how the poor, abused,
beaten, and wounded Saviour
must have suffered for water as He
hung on the cross under the blaz-
ing sun, and then in the three
hours of darkness as His blood
dripped away. No wonder that
Jesus cried out, "I thirst!" (John
19:28).

* * *

The Greatest Glad News. I
remember Camp MacArthur near
Waco, Texas, in November, 1918.
The weather was uncomfortable,
the mud was deep. Camp life was
dreary. We were citizen-soldiers
snatched out of homes and
business, postponing education
and marriage and professions to
serve our country. The bloody war
which involved half the world held
us in chains of circumstances, and
headed us toward the bloody
trenches of France.

Then came Armistice Day!
First, there was a false report, then
a true one. The Germans had surrendered! World War I was over!
Now we would soon go home, back
to school and farm and city; back
to wedding bells, careers and jobs.

I have never seen such a time of
pandemonium and praise. Guns
firing! Tubs and dish pans skid-
ding, banging, tied behind cars!
Anvils ringing, galvanized iron
tanks pounding, soldiers yelling,
singing!

It was good news to me. In a few
weeks I was out of the army and
had entered the university to finish
my education.

But that was no glad news such
as the angel gave in Judaea that
night when the glory of the Lord
shone round about the shepherds
and they heard the glad tidings of
great joy for all people. A Saviour
was born!

* * *

The Black Preacher's Triumph.
An old black man preaching on the radio in Chicago years ago said, "If you trust in things of this world, they will fail you. You trust in yo' pretty clothes, and dey gets raggedy. You trust in yo' boss, and he fires you. You trust in yo' strength of youth, and you gets old and tottery." Then his voice broke as he said, "You trust in yo' good wife, and she dies and leaves you!" Then, with a shout of triumph, he said, "You trust in Jesus Christ— Amen! He's all right!"

This world needs a Saviour to heal the brokenhearted.

* * *

Homecoming! I have heard my uncle tell of his homecoming after the four years' absence and struggle in the Confederate Army during the Civil War. I saw a letter the other day from a man in the Texas Penitentiary who was now eligible for parole and so expected to be released after many years of imprisonment. The eagerness with which he awaited the day when he would go free was tremendously moving.

I remember the day when we soldiers in the camp knew that the first World War had ended on November 11, 1918. What laughing and crying and praising and rejoicing! Horns and whistles blew, bells rang, wash tubs were tied on behind automobiles, and every noise-making device men could think of were used to express our tremendous relief that the war, the bloodshed, separation from loved ones, the dark uncertainties were finished, or soon would be! I have read of the escape from Devil's Island of a convict who had spent most of his adult years there. These things can only picture faintly the tremendous relief, the joy unspeakable that our Saviour must have felt when the suffering, the exile from Heaven and the weakness of His human incarnation were finished.

* * *

"The Man in the Glory!" My good friend, Dr. H. A. Ironside, who has now gone on to Heaven, used to talk often about "The Man in the Glory." "The Man in the Glory!" When I see Jesus, He will have wounds in His side and in His hands and feet. I want to kiss those scars in His hands. When I see Jesus, He will have a real body. I hope maybe He will let me touch Him. You remember that John leaned on His breast at supper. Even to doubting Thomas, Jesus invited him to "Reach hither thy finger, and behold my hands; and reach hither thy hand, and thrust it into my side: and be not faithless, but believing" (John 20:27). I'll see Jesus with a human body.

* * *

The Virgin-Born Saviour. Some years ago when I put a series of articles in THE SWORD OF THE LORD, a man who had been president of the General Assembly of the Presbyterian Church in America, and one of their leading men, wrote and said, "You have convinced me." Yes, but I don't have to convince you, if you are willing to take what God says about it. He says "virgin"—it was a virgin-born Saviour that was born. Mary *was* a virgin, and God insists on that.

* * *

Somebody With Skin. It is said that once when a little girl was put to bed she said, "I am afraid of the dark! Mother, can't you come to bed with me?" The mother said, "Now, God is with you, and the angels are with you. Never mind the dark now. Go to sleep." The little girl said, "Yes, but I want somebody here that's got skin on."

That is the kind of Saviour I want, too; One who knows all my temptations, One who "was in all points tempted like as we are, yet without sin" (Heb. 4:15). I want a Saviour who has been hungry, who has been tired, who has been abused and offended. I want a Saviour who suffered as a man. I want a Saviour who can always have sympathy with my weakness and frailty.

* * *

Paying for Another. Someone says, "One man can't pay for another!"

Oh, yes, he can. I knew a man whose son went wrong. I knew of a post office employee who stole again and again. His father who loved him, with great sacrifice raked and scraped to pay the money back. The father told the judge, "I will make everything good." And the father paid for the son's misdeed.

You know how a mother does for a baby what the baby can't do for himself. Her love makes her wash the diapers and wipe the dirty nose and kiss the bumps and teach the little mind and feed him who can't pay for the food. You have never paid your mother back for her toil, her love, her tears, for the dressing, bathing, cooking, preparation and protection. Oh, love! And if the love of a mother could do all that for a guilty one, couldn't the love of God do more?

Before Nathan Hale, who was caught as a spy in the service of his country, was shot, he said, "My only regret is that I have only one life to give for my country."

You and I have had purchased for us freedom that other men died for. Some men do pay for other men's debts. Near Murfreesboro, Tennessee, where I live, is the home of Sam Davis, a young man in his early twenties who died when he could have had his life saved. Because he would not tell the names of those from whom he got information for the Confederate Army, he was hanged as a spy. He gave his life rather than tell on others. He died for others.

God made a way for Jesus, the Innocent One, to die for us, the guilty ones.

* * *

"Mister, They Killed Him!" It is said that at Easter in the great department store founded by John Wanamaker in Philadelphia, they hung on one of the walls a large painting of the crucifixion of the Saviour. A newsboy came there often to see it. Many other people crowded into the store at Easter to see the beautiful painting. It is said that a preacher came one day and as he stood gazing at that picture, the newsboy spoke: "Yes, Mister, they killed Him! He hadn't done anything wrong at all, but they killed Him! They oughtn't to have done it. It was a wicked thing! But, Mister, they killed Him!" The boy started away, but then came running back to say, "Mister, I forgot to tell you, He didn't stay dead!"

* * *

No Rest But in Jesus. I talked to a man about his soul and he told me he was unsaved. I said, "You have no peace in your heart, you need Jesus." He said, "Oh, yes, I do, I am very happy." But I answered again, "No, you do not. I have proof that you have no peace. I know your heart is not content." Rather angrily he asked me how I knew, and I said, "Because the Bible says, 'There is no peace, saith my God, to the wicked' " (Isa. 57:21). With downcast eyes and humble heart then he admitted that he was not happy, that his heart was not content, that he had no rest of soul. Dear friends, you cannot have this rest, this peace unless you find it in Jesus.

Saint Augustine said, "O Lord, our souls are restless until they find their rest in Thee!" Jesus has promised soul rest.

* * *

The Holy Stairs. In Rome, Italy, I went to see the Holy Stairs, the Scala Santa. Deeply moved, as I have been each time I see it, I saw people climbing on their knees up the twenty-eight steps of the Holy Stairs, many of them weeping and many stopping to kiss each step before raising bruised knees to another. I counted twenty-eight people on the stairs at one time, and two more began the painful climb as I watched. I suppose that 200 or 300 people each day normally go through this act of veneration or this deed of penance. Only God knows what deep distresses, what longing of soul, what hope of forgiveness or for the favor of God are pictured in the sad faces of these worshipers climbing the "Holy Stairs" at Rome.

Why are they holy? Well, tradition says that these are the same marble steps leading to the Fortress of Antonia at Jerusalem, in the place of Pilate's Judgment Hall where the Jews brought Jesus to be tried. They say that up these steps came the feet of the Saviour who was tried and crucified, therefore they are especially holy. Tradition says that Queen Helena, the mother of Constantine, the first nominally Christian Emperor of Rome, discovered these steps and had them shipped to Rome. There they were preserved in one way or another and eventually this church was built around them.

There is no doubt that these steps have been watered by the tears of thousands, so they are steps of tears. And the guides are taught to say that on these steps was sprinkled the blood of the Saviour as He was scourged before Pilate and led away to be crucified. Yes, they are steps of blood and tears, but are the "Holy Stairs" the way to Heaven?

I do not wonder that tradition tells us Martin Luther, the young Catholic monk, greatly distressed over his sins, went to Rome and climbed these Holy Stairs which I saw. But we are told that in the midst of them a verse of Scripture he had memorized kept coming back to his heart, "The just shall live by faith!" "The just shall live by faith!" "The just shall live by faith!" Then if one can have eternal life by faith, why bruise these knees, why scourge one's heart in lamentations, why try to buy that which is already bought and freely given to us? So the tradition says Martin Luther rose from his knees, walked down those stairs and started the Reformation, crying out in every way he could that "the just shall live by faith," that the blood and tears that pay the way to Heaven are the blood and tears of the Lord Jesus Himself.

* * *

Beautiful Hands. It is said that once a mother with gnarled, misshapen, scarred hands, raised a beautiful daughter. The daughter was at first ashamed of those ugly, misshapen hands, those hands that had done so much for her. But one day the mother told her the story.

When the daughter was a baby, the house was on fire. The mother went into the burning room, caught the baby and beat out the flames on her blankets with her own bare hands and carried the little one to safety. But the mother's burned hands always showed the scar. Oh, how the daughter took those hands and kissed them! How beautiful they were now always to her! So ought the wounded hands of Jesus be to us who are saved by His sacrifice on the cross.

* * *

Since Jesus Rose. . . . My mother was buried, but she will rise again one day, as did Jesus rise from the dead. I stood by the grave of my mother years later. Now I was a preacher, and by that grave in a little sandy-land cemetery out near Gainesville, Texas, I said, "Mother, one of these days the trump will sound, and the dead in Christ shall rise, and I will see you again. We will go to meet the Lord together." I rejoiced. And I know my mother wasn't in that grave. That body that suffered, that young mother who died at about thirty years of age, leaving her four children, rejoiced in Heaven. And one day that body will rise. We can be glad. Since Jesus rose from the dead, so also we shall rise.

* * *

Only the Blood of Jesus!

Once in Dallas, Texas, when I was pastor of the Galilean Baptist Church, the telephone in my study rang. When I answered, a woman in troubled voice said, "O Brother Rice, I'm at my wits' end! I'm in such trouble I don't know what to do!"

"What is it, Mrs. Hunter?" I asked.

"Pastor, you know that little Jackie, six years old, has had pneumonia. Now, after long weeks, his lungs have cleared. But he is so weak and frail. His blood is so thin. The doctor feels he cannot get well without a blood transfusion. I have a new baby and they will not let me give my blood. I have asked all the people I know, and no one wants to give blood for a transfusion. What shall I do? What shall I do?"

"I will take care of that," I answered. "Don't fret. We will have somebody at the hospital to have their blood typed at the hour appointed," I promised.

I found it difficult to get others to help. Everybody was busy. So in my own office I asked my brother, Bill, one of my secretaries, and in my home the Christian girl who helped Mrs. Rice. I went with them, and with the boy's father there were five of us. The doctor took samples of blood with a syringe from each of us. We were told that soon we would have a report and know which one, if any of us, would have the right type of blood for the transfusion.

"Doctor," I said, "I am glad to give blood for the transfusion if my blood will do, but I am promised to preach eighty miles away, at Bridgeport, Texas, tonight. So what you do, please do quickly and let me know."

The doctor agreed and I went to my home. As I sat at lunch the telephone rang. Of the five of us whose blood was tested, only my blood was sufficient and compatible. So I went to the hospital.

Little Jackie, the doctor, the nurses and Jackie's mother were waiting in the operating room when I went in. I pulled off my shirt and lay on an operating table. As the nurse prepared my arm for the needle through which the blood was to be drawn, little Jackie was rolled up beside me. A nurse put alcohol on his arm, too. The little fellow was frightened. He cried, "Mamma! What are they going to do to me? Mamma, make her quit!"

The mother knelt by the little fellow's side. "Now, Jackie, be a little man; don't break Mother's heart. The doctor says that you need more blood to give you strength and to get you well. Daddy's blood wouldn't do. Miss Viola's blood wouldn't do. Miss Lillian's blood wouldn't do. Brother Bill's blood wouldn't do. Only Brother Rice's would do. So our pastor is going to give you some of his blood, and you will be strong and get well. Now be a brave little man for Mother."

The little fellow straightened up his face and there was hardly a whimper when the needle was put into the vein in his arm.

One nurse handled the transfusion equipment, the tube and measuring device between the two needles in my arm and in his arm.

"Twenty cubic centimeters, Doctor," she said. Another nurse wrote it down.

Again, "Twenty cubic centimeters, Doctor." The nurse recorded it.

After this the other nurse said, "Look at his cheeks becoming pink! His lips were so pale and now they are turning red again."

The doctor said, "His pulse is coming back good and strong. This little fellow is going to live and get well."

At last the nurse said, "That makes two hundred cubic centimeters, Doctor."

He said, "That is enough!" They drained the last blood from the tube into the little fellow's arm and as they were removing the needle and taping a bit of cotton over the place where the needle penetrated, the mother came to the little fellow's side and said to him, "Don't forget to thank

Brother Rice. Wasn't he good to give you his blood when nobody else's blood would do?"

I thought to hurry away but the doctor insisted that I lie still for a bit, drink a glass of warm milk and be refreshed before I started to drive eighty miles to preach. As they pushed the wheeled cot through the door, little Jackie turned and waved to me and said, "Goodbye, Brother Rice! You're welcome."

I could not get the matter off my mind. That night I could preach on nothing but the precious blood, the only blood that would ever do anybody any good, the blood of Jesus Christ! I remember a woman with a sad and sin-marked face, with a baby in her arms. She tossed the baby to the woman next to her and trembling and weeping came to take Christ as her Saviour. Only the blood of Jesus Christ could make such a sinner clean and whole.

* * *

"I Jist Loves to Pint Him Out!" I would like to be like the old colored man on the dock at Memphis, Tennessee. Down the Mississippi River there came a steamboat, and as the ship whistled, the old Negro always ran to the dock, and as that big side-wheeler boat passed, he cried out, "Dar he goes! Dar he goes! Look at the captain on the bridge!" When the boat had passed, the old fellow would wipe his eyes and say to somebody, "I jist loves to pint him out!"

The story is that this black man was in a little rowboat in the muddy waters of the Mississippi. One day a larger ship came too close to his rowboat and it turned over, throwing him in the muddy waters, and he didn't know how to swim. The captain of the larger boat jumped off his ship and pulled the old man to shore, saving his life. This old black man couldn't forget him. He said, "I jist loves to pint him out!"

You had better get fixed up inside so the fire is burning and so you will have something to talk about, then you can talk for Jesus. You can point Him out to others. You surely can.

* * *

"Even So, Come, Lord Jesus!" (Rev. 22:20). When Handel had finished his oratorio, "The Messiah," and the glorious climax of the Hallelujah Chorus rang in his mind and heart and ears, he was transported with joy, and almost he could see the glorious coming of the Lord Jesus Christ.

I remember when after five years of toil I completed preparation of a correspondence course on the whole Bible with my lessons on the Book of Revelation. As I dictated the comments on the last two chapters I was so exalted and so thrilled I walked up and down in my study as I dictated. Tears ran down my face, and my voice trembled as I realized a little of the marvel of the glorious rapture of Christians.

*   *   *

Homecoming! An old Civil War veteran of the Confederate Army told how he got home to Mississippi after the long, sad years of war. He said,

"After the war was over, a group of us boys from Mississippi struck out for home. We had no horses, almost no clothes, no shoes; our feet were bleeding and frost-bitten, tied up with gunny sacks.

"Through a wrecked Southland, we trudged our way. Finally, we were within a few miles of home in 'ole Mississippi,' footsore, tired and weary."

The other gaunt soldiers wanted to lie down and sleep and go on the rest of the way in the morning, but Bill said, "I am on familiar ground; just a few more miles and we will be home for breakfast."

The others said, "We are too tired; let's sleep."

But Bill said, "No, I am going home, going to eat breakfast at home in the morning!"

He left the group, dragged on through the night, and when the first break of day came, he stood on the last hill from home! He saw the smoke going up from the chimney where his mother was getting breakfast.

He forgot he was tired, forgot his bleeding feet. He quickened his pace, ran, came to the foot of the hill, to the lane leading up to the house. His young brother, Jim, sitting on the rail fence, happened to look his way and saw him. Jim shouted to those in the house, "YONDER COMES BILLY! YONDER COMES BILLY!"

Out came father and mother and all the family! The slaves and all came running. Whites and blacks together struck out down the long lane. They grabbed him, hugged him, carried him up to the house, took off his rags. They bathed him and gave him clean clothes. And all together shouted and laughed and praised God for Billy's homecoming!

Well, Jesus' coming for His own will be as unexpected as that. When we hear the glad shout, "Behold, the bridegroom cometh; go ye out to meet him," it will be a glad surprise. Like a sweetheart who has so long looked for the homecoming of her soldier and finds him suddenly come and knocking on her door, so will the saints of God meet our Saviour, our Beloved, our Redeemer, our King!

* * *

The Man at the Door. It is said that Holman Hunt, famous painter, once invited a friend to see a painting he had just completed. "It has come very close to my heart," said the artist. "I hope it may be my masterpiece. Tell me how you are impressed by it." Thus saying, he drew the curtain from the new picture and the friend gazed upon it. "What do you think of it?" asked Mr. Hunt.

"It is a beautiful picture, but I think you have forgotten something," answered the friend.

"Forgotten something? What do you think I have forgotten?" His friend replied, "There is a man at the door knocking. Vines are growing up around the door. The man has an ancient lantern in his hand, but, strangely, you seem to have forgotten something. There is no latch on the door! He could not get in if he wanted to!"

"Ah, but you have missed the point of the picture," said the artist. "The man at the door is the Lord Jesus Christ. The door is the door to the human heart, and the latch is on the inside. Unless the one inside opens the door, Jesus can never come in!"

That illustrates the blessed statement of the Lord Jesus when He said, "Behold, I stand at the door and knock: if any man hear my voice, and open the door, I will come in to him, and will sup with him, and he with me" (Rev. 3:20).

* * *

Brokenhearted   Saviour. I received a letter from a sixteen-year-old girl who wrote to say she was trusting Christ to save her. Brokenhearted over her sins, she wrote, "I don't want that Man crying over my sins any more!" Oh, brokenhearted Saviour, who died for our sins! He is anxious to save you.

⌇⌇⌇⌇⌇

Judgment

Conspiracy Against the Pastor. In a church four men conspired against the pastor. The building program seemed too slow paying cash as the church could raise it. They decided they must borrow money and proceed. They must set certain rules for the pastor. They were good men, but they took a strong stand against a leadership that had been wonderfully blessed of God in the saving of thousands of souls.

One of his men walked into a place of business and fell dead with a heart attack.

Another of the four was rushed to a hospital desperately sick. The doctors could not diagnose his trouble, never knew what was wrong with him. He died in two days.

Another, strangely enough, a man with a big family, was suddenly drafted into the air force. The air force then started to move him from one camp to another. The plane fell and he was killed. All this in a few weeks!

The blessed, anointed ministry of that pastor continued. God interceded for His own.

I was that pastor!

* * *

God's Immediate Punishment

Often men die in immediate punishment for some great sin. Sometimes one who is spiritually-minded and knows the facts can trace the hand of God and can sense the spiritual reason for sudden death on a sinner.

In Waxahachie, Texas, in the midst of a great revival campaign in which I was the preacher, several remarkable incidents came which seemed clearly to be immediate punishment of God for sin.

Two young men drove about in a car one afternoon drinking, breaking the speed laws, endangering the lives of others. One at least was active in a church young people's society. I do not suppose he claimed to have been converted.

They drove into a filling station to fill their gas tank again. The kindly operator pleaded with them, "Go home and sleep off your drunk. You will kill yourselves or somebody else. If you will promise to go home at once without any more racing through the streets, I will take the hose and wash out the vomit in the front of the car, fill the gas tank and charge it to your dad. But promise me, will you?"

They promised, so he filled the gas tank. The two young men under the influence of liquor started home. "But let us have just one more run down East Marvin Street before we go in," one of them said. The other agreed. They raced down East Marvin Street at seventy miles an hour, according to the one boy who lived to tell the story. At a thirty-degree turn in the street the car skidded to the left side of the street, hit the curbing, turned on its side, skidded into a telephone pole, breaking it off at the base. The young men were rushed to the hospital. One of them died at four o'clock the next morning after saying over and over again in delirium, "O God, have mercy!" and never, as far as we know, coming to clear consciousness.

A few days later a young man who had been to the revival the night before and had been deeply concerned as friends pleaded with him to be saved, stayed to keep the garage. When he went out with the wrecker to pull a car out of the ditch, a bus hit the wrecker, knocked it over on him, and crushed him instantly.

In the same twelve weeks of revival, another man who had heard me preach and had been solemnly warned was found shot through the heart at the town waterworks. Many believed, as did I, that all this was the hand of God. He does sometimes bring people to sudden judgment and death because of some immediate sin.

*   *   *

Death of a Deacon. I was invited for a revival campaign in a large Southern Baptist church. A prominent deacon who disliked my strong stand against modernism and did not want me to come, confronted the pastor. He feared it would stop some support of the denominational program. He planned to call a meeting of the deacons and bring the matter before the church—to stop or to bring to an early close the revival effort.

Within a few minutes of my plane's arrival in that city, he died with a heart attack. The revival progressed with great blessing and many were saved.

*   *   *

God Protects His Own Servant. I went for a revival campaign in the little town of Hartley, in the panhandle of Texas. It was harvesttime; the crowds were small; the people indifferent. I preached and led the singing. My wife played the piano. Once when our second baby, Mary Lloys, had interrupted the service twice by crying and her mother must go back from the piano to comfort her, I stopped and gave her two or three resounding spanks and told her to hush. She stuffed her fingers in her mouth and snuffed, but got quiet.

After the service a woman came to me and said, "If I don't come back anymore, I guess you'll know why."

I said, "I suppose you are not burdened about revival and soul winning."

"No," she said. "I don't care about hearing anybody preach the Gospel who is as brutal as you are with your children."

A crowd was about. What should I say? I simply silently called on the Lord. "Lord, take care of this case." I stood there a moment and that woman fell in the aisle as if someone had hit her in the head!

When she had begun to talk to me, her husband, accustomed, I suppose, to her sharp tongue, had left the building. I called him and told him to get some water, that his wife needed help. They sprinkled water in her face, bathed her face, and she regained consciousness. She was the nicest lady you ever saw after that! She was in every service. She listened earnestly. After the week of meetings she came to tell me how wonderfully she had been blessed.

But one little thing God allowed to remain as a reminder to her and to me, that He was taking care of His preacher. She stood in the aisle and talked to other women with her back to me. As I drew near she, with her back to me, suddenly began to stutter, and became speechless until I passed. All that week, whenever I came near her, she began to stutter and could hardly speak.

I am saying that God has a right to protect His own.

*   *   *

Shake Off the Dust! Jesus told His disciples in Matthew 10:14, "And whosoever shall not receive you, nor hear your words, when ye depart out of that house or city, shake off the dust of your feet."

Early in 1936 I had a citywide campaign in Binghamton, New York, in the Binghamton Theater, seating 1,700. Although we had great crowds and many, many people saved, the Pastors' Conference,

principally liberal, unbelieving men, scoffed publicly and in the newspapers about the revival. When I likened Binghamton to Sodom and Gomorrah, they were shocked, saying that Binghamton was the Athens of New York State. The police department wired back to Dallas to find if there were any criminal charges against this preacher!

Before I drove out of the city, after five weeks, I stood out on the snow, shook the dust off my feet and asked God to hold the city accountable for the preaching they had heard and the great number of conversions they had seen. Within a day a great thaw came and the nineteen inches of accumulated snow up and down that valley melted and a great flood inundated much of the city. There were millions of dollars of damage, and some deaths.

*   *   *

Sin Calls for Judgment. There was a Baptist preacher in Philadelphia, Mississippi. A certain man came to that preacher's father and said, "We've got a plan whereby we can make some money. Have you got money to invest?"

"What is it?"

"We can build a row of shotgun houses down here. Some women will take them over as houses of prostitution. We can charge big rates. We have enough influence to get it decent and legal, and we will make plenty of money."

The man said no, he would not put his money in that kind of thing. But the houses were built and used anyway.

A little bit later the man came back to this preacher's father and said, "Say, you do construction work, don't you?"

"Yes."

He asked, "Do you have any dynamite?"

"Yes. I got it under regular agreement and I save it for blasting purposes."

This man said, "Let me have a couple sticks."

"What for?"

He wanted to blow up that row of houses down there because his own daughter had been gone night after night. She was working in that place as a prostitute. Now he wanted to blow it up!

Do you think God will let us get by with the lewdness and filth of the movies, the way women dress, the dirty magazines and paperbound books in your airports and drug stores, and the lewdness of the stories and pictures, and the comic books? Do you think the all-seeing eye of God is going to let that get by in America? These are sins of America that call for judgment.

* * *

Is the Equation Equal?

In Lubbock, Texas, it is said a man sat by the sidewalk in a wheel chair. A strong young fellow came clicking his heels down the walk, and since it was down in Texas where people can be friendly with strangers, the cripple called out to him, "Stranger, are you good at mathematics?"

"Well, what is the problem?" the young man smiled.

"Here is an equation," the man in the wheel chair said. "On one side was fifteen minutes' pleasure down on the Mexican border with a little Spanish girl. On the other side is twenty-two years of disease, having to be rolled in a wheel chair. Now are they equal? Was it worth it?"

"My God, no!" exclaimed the horrified lad.

"Then remember," said the sufferer, "be sure your sin will find you out!"

The young man never forgot the question. No, no! it was not worth it. Sin costs too much—it finds you out in your body.

* * *

A Wild Beast on Your Trail.

Late one afternoon in West Texas, about 1880, a lone cowboy rode across the prairie. Far ahead lay the west fork of the Brazos River, and the dim trail down that wooded stream led to the camp, which he must reach tonight. Soon he came across the freshly killed carcass of a two-year-old steer. Great, slashing cuts across the side proved that the beast had been killed by the attack of a panther, a mountain lion. The body was still warm. This was the work of a blood-thirsty killer who killed for devilment and not just for food.

Soon the lone horseman rode into the wooded creek-bottom, found and followed the trail toward camp. The sun went down, and as dusk settled over the land, there came behind him the shrill scream of a panther. The tired horse quickened his step. Soon, to the right, and not far away, the wailing cry was heard again. The beast was circling ahead! A little later, and far ahead, somewhere near the trail, it seemed, came that dismal and blood-curdling cry. The cowboy was my father. He said that as he rode among the darkness of the trees, he knew that at any moment there might come hurtling upon him from some branch above, the clawing, killing body of the big cat. Panthers had been known to leap upon and kill a full-grown horse. With what relief he came to the campfire, the chuck wagon and his companions!

Perhaps you have never been stalked by a blood-thirsty beast of prey. Nevertheless, dear friends, there is a wild beast on your trail. Swift and pitiless, retribution trails you. "Be sure your sin will find you out!" (Numbers 32:23).

* * *

The Danger of Rejection

I remember with deep emotion a visit I made to a woman in Amarillo, Texas. She had, only two or three hours before, shot to death another woman, and tried to kill her husband. It was a terrible thing, but she unburdened her heart to me. She told me how she had loved her husband, loved him with a holy love, loved him with self-abandonment. When he drank, she forgave him. When he neglected her, she loved him still. When she began to hear that he was keeping company with another woman, she did not believe it. Later, when she knew it was so, she still clung to him, pleaded with him for the sake of her children and their home. With wretched heart she wondered what to do. She asked counsel of her pastor. She sent good men to see her husband, to pray with him. She continued to live in her husband's home.

But the husband became bolder in his adulterous attachment to a wicked woman. He would take his car from the home for the woman of his shameful love to use while he worked, and let his wife walk. The wicked woman made a public joke of the fact that she had the affection and most of the money of the false husband. The husband called the wicked woman his sweetheart, told his wife she could have what was left of his affection or none. That woman who had gone with her husband through the days of his poverty, had forgiven him his failures, had exalted him before the children, had loved him with a woman's measureless love, reached the limit of her strength. One day when the shameless thief of her husband's affection sneered in her face on the sidewalk, then drove off with her husband's car, she came to the breaking point. She bought a gun and waited and when her husband and the other woman drove up together, she began to shoot. The wicked, shameless harlot woman was killed, the husband was not.

As I talked to that poor distraught woman two or three hours after she had fired the fatal bullets, the doctor who examined the dying woman telephoned to say that a little life, conceived in sin, had gone out with the life of the dying woman. And as I looked into the tear-stained, agonized face of that woman whose love had been scorned, whose womanhood had been abused, whose pleadings had been ignored, I could understand what she meant when she told me simply, "There was nothing else I could do. I reached the end of forgiveness, the end of mercy, the end of my love."

I do not excuse her, but every sensible person can understand how she felt.

And do you think that the Almighty God, the God who sent His Son, Jesus Christ, to die on the cross for you, will let you go on week after week, month in, month out, year after year, treading under your foot His Son, who was offered on the cross as a price for your sins? Do you believe that God will allow the sweet Holy Spirit to strive forever with you, and never be angry, never turn away? How many insults do you think God will take from your wicked, unbelieving, Christ-rejecting heart before He will let you go to Hell?

* * *

Sins Come Out Publicly, With Open Shame. We cannot select the time and place when sin is to catch up with us. It is a part of the tragic bitterness of sin that it must come out openly, publicly. Remember that which was whispered in secret will be shouted from the housetops. There is something in the very nature of sin that makes it show itself. Sin is like a cancer that eats its way to the surface and becomes apparent after it has poisoned the whole body. Sin is like the smallpox which marks its victim publicly. Sin does not always bring judgment immediately, and sometimes the punishment is long delayed. But sooner or later, according to the plain warning of God, sin must come to judgment, and often, to *public* judgment.

I remember that Rev. W. W. Melton of Waco, Texas, told how, as a boy, he planted cotton seed for his older brother. He begged to get off and planned to go swimming, but the older brother insisted that the boy could not go swimming until he had planted all the cotton seed. The sun kept getting lower, and the cotton seed did not diminish very rapidly. Finally the lad dug a hole in the ground and planted all the cotton seed in one place and covered them up and went swimming. But a little while after there came a big rain, and the cotton seed sprouted, and those planted all in one hole sprouted, too. The crusted ground buckled where they were, and some cotton plants began to appear. Finally the older brother found the place and the whole story came out. So sin reveals itself and comes out in public shame and public disgrace. Be sure your sins will find you out!

The God who hears the prayers in secret closets and answers them openly, is the same God who sees the sly sin hidden in the wicked heart and brings it to open and public judgment.

Some years ago, I remember, a man prominent in the church life in a North Texas town, a well-known citizen, a grocer, was arrested and charged with systematic looting of express packages. He was tried and convicted and sent for five years to the penitentiary. How shocked were all his friends, including my own father. His sin was secret, probably small at first, until it grew and grew and got a deadly hold upon him. And then, finally it dragged him out to open shame before his family and church, and to disgrace before the world. Sin finds one out in public!

* * *

Sin Must Be Punished and Murderers Must Pay. In that moving book, *The Seven Pillars of Wisdom*, Lawrence of Arabia tells how he and the Arabs, striking for independence from the unspeakable Turk during World War I took the village of Tafas from the retreating but blood-thirsty and murderous Turks. Among the corpses on the ground, a little figure tottered off as if trying to escape, a girl three or four years old, soiled dress red with blood down one shoulder and side. She had been wounded, a lance going deeply into her body at the neck. She begged, "Don't hit me, Baba!" A choking friend who lived in the village fell from his camel, knelt beside the child. Fearful, she tried to scream and died.

On the mud wall of a sheepfold, a pregnant woman, naked, had been pinned with a saw bayonet. Some twenty other innocent ones butchered were "set out in accord with an obscene taste, " Lawrence tells us.

Lawrence told his men that he would regard best the soldiers who would bring in most of the Turkish dead. Nearly insane with grief and righteous rage, they pursued the Turks, killing, killing. Part of Lawrence's Arabs had taken prisoner the last two hundred men, and had them huddled under guard. Lawrence would have saved them. But he was called to find one of his own men with thigh shattered and dying; yet heartless Turks had hammered bayonets through his shoulder and the other leg, pinning him to the ground. When they saw this last barbarism and asked who did it, Hassan, dying, motioned toward the prisoners. Is it any wonder that they turned guns upon the prisoners, and shot them down in a heap?

Under other circumstances that would seem horrible. But Lawrence and his men had fought honorably for freedom, by high standards of warfare, only to have women and children, old men and prisoners, tormented, violated and murdered. Say what you will, the conscience of decent men cries out that such sin must be punished and that such murderers must pay.

Love

Love Till the End

A mother said to her son, accused and convicted of murder, "Tell me, Son. If you will confess it, the judge said he would be lenient with you. The court will give a lighter sentence if you confess the crime."

"I did not do it, Mother." And he solemnly protested innocence to the end.

The mother proudly said, "My son did not do it! I know he didn't. He told me he didn't do it!"

The boy was put in the death cell. At last the chaplain came to lead him to the electric chair. "Have you any word for your mother?" the chaplain asked.

The lad, facing death, said, "Tell Mother I did it. I am guilty."

The chaplain hurried to tell the mother. "He is guilty. He says he did it."

Turning to the chaplain, the mother said, "Hurry, then; go back and tell him before he goes to the chair that I love him still!"

God loves the sinner even in Hell. God would save every sinner in the world if He could on righteous terms. He is "not willing that any should perish, but that all should come to repentance" (II Pet. 3:9).

* * *

The Love of God. I talked to an arrogant, proud woman, a woman who had been deliberately rebellious against God. She told me she did not believe what I preached. She was angry at God over the death of a loved one. She had been proud and haughty about her good deeds. But when I looked into her wan, sad face and told her that God loved her, her lips began to tremble and she said, "He does not! He *could not!*"

"Yes," I said, "God loves you. He loved you so much that He let Jesus die for you to keep you out of Hell. He loves you!"

Again she insisted, "I don't see how He could!" But suddenly she began to sob and in a few moments her rebellion was melted away and she surrendered to Christ. She could not continue to fight against the love that God has as proven by the death of His Son on Calvary. "God commendeth his love toward us, in that, while we were yet sinners, Christ died for us" (Rom. 5:8).

* * *

God's Love Should Awaken Love in Every Heart

God's goodness is like the continual wooing of a lover. "The goodness of God leadeth thee to repentance" (Rom. 2:4). How well I remember when I wooed and won my dear wife. When we were students in Baylor University together at Waco, Texas, I worked hard to earn my tuition and board and other expenses. I carried the mail for the University Post Office Sub-Station, I milked cows, I dried dishes, I clerked in the book store. Sometimes I wore patched clothing to classes. Sometimes in the cafeteria my lunch was buns and potatoes and gravy; and yet I found ways and means to carry the gifts that my love dictated to the girl that I loved and whose hand was even then promised me.

She liked candy—not a little bag of gumdrops, nor a 5¢ bar. No, her favorite was "King's Nut Trio." It came in golden three-decked boxes, Brazil nuts and almonds and pecans dipped in the richest chocolate, and it cost me one dollar and a half per pound! But, bless her dear heart, she got her candy many the time, and I felt that if she would but love me she might have all that my labor and planning and devotion could provide.

I will never forget when we went to the Junior-Senior banquet. I was a senior and she was a junior. The juniors entertained the seniors in the Gold Room of the Raleigh Hotel. She would be beautifully gowned and no one must outshine my sweetheart on that great night. I will never forget the long-stemmed hot-house American Beauty roses that I bought her for that occasion, though they cost me three dollars per half dozen! I never read a book that I delighted in but I marked it for her. I never was moved by a glowing sunset but I must tell her about it. I never thanked God for a blessing, I think, without pouring out to her my joys. No work was hard if she were pleased with it, and no road was long if she were at the end of it! I wrote her daily, month in and month out for four years, when we were away from each other. Unworthy as I am, I do not see how she could have helped loving me. My love gave all it had and demanded love in return.

And I think in some small measure this is a parable of the love of God for sinners. His tender compassion never sleeps in the night. His love knows no bounds of time or distance or even of wickedness.

*   *   *

Christian Love Sometimes Varies and Wanes. It is a sad thing that the love of a Christian is not perfect, since Christians are not perfect. In these last wicked days we are in it is prophesied that "the love of many shall wax cold" (Matt. 24:12). To such people Jesus sent the message, "Nevertheless I have somewhat against thee, because thou hast left thy first love" (Rev. 2:4). Though Christians do not lose their love, they sometimes lose the joy they had at first, the freshness and sweetness that was in their first love. But every saved person still has love for God, whether it is his first love or a love somewhat cooled down by the care and deceitfulness of this world.

When I was a boy, in a revival meeting a man for whom Christians had long prayed came back to God. We had supposed him an unregenerate sinner, but weeping, he stood before the congregation and said, "Twenty years ago I was saved. Since that time I have wandered far in sin. Sometimes I myself doubted if I were saved. But always in my heart, unseen by the world, there was a little flame that never went out. I could not destroy it. God would not let me go!" Surely that must be the experience of many a child of God.

*   *   *

"I Loved You Even if You Did Get Drunk!" Years ago, I am told, in the First Baptist Church of Dallas, Texas, there was a little boy six or seven years old. He was won to Christ in the Sunday school and was a happy-hearted little Christian. He was accidentally shot, and the doctor told the father that the little one could not live. Dr. Truett went with the father to the child's bedside to break the news gently. The father was not a Christian, a drinking man who had made life miserable at home many a time by his drunkenness. Yet he loved his child and wept with a broken heart to think he must lose the little one.

The boy called his father to lean down over the bed and lifted up his head and put his arms around his neck and said, "Daddy, I want you to remember this: I loved you even if you did get drunk!"

This broke the father's heart. Abruptly he turned and left the room, going out the front door, around the house and into an outhouse at the back. Dr. Truett followed him and found him on his face on the floor weeping out his heart. There the man of God put his arm around him and said, "And I have something to tell you. Your little boy loves you and I want you to know, God loves you, too, even if you do get drunk!" The drunkard was won to Christ. And I tell you, dear, unworthy, Hell-deserving sinner, God loves you, too. You ought to be in Hell as I ought; but God loves you and sent Jesus, not to condemn you but, to save you!

* * *

Love Triumphs! In my boyhood we had every year a Christmas tree at one of the two churches in our little town. One year it would be at the Baptist church, and the next year at the Methodist church. The entire town and countryside would attend. There each one brought his gifts for those he loved.

One year a certain young man had worked long and hard, month after month, saving money for the girl that he loved. And it was an open secret, we thought, that his love was not returned. On the Christmas tree that year his were the most expensive gifts, and there were many of them. As I remember, there were some fifteen or sixteen presents that he shamelessly had put on the tree so that everybody in the community might know how he loved her! That seemed then a little silly. However when a year or so later he got the girl, I revised my estimate!

Love does often tell, after all. But I will tell you now that that lovesick lad did not pursue the object of his affections with one half of the bounty of gifts that God pours out upon lost sinners who despise Him and hate Him and ignore Him, every day. God in His goodness seeks to woo and win the love of sinners by His mercy. The goodness of God is simply calling you to repentance. Every meal that you eat is the call of God to love Him. Every night's rest that leaves you fresh and vigorous is God's plea that you turn your face toward Him and serve Him. If you have a job, if you have good health, if you have a good name, if you have a home—whatever the mercy your heart is grateful for today, then remember that God gave it, gave it as a love gift to turn your heart toward Him!

*   *   *

Love the Other Sheep. *"And other sheep I have, which are not of this fold: them also I must bring, and they shall hear my voice; and there shall be one fold, and one shepherd."*—John 10:16.

Joe Trigger is a registered Tennessee Walking Horse. My, what a magnificent animal! Over sixteen hands high, tall, high-headed, with a flowing blond mane and a tail that reaches nearly to the ground. He has beautiful saddle gaits, foxtrot pace, singlefoot. I bought him for Mrs. Rice to ride along beside my fine Tennessee Walking saddle horse, MacArthur.

When I first brought Joe Trigger on the place, he was not well received. MacArthur was king of the farm and knew it. All the other horses respected him, followed his leadership. But Joe Trigger, so anxious to be friends with MacArthur, had to keep his distance. MacArthur saw to that. The new horse was not allowed in the bunch, so he grazed fifty or a hundred yards away until the others gradually came to recognize him as a member of the family, with all the same rights they had.

Sometimes we, like MacArthur, are not quick to recognize Christ's other sheep! All over the world He has millions of born-again people, dear to the heart of God, redeemed by the blood of Christ, loving Him and being loved by the Saviour. And Jesus reminds us, "Other sheep I have, which are not of this fold: them also I must bring, and they shall hear my voice; and there shall be one fold, and one shepherd."

*   *   *

"A Companion of All Them That Fear Thee." In Springfield, Missouri, the headquarters of the Assemblies of God in America, I had a citywide revival campaign in a big four-pole tent. I was invited to speak in the headquarters of the Assemblies of God and did. One night in the campaign twenty-six Assemblies of God preachers were on my platform as special guests. They did not talk in tongues, they did not make division and strife. They were glad to see a blessed revival and help get many people saved. They could cooperate in that.

I am saying that good Christians ought to have loving fellowship with other good Christians.

When I started out in the work of an evangelist, I earnestly sought from the Scriptures and in waiting on the Lord to know whether I should have campaigns only in Baptist churches or whether I should have united cooperative campaigns. One sweet verse of Scripture helped settle that—

Psalm 119:63: "I am a companion of all them that fear thee, and of them that keep thy precepts." Of course there are none who perfectly, without a sin or failure, keep the precepts of God. But God loves and counts the heart intent and the holy desire here, and so should we.

In other words, I am for God's people who believe the Bible, who love Jesus Christ, who try to win souls. I am against the crowd that is against Christ and the Bible.

*   *   *

Learning to Please

Let us say that a country boy moved to town. I knew such a case. He went to a nice church, and, oh, he saw the loveliest girl. She sang in the choir. She was sweet-faced and reverent. She was lovely in form and face and character. When he found that she attended the young people's meeting, he attended too. He took particular pains to get acquainted. He was more impressed with her than ever. He worked hard to get to sing in the choir so that he could be with her more. At last he got courage to ask if he could walk home with her. She was gracious and accepted his kindness.

Two or three times he had dates with her, then one day he telephoned saying, "May I see you Friday night?" But she was all excuses, she had other engagements, she was sorry.

"Well, what about Saturday night?" he asked. Oh, she was so busy she didn't see how she could go with him at this time at all.

Again he called for a date another night and was refused. Finally, in great distress of mind, he met her on the street and demanded to know what was the matter. Why would she not see him any more?

Red-faced she told him, "When we ate together you made noises with your soup. Your fingernails were dirty. You did not open the door of the car for me to get in."

The crude, country fellow, well-meaning but without the niceties and good manners to which she was accustomed, displeased her. She saw a genuine worth and character in the lad, but she was distressed by his crudity.

"Well, just give me a chance!" he pleaded. "I know I am from the country, and I have been poorly raised. But I will learn good manners if you will just be patient with me."

Well, she was forbearing. He went with the girl for two years, then they got married and by that time he had become a Lord Chesterfield in good manners!

You see, in waiting on her and learning to please her, he grew to be the kind of a companion she wanted.

So as a Christian waits on God and pleads with Him, the things that are wrong show up very glaringly in his own conscience, and he begins to find what God wants and what would be right. So, little by little, those things that were in the way vanish and God can answer his prayers!

*   *   *

Fellowship. I remember that, years ago, P. B. Chenault, pastor of the Walnut Street Baptist Church of Waterloo, Iowa, came to the Galilean Baptist Church in Dallas of which I was pastor, for two weeks of revival services. The night he closed that campaign he met his tragic death on the highway at the hands of a drunken driver, but I have always remembered how Brother Chenault came to my home. We had secured a nice little apartment for him and his wife and little girl for the meeting, but he simply drove up into my driveway, took out his bags, and said, "No, we want to stay with you." So he came with his wife to bring us great joy and comfort in the fellowship of those two happy weeks. So Jesus came into the home of Zacchaeus, the crooked tax collector, and fellowshiped.

~~~~~~~~~

Marriage

"Fifty-Fifty." I don't believe in women and men going fifty-fifty in the home. That is like the Italian who got a permit to make rabbit sausage. After a while he was arrested for selling adulterated sausage. Somebody accused him of putting dead horse meat with it.

He was called up before the court and the judge asked him, "Is that really rabbit sausage?"

"Yes," he replied.

"But somebody said it had horse meat in it."

"Well," he answered, "it is 'fifty-fifty.' "

"What do you mean, 'fifty-fifty'?" they asked him.

He answered, "Fifty-fifty—one horse and one rabbit!"

Any time you have a home on the basis of "fifty-fifty," you can put it down—one horse and one rabbit, and the man is the rabbit, as sure as the world! God didn't plan it that way.

* * *

God Put "Obey" in the Ceremony.
Once I was asked to marry a young couple whom I loved very dearly. The young bride-to-be asked me, "You are not going to put *obey* in the marriage ceremony, are you?" I answered back that of course I would not want to make up my own kind of marriage ceremony. "But," I said, "if I leave it out, God has put it in. It is in the Bible that wives are to be 'obedient to their own husbands.' You don't want me to leave out what God put in, do you?" And since she was a good Christian girl, she agreed.

Preachers, to please a modern world, may leave *obey* out of the marriage ceremony. But God puts it in just the same and preachers ought to, too, and no Christian wife pleases Him who does not take the solemn vow to obey her husband and who does not prayerfully, with God's help, seek to fulfill that vow.

* * *

Engagement Broken for God's Standard.
In 1963 we moved from Wheaton, Illinois, to Murfreesboro, Tennessee. I remember that as we packed and laid aside things we would not need, I came upon a great box of engraved wedding invitations. They brought to mind a strange but wonderful story. One of my daughters was engaged to a young man who planned to be a preacher, he said. His mother was well-to-do. Once when they were on a date, he said, "I will be so glad when we are married and we can cut off that long hair of yours so you will look like other women." My daughter said, "I am not going to cut my hair so I can look like other women. I am going to do what the Bible teaches, and that is that if a woman have long hair, it is a glory to her."

He insisted, "Oh, yes, you will. When you are my wife, you are going to dress like others and have your hair look like others." She solemnly pulled off the engagement ring, and though the wedding was already announced and the wedding invitations already printed, it was called off.

Later God gave her the love of another man who is now a godly preacher.

Oh, marriage out of the will of God is a tragedy unspeakable. And always a marriage of a saved person and a lost person is out of the will of God.

*   *   *

"This Is the End"

Some years ago I was to speak at Winona Lake Christian Assembly one Sunday afternoon. As I dressed in the hotel before going to the platform, the telephone rang. A preacher from South Bend said, "I must see you at once," I told him that I would be on the platform in ten minutes but if he would come to the room we would walk over to the auditorium together.

He told me a beautiful story.

"You remember last August you preached in the Wheaton Bible Church?"

"Yes," I said.

"Do you remember that you preached on 'Leaving All for Jesus'?"

I replied that I did not remember what the text or sermon was.

He said, "I know what it was, for one of the young women in my church came home and said, 'Pastor, we must get Jim saved.' She was engaged to marry Jim.

"We went to see this unsaved young man and pleaded with him. He said to his sweetheart, 'I'm not going to become a Christian now. I am glad you are a Christian. I want that kind of a wife. You may go to church, and sometimes I will go with you. I may even one day get saved, but not now.' And when we pressed the matter upon him, he turned rather angrily and said, 'No, you must drop that subject. I am not going to be a Christian now.' "

Then the pastor told me the young woman took the ring off her finger, handed it to her fiance and said, "This is the end."

Shocked, the young man said, "What do you mean?"

"I promised God that my life belonged wholly to Him at any cost. I am not going to marry a man who won't have Christ in my home and Christ in the marriage."

He protested that the invitations were already out and that already wedding presents were coming in.

She replied that most of them were within a radius of a few miles, so they could take the wedding presents back and she would tell them plainly it was her mistake and the marriage was off.

Glumly they made the rounds and returned the wedding gifts. Once back at her home he did not even get out to open the car door for her. She stumbled up the sidewalk and fell in a heap, unconscious. They rushed her to the hospital. She nearly died. But when she was well, people found God had given a great sweetness to her singing voice and she was blessing multitudes. Then God sent a Spirit-filled young preacher to this beautiful Christian who would not marry out of the will of God.

* * *

The Symbol or the Submission?

A devout man of another denomination came to Dr. Jack Hyles in Hammond, Indiana, wishing to go with him from house to house and learn how to do personal soul winning. But he was dressed in the traditional clerical garb of a collar turned around backwards, making him look like a Roman priest. Dr. Hyles said, "I will be glad to have you go with me soul winning, but you would be misunderstood with that garb. If you will change into a business suit so you will not mislead people, then you can go with me to win souls."

But his wife interrupted boldly and said, "He will do nothing of the sort! He will not take off his minister's garb!"

Dr. Hyles said, "What is the meaning of that little lace cap you wear?"

She replied, "It is a sign of my submission to my husband."

Dr. Hyles replied, "I would rather have the submission than the lace cap."

Oh, Christian women, what treasure is that adornment of a meek and quiet spirit which in the sight of God is of great price (I Pet. 3:4).

* * *

"Why Didn't Some Preacher Show Me That Fifteen Years Ago?"

I once held revival services in a small town in North Texas and preached on "Be Ye Not Unequally Yoked Together With Unbelievers." The next day a woman who was not present at the preceding service chided me saying, "I know what you preached last night and I don't believe it." From hearsay she had been displeased with my sermon. However, I told her that it was not my message but God's, and I turned in the Bible to II Corinthians 6:14 and had her read the plain command of God not to be yoked up with unbelievers. I knew her case. She had married an unsaved man. A fourteen-year-old son was already grieving his mother's heart and following in the footsteps of his un-saved father.

When she read the Scripture she turned to me and her eyes filled with tears. This is what she said— "Why didn't some preacher show me that fifteen years ago?" I answered back that I could not say for other preachers but for my part I wanted no brokenhearted woman, because of ignorance of the Word of God, blaming me for her sin and unhappiness when it was fifteen years too late! Therefore I am warning people not to be yoked up with unbelievers.

* * *

God Wants Submission More Than Money. I recall that once in Dallas, Texas, I received a money order for $6.00 from a woman in Oklahoma. She asked that the money be applied on the radio broadcast expense and said, "Please do not acknowledge this gift over the radio nor by letter. I will be sure that you have received it anyway. If you should write a let-ter or announce it over the radio my husband might learn of my gift. He told me never to send any money to radio preachers. I took this money from that which he gave me for household expenses. I want the Lord to have it for the radio broadcast which has blessed so many people."

I wrote the lady that I could not receive the gift and returned her money order, telling her why. She wrote me again and said, "I gave fifty dollars this way on our new church building, taking the money out a little at a time from that which my husband gave me for the expense of the household. Other preachers have taken money given in this way without any protest." But I replied that however much the money would be appreciated as a gift for the Lord's work under other circumstances, I could not be a party to her disobedience to her husband in this matter.

God is not pleased with rebel-lion, even though it be, ostensibly, because of love for Him. God wanted a meek and quiet spirit in the heart of that Christian woman, wanted her to be subject to her husband, more than he wanted $6.00 for a gospel radio program.

Missionary Service

The Universal Appeal of the Prodigal Son. In a Japanese town of some thirty thousand people, north of Tokyo, I preached under the little tent. Benches were without backs; a missionary played an accordion and people sang, not from songbooks but from sheets of paper held high by a young evangelist on which were written in Japanese characters a verse of the song. Many of the people had stooped in the rice paddies for a long, hard, back-breaking day, then came down the hills to the little tent. I preached through an interpreter that moving story of the boy who did not respect his father (a great sin among the Japanese), who got drunk on "sake" (the Japanese rice wine), wasted his father's money and came to want. They listened, entranced!

How universal is the appeal and the warning in this charming, moving story of the prodigal son! I found that in Japan this was an old, old story as it is in every land since Cain broke the heart of his mother and father.

"And do you know who that wild, rebellious boy was?" I asked one, then another. They were deeply interested. When I said, "I was that poor, lost boy who left the father's house and went into sin," they shook their heads partly in pity for the father, and partly in embarrassment for me that I should confess such a sin! But then I selected an old, long-bearded grandfather. "You were the prodigal boy! You went into sin. You wasted opportunity, wasted happiness. You were rebellious and sinful!" And I pointed to them one by one. They first looked in shocked surprise, then some of them began to nod their heads,

and some, with downcast eyes, showed deepest conviction.

How well the Lord Jesus fitted the Gospel to the frail, human heart! And wherever men and women are, there the story of the prodigal son is repeated and there men need the Gospel Jesus brought. So in that little tent that night, after long instruction, five people came to know Christ and trust Him and claim Him openly.

* * *

The Perfect Gentleman. David Livingstone opened Africa, the dark continent, to trade and to missionaries and the Gospel. He was in such constant danger, he endured so many privations that only an iron will and strong faith enabled him to press on through the almost insuperable difficulties until he had accomplished his purpose and made contact with the heathen black tribes across the continent. Livingstone said, "I was enabled to go on because I had the word of a perfect Gentleman, never known to break a promise, that He would be with me always."

The promise referred to is that of Christ in the Great Commission, "Lo, I am with you alway, even unto the end of the world" (Matt. 28:20). Livingstone, obeying that Great Commission and taking the Gospel to Africa, knew that Christ was with him as He had promised. And every Christian has this same promise, "I will never leave thee, nor forsake thee" (Heb. 13:5), and "Lo, I am with you alway, even unto the end of the world."

* * *

C. T. Studd: Nothing Left to Sacrifice.
C. T. Studd in England had inherited wealth. He had fame as the greatest athlete of his day. He had social standing. Practically anything in England that he wanted he could have. Yet he gave up his cricket playing, went to China as a missionary, gave away all his fortune deliberately and carefully, and then gave himself to a life of self-renunciation and self-denial to get the Gospel to poor sinners. He served in China, later he went into the interior of Africa and opened a new mission field. For some fourteen years he was kept away from wife and child by the call of preaching the Gospel to the heathen.

At last he died, away in the interior of Africa. Career and fortune had early gone to the altar. Health and home and family life went also. Indeed C. T. Studd once said, "I have searched into my life and I do not know of anything else left that I can sacrifice to the Lord Jesus Christ."

I say to you, God requires the same surrender of you as He re-

quired of C. T. Studd. It may not be Africa for you, but it means exactly the same surrender. I do not know whether you ought to give away all your money, but I know that you ought to be willing to do it any minute that you find it would please the Lord Jesus.

* * *

My "Missionary."
Each of my six lovely and gifted daughters is specially dear to me in her own way. One of them is specially dear to my heart because I gave her to God for the foreign mission field and always, between God and me, she is my "missionary." Mary Lloys and Chuck Himes were accepted by the China Inland Mission for work on the borders of Tibet, on the back side of China. They went to Philadelphia for a season of orientation. They were to wait a little while and Mary's health was to be built up, then they were to go to that far-off country where so many missionaries have died for Christ and the Gospel. I had quite a catch in my heart to remember that there were more graves of missionaries on the border of Tibet than there were Christians in the entire country! But God knows how gladly I gave my consent, and how fondly I planned to help pay the expenses of my daughter and son-in-law on the foreign mission field.

But communism overran China; the doors were closed. They went into the pastorate, and now Chuck is pastor of a soul-winning church and Mary has five beloved children. But down in my heart, between God and me, she is my dedicated and surrendered "missionary." I sometimes remind the Lord, very close to tears, that I did not seek to withhold her when she would have gone to that dangerous country on the roof of the world, from whence there was a good prospect that she would never return alive and that I might never see her until we should meet in Heaven. You see, I have a heart for missions.

* * *

A Martyr's Covenant

A few years ago a young couple went to China as missionaries. First Betty Scott went with her father, a Presbyterian missionary. She had been educated in an American college and at Moody Bible Institute. There she had fallen in love with John Stam. And John loved her with all his heart. They hoped and prayed and dreamed that God would allow them to live and work together. John was accepted as a missionary and went to China. There he saw Betty again, and soon they were married. In a year God sent a lovely baby, Priscilla. Then they went into the interior to open a new field. Soon communistic bandits came to take the town and sack it. They took John and Betty Stam and cut off their heads. Only the baby, Priscilla, lived to be brought back to America.

Many people thought, "Oh, what a tragedy!" No doubt many said, "What a waste of young lives and talent and training!" I can well imagine that some people thought, "Oh, if John and Betty had known the terrible cost, I wonder if they would have gone to China?"

Well, happily, I can answer that question. Do you suppose that God would take people to a martyr's death when they had not themselves surrendered to Him? Oh, no! Dr. Scott, Betty's father, sat by me at the faculty table for lunch at Moody Bible Institute several years ago and showed me a Bible that had been recovered many months after this martyrdom from Betty's effects, stolen by the communists. In the back of this Bible which he, Dr. Scott, had given to his daughter when she was a sophomore in college, he showed me in Betty's handwriting this solemn vow:

"MY COVENANT"

"Lord, I give up my own purposes and plans, all my own desires, hopes and ambitions (whether they be fleshly or soulish), and accept Thy will for my life. I give myself, my life, my all, utterly to Thee, to be Thine forever. I hand over to Thy keeping all of my friendships, my love.

"All the people whom I love are to take second place in my heart.

"Fill me and seal me with Thy Holy Spirit. Work out Thy whole will in my life, at any cost, now and forever. 'To me to live is Christ and to die is gain' (Phil. 1:21).

"Elizabeth Alden Scott
August 3, 1925."

So I was not surprised when I read excerpts from the diary of John Stam, her young husband, and found that he, too, had made a definite covenant, years before when he was a student at the Moody Bible Institute, asking God to glorify Himself in his young life "whether by life or by death" (Phil. 1:20). These two young people had a rendezvous with death. They had offered themselves for martyrdom. God in His infinite mercy granted to them that high and holy privilege, to die for the Gospel. How high their honor! How great their reward! Remember, it was voluntary. They gave themselves up to die for Jesus, and He accepted their gracious surrender and set His seal upon it and blessed it!

*   *   *

Crossing the Ocean Does Not Make Soul Winners!

Once I spent a month broadcasting with a noble radio preacher who is greatly loved and honored all over America. This good radio preacher raised thousands of dollars for a missionary society. A missionary representative who came to take part in one or two broadcasts and to receive the gifts raised by the radio evangelist said to me one day, "Dr. Rice, you ought to have a missionary to support."

I replied that I had long felt so myself, and that I had been continually looking for some missionary who would be as sacrificial and earnest about soul winning on the foreign mission field as I myself tried to be in the homeland, and that I wanted to take such a missionary and support him completely.

"I have just the missionary for you," he said. And then he introduced me to a young man he had with him. This young man was a graduate of a Bible institute. He had volunteered for the foreign field, and was under appointment. This missionary representative now sought support for him.

I took the young man aside and talked with him earnestly. I said to him, "Are you a soul winner?"

He replied that he wanted to win souls but had had very little experience in that.

"But have you ever won anybody to Christ?" I asked him.

He answered that he had been a member of a gospel team for two summers of his Bible institute training. In services conducted by a quartet during two summers, two different people had claimed Christ as Saviour. "I think I could claim part of the credit for those two, since I sang in the quartet," he said.

Without intending any reflection on the sincerity of the young man, I say frankly that I was astonished! How anyone could think that he would be equipped and qualified as a missionary in Africa when he had never personally led one soul to Christ, I could not see. I still feel the same way. I think that young man ought never to have been accepted as a foreign missionary candidate until he had proved himself a soul winner. Whether he lacked in concern or whether he did not understand the Scriptures well enough to use them in soul winning, or whether he knew nothing of the power of the Holy Spirit, I cannot say. I simply know that he was not a very good Christian if he did not win souls, and he dead certain could not be a very good missionary. Crossing the ocean does not make soul winners!

* * *

The Need Is Not the Call

I was once in special services in Omaha, Nebraska. A young pastor had been led of God to take the leadership in a church which was run down. The attendance had greatly increased. The power of God had come upon the church and week after week saw a moving of the Spirit of God. A great many people were saved. A flock of young people, particularly, gathered around the pastor. I saw abundant evidence that he was where God wanted him to be. He felt so himself. God had seemed to lead clearly in the work. His heart was happy in it. The results were blessed and satisfied him more and more that it was the place God had for him.

But a missionary leader challenged him, urged him to go to the foreign mission field. He reminded the young pastor that there were other churches in Omaha. If a sinner wanted to be saved, he could look up one of the churches and get saved. But, he said, in heathen countries there were many people who had never heard the Gospel and who never would. Therefore he urged the young pastor to resign his church and go to the foreign mission field.

"But I do not feel any call to the foreign mission field," replied the young pastor. "All the moving of the Spirit on my heart seems to lead me to stay here and do the work now given me, instead of going to the foreign mission field."

"But," said the missionary secretary, "you do not need to feel the call. The need itself is sufficient call. There are lost people who have not heard the Gospel. You ought to go and take them the Gospel."

The pastor then asked the missionary leader what course he would recommend. The pastor was urged to go at once to the missionary headquarters in the east and offer himself as a candidate for the mission field.

"But," protested the young pastor, "I do not have the money for a trip to New York."

The missionary secretary brushed this aside very lightly. "Sell your car and get the money," he said. "The fact that there is a great need is call enough."

All this had occurred just a few days before I was engaged in special services in the church. The young pastor asked me what he should do. Would not God tell him if He wanted him on the foreign field? Could a man not ask and have the clear leading of God about where he should minister? Was it lack of vision or lack of faith that made him hesitate to sell his car and go offer himself as a candidate for the foreign mission field?

I told him, as I tell you, that any such advice is foolish tommyrot. It is worldly wisdom, not spiritual wisdom. God can show people where they ought to serve, and one who goes to the foreign field or anywhere else to serve God without clear leading will most likely go to disaster and failure.

Persecution

Be Glad to Suffer for Jesus. For several years I have taken, each year, a group to the Holy Land, and we always, in Rome, visit the Mamertine prison where we believe Paul was in his second imprisonment and from which he went out to be beheaded. It is a little underground room, with ceiling about seven feet and about seven-teen feet across and there is a round hole about two feet in diameter through which they then let down the prisoner and through which they led down his food and such. Now they have a stairway for tourists.

As we met once, a great crowd of us, in that dungeon, I read those farewell words of Paul in II Timothy, how he hoped that Timothy could come soon, that he should try to come before winter and that he should bring the cloak Paul needed. And we read how Paul so gladly faced death and we sang,

"Faith of our fathers! living still
In spite of dungeon, fire, and sword:"

and then I called on a godly, small-town preacher from Tennessee to lead in prayer. He prayed, with tears, "Lord, don't let us ever complain about anything any more!" Oh, Christians should be glad to suffer for Jesus.

These days are not crowning days; these are cross days. And these are days to go outside the camp to Jesus bearing His reproach. And "if we suffer, we shall also reign with him" (II Tim. 2:12).

* * *

The Curse of Being Well Spoken of. I was once in a city-wide campaign with forty churches in Miami, Florida, with services in the new auditorium in Lakeside Park. I was introduced by Dr. Roy Angell in most kindly terms. I remember that he said, "Everybody loves Brother Rice. Southern Baptists love him. Northern Baptists love him. We are glad to have this man of God to lead a great revival campaign in our city."

All that came from a kindly heart of love and I appreciated the spirit of it.

But in preaching on this scene, later, I was led to say the following:

"Suppose that in the midst of this campaign I am stricken down by death. Mrs. Rice might come to the city and say, 'Since Dr. Rice was preaching here and his heart was so exercised for revival, let us have the funeral service from this same auditorium.' "

I said, "Suppose that in this auditorium the crowds come by to look on my cold, dead face. Here is a drunkard saved from his drink and from his misery and enslavement; he will come by and shed a tear of gratitude for the man who won him to Christ. Others will come by with scornful look and say, 'Now the old loud mouth is dead. He'll never condemn my sin any more. He'll never hurt my feelings any more!' "

I said further, "And suppose Dr. Angell is selected to preach the funeral sermon and suppose he should say, 'Here lies a man who had not an enemy in the world.' " And then turning to Dr. Angell I said, "Dr. Angell, if you should say that I would rise up again from that coffin and call you a liar! I would have to say that poor and weak as I am, thank God I've made some enemies for Jesus Christ's sake. I do not have the woe, the curse upon me which is pronounced upon those of whom all men speak well" Luke 6:26

* * *

"Dr. Torrey, Jump!" Dr. R. A. Torrey said when he was pastor of Moody Church, they once had many people saved. One night he stayed to wait and pray and talk with the others. As Dr. Torrey started to leave the building a man back at the door said, "Dr. Torrey, jump! Jump!"

"Why should I jump?"

"If you had heard what that man said about you who just left, you would have jumped, for the Bible says, 'Rejoice ye in that day, and leap for joy: for, behold, your reward is great in heaven: for in the like manner did their fathers unto the prophets' (Luke 6:23). Jump, Dr. Torrey!"

You have not much to jump about, do you? You fit into the world very nicely, don't you? You are interested in what the world is interested in—three bedrooms and bath and wall-to-wall carpeting and a paid vacation. So you fit in very well.

* * *

Between the Lines in Acts 16

Reading between the lines in Acts 16:25-34 I find a strange fact. "And at midnight Paul and Silas prayed, and sang praises unto God." But what happened the first part of the night? Why no songs of praises at ten o'clock and at eleven o'clock? Why those long hours before the time of praises and before the prayer of faith which delivered them?

I can imagine that the first half of the night was a time of soul-testing for Paul and Silas. Perhaps Paul said, "Silas, the people are meeting tonight for services and we are not there! Now the whole revival effort is ruined, because we healed this slave girl's demon-possession and got her saved."

I can imagine that Silas said, "Well, Paul, I'm for plain preaching, but don't you think you carried the thing too far? Now we are in disgrace. Everybody in town has heard that we have been arrested, that we have been publicly beaten, that we are in jail. Even the sinners have been told we are teaching customs that are wrong and wicked and unlawful."

I do not know all that went on in the hearts of Paul and Silas. But at last I imagine Paul looked up and said, "Well, bless God, that slave girl is saved! She will never tell any more fortunes. She has peace and forgiveness. Thank God, we did right and God answered prayer. So I'm going to rejoice. God can take care of the ruined revival. God can take care of the public disgrace and the bad reputation. Let's have a good song."

So they prayed and sang praises to God.

The prisoners heard them, we are told.

But somebody else heard them too. Let us imagine a scene in Heaven.

I can imagine that near the throne of God, Gabriel stands rather anxiously waiting to see what God would do. I can imagine that the Lord turns to him and says, "Gabriel, what is wrong? Why are you troubled? You seem upset!"

And I can imagine that Gabriel answers back, "Lord, aren't You going to do anything about those two preachers in jail? They were true to You. They preached the truth. They won that slave girl and cast out the demon. Now they have been abused and beaten; their clothes are torn, and they are sitting there in a dark dungeon with their feet fast in the stocks. They had no supper. They're sitting on a cold, stone floor. Their backs ache. Lord, aren't You going to do anything about it?"

And let us imagine further. I imagine that the Lord turns to the Angel Gabriel and says, "Well, what would you like to do about it?"

And Gabriel answers, "I'd like to go down there and shake that jail to pieces! I'd like to break those stocks open and turn Paul and Silas loose and break every lock on the doors in that old jail. I'd like to shake that old jailer out of his bed and bring him to his senses!"

I can imagine that the Lord turns and says to Gabriel, "All right, Gabriel, but take it easy, don't hurt anybody!"

It may not have happened just that way in Heaven, but something happened! For suddenly God shook the old jail with an earthquake. The stocks were broken and Paul withdrew his aching ankles from them, and so did Silas. The doors flew open, the chains fell off. The keeper of the prison awoke out of sleep and saw the prison doors open. He thought, "Every prisoner has escaped! They will hold me accountable for this and put me to death tomorrow!" So he drew a sword and would have killed himself.

But Paul cried with a loud voice, saying, "Do thyself no harm: for we are all here."

So the old jailer called for a light and came in with great trembling and fell down on his knees before Paul and Silas. I suppose he admitted the wickedness of beating the apostles. At any rate, he brought them out of the jail and said, "Sirs, what must I do to be saved?" Paul and Silas told him how to trust Christ, and the jailer and his whole family were saved!

Prayer

Power in Prayer. Do you want to pray for power? Then how encouraged we are when we find how Jesus insisted that the disciples tarry in Jerusalem until they be endued with power from on High. How it ought to strengthen our faith!

This is why all the great evangelists were mighty men of prayer. Charles G. Finney would frequently feel some lack of power and blessing and would set apart a day of fasting and prayer "for a new baptism of the Holy Ghost," as he was wont to say. Moody sought God unceasingly for two years, until he was mightily endued with power. Dr. R. A. Torrey started the prayer meeting in Moody Church in Chicago and there prayed for two years that God would send a great revival. Then suddenly a committee from Australia came and sought out Torrey, the Bible teacher who had never been much thought of as an evangelist, and Torrey began the mighty campaigns in Australia that led him finally around the world, with hundreds of thousands of souls saved under his great ministry. Torrey learned to pray, so he learned to have revivals. If you want to know the simplicity of Torrey's prayer life and his teaching on prayer, read the little book, *How to Pray* (Moody Colportage Library), or *The Power of Prayer and the Prayer of Power* (Fleming H. Revell).

* * *

Prayer Meetings of Two Country Boys. I had a letter one day that blessed my heart. It was from Dr. Wallace Noles in California. He and I had been out of touch with each other for many years until he saw a copy of THE SWORD OF THE LORD given him by his pastor. "I wonder if that is the John Rice with whom I used to have prayer meetings when we were boys together in West Texas?"

My heart rejoiced as I remembered those prayer meetings, attended by two country boys who rode into town on horseback to pray together at the little Baptist church. Often we were there alone. Sometimes we told how God had answered our prayers and told each other what we had found new in the Bible during the week, and prayed there in the dark. Sometimes, in the summer we sat out on the church steps together under the stars. We had other prayer meetings off alone at the noon hour when we worked together in the threshing crew. We believe that, in God's mercy, the salvation of many souls can be traced back in the heavenly records to those prayer meetings held by two boys, fifteen or sixteen years old.

* * *

Charge It to My Father. When I was a boy, I drove to the general store in the little cowtown of Dundee, Texas, and I said, "We want a 24-pound sack of flour, and we want a gallon of syrup, ten pounds of sugar and we want this and this and this." I would say, "Charge that to Will Rice." My dad who sent me for these things, gave me authority to charge it to him. I asked it in his name and got it. Now, my name wasn't good at the store, but my dad's was; he had an account there.

And when I come to ask things from God, I am a poor, weak kind of a child, and I don't always know God's will and don't know what is right. But when I find out what Jesus wants and ask that of my Father, wanting just what Jesus wants, I can honestly ask it in Jesus' name.

* * *

When to Ask for $10,000. A young minister's wife read my book, *Prayer—Asking and Receiving,* and was thrilled to be reminded how often God had answered prayer, even this poor preacher's prayers. So she wrote to me and said something like this:

"Brother Rice, I have read your book on *Prayer* and I see that you can get things from God. I want you to join with me in prayer that God will give my husband $10,000. For $10,000 he can buy a good car, and can pay his expenses of four years of college, and he can be free from any trouble and concern about finances during these college days. Thus he will do better school work, and have greater peace of mind. I am asking you to agree with me to ask for $10,000 now for my husband."

I wrote her that I could not join in any such request. I did not believe it the will of God. I did not believe that is the way God takes care of His preachers. I told her that if I had the $10,000 to give away I would not give it for that purpose. I told her that if her husband had a rich father with millions, and who gave away thousands of dollars each year, I still thought it would be folly for that indulgent father to put $10,000 cash in his son's hands at one time, to prepare for four years in the future.

It might be that if that young preacher learned the lessons God teaches preachers by poverty and daily waiting on God and living with some hardship, but with constant evidence of God's care, that later he might have some enterprise for God that would justify asking for $10,000 at one time and that God might give it.

* * *

"Pray Without Ceasing" (I Thess. 5:17). How could one pray without ceasing? Is not that an impossible standard? I answer no, that the Bibile can be taken at face value. God's standards are proper standards, and God's words say what they mean and mean what they say. Prayer ought to arise from the heart like the fragrance from burning incense on an altar day and night, all the time. The soul of a Christian can be so possessed of God, so hungry for His presence that both the conscious and the subconscious mind carry on the pleading, the searching for God's face and His will and way and work.

Here is an example. The baby sleeps in his crib, and when all the household is abed, mother settles down to rest. In the night there is a tiny whimper, and instantly the mother is awake. She was *listening!* She was watching over the little one, even while she slept. Her soul was so set on the care of the little one that while her conscious mind slept, the subconscious being took over the listening post at her ear and watched through the darkness.

In the West Texas cattle country where I grew up, much of my boyhood work was done on a horse. Many a day I rode long hours, sometimes ten or twelve hours a day. Once after a long, heavy day it was far into the night when I, wearied to exhaustion, turned my sorrel horse homeward. As he followed the long road across a ranch pasture, I sat upright in the saddle, sound asleep. When he came to the gate and stopped, I awoke. When I had opened the gate, gone through and closed it, again I slept in the saddle until the tired horse stopped at the corral gate. My muscles did their accustomed work of years when my eyelids shut and I slept. But part of me was conscious of my horse, my feet in the stirrups, and the accustomed motion; and I awoke instantly when the horse stopped.

And, dear friend, if a mother can be conscious of her babe when she sleeps, and a horseman can be conscious of his horse and maintain his equilibrium when he sleeps, cannot a Christian who with all his soul loves the Lord and longs for certain blessings which he seeks— cannot such a Christian still be conscious of God when he sleeps? One hypnotized carries out certain orders through the control of the subconscious mind. So it is foolish to say that we cannot do what God commands about prayer simply because our consciousness is directed to other business or because we sleep.

*   *   *

A Hole for Each One. I think this illustration will help you to understand how eager God is to hear our prayers, and how He has provided many, many various promises, trying to encourage us to pray. A visitor at a farmhouse, it is said, saw one large hole and three smaller holes at the bottom of an outside door. So he curiously asked the farmer what the holes were for.

"They are for the cat and the kittens," replied the farmer.

"But," said the visitor, "why wouldn't one large hole do? Why can't the kitten go through the same hole as the mother cat?"

"No, that wouldn't do," said the farmer, "when I say, 'Scat,' I mean scat, and every kitten needs his own hole!"

And so every Christian needs his own promise. The blessed promise of God in one verse is just what one Christian needs to stir his faith. But the same promise arouses no spark of hope and faith in the breast of another. So God gives the other Christian another promise.

* * *

"Amen!" "Amen!" "Amen!" When my oldest daughter was three years old, she taught me a shocking lesson. In our prayer at the table I found that she waited until I drew near the end of my prayer and then she began to say, "Amen!" "Amen!" "Amen!" It seemed strange. I was puzzled. How did she know when I was drawing near the end of my prayer?

And upon careful examination I found I was saying approximately the same thing in every prayer. I could start my prayer and let it go like a phonograph record, and my mind could wander here or there while my lips went through the pious phrases and the platitudes that long before had meant something but now had become a commonplace form with no heart-cry to God. And my three-year-old baby girl, who was hungry, and glad when the prayer was through, could anticipate the close of the prayer. She knew just what came next because I had said the same thing so many times!

My spiritual face was certainly red! I found with shame that I had drifted into a kind of formalism in my thanks at the table. I was a Pharisee, a hypocrite. Of course, I was a very well-meaning hypocrite, as all Pharisees are, but nevertheless there was a fundamental insincerity in the following a certain form and using pious terms which had more or less lost their meaning. Shame, shame on us that when we pretend to pray we usually do not really ask anything from God!

* * *

The Exercise of Prayer. I once visited a home in Chicago where for purposes of exercise they had an "electric horse." As a horseman of long experience in my youth I was asked to ride the electric horse. I got on, pressed the button, and presto, galloped and galloped, arms flapping, coattail waving! The action was a fine imitation of the gallop of a horse. But it was only an imitation after all, for I pressed the button, the galloping stopped, and I got off exactly where I got on! I had not been anywhere at all! And that is exactly like the prayer of a modernist, purely for exercise, and not to get things from a prayer-hearing, prayer-answering God!

Prayer is not meditation, not adoration, not even communion in the ordinary sense. Pray is *asking God for something.*

*   *   *

Keep on Asking

I went to Chicago University in 1921 for graduate work. I left my teaching work at Wayland College to work on the M. A. degree in Chicago. I went to the University book store for a job to pay expenses. (I had worked in a book store at Baylor University.) I said to Mr. Fred Tracht, "I want a job in the book store here."

He answered, "We are already filled up and I have another fellow in mind when we need anybody."

But I said, "Well, you might need me. I will come back tomorrow."

He said I needn't come back. But I did—the next day. I said, "Mr. Tracht, anything open yet?"

"No, I guess not."

"Well, I just wanted to remind you that I have had experience in a book store. I love books. I am dependable and I want the job. I am going to work my way through here."

He answered, "Well, never mind. I have another fellow in mind if we need someone."

"That is all right," I said. "I will come back tomorrow."

He softened a bit and said, "Come back in a couple of weeks and we will see."

"I will be back tomorrow," I said.

I went back the next day. "I came by to see if anything had turned up."

"You say you worked in the Baylor University book store and you know books pretty well?"

"Yes, I have —yes, I think so."

"We will see about that," he said. "I might need you; I don't know. Give me your phone number and I will call you."

The next day I came back to ask if anything had turned up. Mr. Tracht said, "When can you go to work?"

I took off my hat and went right to work! That other fellow wasn't hanging around like I was, and I got the job.

When a man is persistent, don't you think God pays more attention? Don't you believe when one of His children comes and says, "Lord, I want so and so; I want to please You about it whether I get anything to eat or not, whether I sleep or not; and if anything needs changing, I want it changed to please You, Lord. I am going to wait until I get it"—the Lord is honor-bound to pay attention? If God says, "Ask, and it shall be given you; seek, and ye shall find; knock, and it shall be opened unto you" (Matt. 7:7), then when someone comes with tears and earnestness and confession, waiting before God, wanting this more than something to eat, don't you know God is willing to hear a prayer like that? To be sure He is!

*   *   *

Bible Preaching Makes People Tremble. In Shenandoah, Iowa, we had a night of prayer. The second man who prayed began to weep. "O God, forgive my sins! I came here tonight, Lord, hoping You would save me. Lord, I am such a sinner! I wish You would save me." We got a preacher to take him to another room, and we went on praying.

There was a young woman in a green suit, back about four or five seats, and she too began to sob. "Lord, save me! Won't You forgive my sin? If I haven't gone too far, Lord, forgive me and save me." As she wept, I had my daughter Grace take her to one side and show her the plan of salvation.

I am just saying that the Bible kind of preaching, like Paul did against sin, "on righteousness and self-control and judgment to come" ought to make people tremble (Acts 24:25).

*   *   *

More Tracks! Out on the Pacific Coast, a Chinaman was cooking for a lumber camp. He went out for a walk in the snow one day on the side of the Sierra Mountains. As he walked along in the snow, he heard a noise behind him, and saw behind him a few yards back a big grizzly bear sniffing along at his tracks. He said, "Vell, you likee my tracks, I makee you some more!"

I tell you what to do: Pray bigger prayers. Oh, let's give God a chance to pour in.

*   *   *

Praying Definitely. I was only a young Christian, about eighteen, in the cattle country of West Texas, when a dear country preacher, R. H. Gibson, took me with him to a rural community for revival services at the Black Flat schoolhouse. The first Monday morning, after one day's services, he and I went out early to pray. He read some verses of Scripture from his little Testament and then said, "Can we agree on something definite to ask God to give us in the service tonight?" We talked it over prayerfully and finally agreed that it seemed that God was laying it on our hearts to pray for five souls to be saved that night. And so we prayed, he first and then I, asking God to give us five souls in the evening service. That night five souls were saved and came out publicly, openly for Christ so definitely that no one doubted their salvation.

The next morning we rejoiced together in our place of quiet prayer out among the rocks and waited on the Lord to see if He would lead us again to know just how many we should ask. After a quiet time of discussion we each felt led to ask for three souls to be saved that night. We prayed, each of us, for three souls. That night three people were happily converted and came out in open profession of faith in Christ. Later

we named particular people in our prayers and felt clearly led to ask for their conversions in the services that evening. The evening we prayed for Bill Palm to be saved he trusted Christ as his Saviour. (Later he was my roommate in college.)

In those few days it dawned upon me that God wanted Christians to pray for *definite objects*, to be explicit in their requests.

* * *

Keep Your Rendezvous With God. The great spiritual victories have been won in secret.

Brainerd, kneeling in the snow, praying for the Indians. Finney, in a hayloft in mid-winter wrapped in a buffalo robe, praying all night.

D. L. Moody, rising at four each morning for an hour alone with God before anyone else awoke.

A group of students meeting in "the haystack prayer meeting" and four men starting the modern mission movement.

John and Charles Wesley with Whitefield and one or two others meeting alone to pray for revival, and seeing the beginning of the marvelous Wesleyan Methodist movement that probably saved England from a French Revolution, and which has been used of God in England and America and around the world to save millions of souls.

George Muller, walking the floor of his study or kneeling by his chair, hours a day, pleading, arguing with God, quoting Scriptures to God, demanding that a good and holy God must keep His promises, that God must not let orphan children go hungry, and so getting millions of dollars for his orphanage without ever taking a collection or asking anyone for a penny.

Those are illustrations of the fact that the biggest deals, the greatest transactions that people ever see completed with God are done with one or a few who go further than others can go in trusting God. Take courage, then, if you are alone. Take courage if your ideas seem radical and over-enthusiastic and impractical to others. It may be if you keep a rendezvous with God at the time and place He has appointed, and if you furnish the vessels, that He will multiply the oil beyond the dream of anybody.

Preaching

"Choose You This Day"

"Now therefore fear the Lord, and serve him in sincerity and in truth: and put away the gods which your fathers served on the other side of the flood, and in Egypt; and serve ye the Lord. And if it seem evil unto you to serve the Lord, choose you this day whom ye will serve; whether the gods which your fathers served that were on the other side of the flood, or the gods of the Amorites, in whose land ye dwell; but as for me and my house, we will serve the Lord."—Josh. 24:14,15

The late beloved Dr. H. A. Ironside, who was for eighteen years pastor of the famous Moody Church in Chicago, told me how devout Christian leaders in England invited him and the late Dr. Mel Trotter of Grand Rapids, a blessed evangelist and founder of rescue missions, to tour England celebrating the one hundredth anniversary of the birth of D. L. Moody. Evangelist Moody's tremendous impact on England was thus to be revived by the evangelistic preaching of two men who were, in some sense, followers of D. L. Moody. Dr. Ironside was pastor of the tremendous Moody Memorial Church in Chicago, founded by Moody, the "cathedral of fundamentalism," with auditorium seating 4,040. Mel

Trotter, a man founding more than 50 rescue missions and winning thousands of the down-and-out and holding blessed citywide revival campaigns, thus, too, represented the evangelism of D. L. Moody in some sense.

Dr. Ironside said that the kindly but timorous English brethren suggested that they be tactful and not "divide the congregation," as they called it. And he, Dr. Ironside, tried to follow that plan, but soon the Spirit-filled Mel Trotter, he said, was boldly calling for everyone who knew he had been born again to stand up or to hold his hand high or otherwise to claim it, and was urging sinners to admit their need for salvation and come to Christ.

And so in the Bible, God's Spirit-filled leaders again and again pressed the matter to divide the crowd into those who are for God or against Him, those who would set out to love and serve the Lord, those who would serve heathen gods or their own selfish will.

* * *

Preach Against Sin! In the midst of a great independent revival campaign in Waxahachie, Texas, a man, just returned from serving five years in the State Penitentiary as a bootlegger, sent for me. I had preached plainly against sin. My wife was frightened and urged me not to go. There had been many threats because of my preaching on the liquor traffic, but I knew God was in it.

I found the man in a wheel chair. He had heart trouble. The doctor told him that he probably wouldn't live but a few months.

He started to complain, telling how he had provided a car for the man who ran for the sheriff's office, had put $200 cash into his support, then he said, "Then he was elected, and then he sent me to five years in hell in the penitentiary!"

I told him frankly, "I am glad to help you any way I can, and I will be glad to pray for you, but let's have it understood from the beginning: I am against the dirty liquor business and everybody who takes part in it, and I am for the law enforcement and the men in authority."

The man looked up to me and very pitifully said, "That is why I sent for you. There are many preachers in this town, but you can't tell what side they are on. You can't trust what they tell you. I have only a few months to live, and I have to get right with God. I want somebody true to God to tell me how." The man soon forgave those he hated and he trusted the Lord and was wonderfully saved. Every week young people would go to his home to sing and pray with him until he died. But he wanted somebody who spoke plainly against sin. He could trust such a man of God.

Oh, how can anybody trust any man of God who doesn't take a plain, sharp stand against sin and wickedness!

* * *

"Don't You Know Where to Go to Find Out?" As assistant pastor of the First Baptist Church of Plainview, Texas, I was to preach on a Sunday night in the absence of the pastor, and I was greatly burdened about facing that crowd of 600 people. A saintly old minister, Rev. G. I. Brittain, and I were walking together, and I hoped he would suggest a sermon theme. I said, hinting, "I do not know what to preach Sunday night." He answered at once, "And don't you know where to go to find out?"

God rebuked me with the dear brother's words. Quickly I answered, "Yes, I DO know where to go to find out what to preach, and I am going there!" I went to God in earnest prayer and God gave me the sermon I was to preach, through the clear leading of the Holy Spirit and through God's Word. We need never be distraught, at the end of our resources. Wait upon the Lord!

* * *

"I Can't Preach!" Sometimes when I preach, I do it so poorly, I can have a great deal of sympathy with the way a preacher friend felt down in Texas. He came in one day after preaching and threw himself across the bed. His wife said, "Jeff, come to dinner."

"I don't want anything."

"Come on to dinner!" she said.

"Go on and eat, I am not coming!"

She said, "I don't want to eat without you."

"Throw it out, then!" he said.

"Jeff, what's the matter with you?"

He said, "Leave me alone!" And Jeff Davis said, "What is the matter is that I can't preach! And I don't know anybody who can preach! Leave me alone!"

I have been there more than once! But I say sometimes when I preach God is in it, and I had rather do it than eat. I had rather do it than sleep. I had rather do it than be President. I had rather do it than trade places with the richest or most powerful man on earth.

* * *

"Take Him Out!" A game is on! On the baseball diamond is a pitcher, and he winds up and pitches.

"*Ball one!*" shouts the umpire. The ball was no good!

And he winds up and pitches another.

"*Ball two!*" says the umpire!

Again he pitches, but again fails to get it over the plate!

"*Ball three!*"

He can't get it over the base.

"*Ball four!*" says the umpire. "Take a walk!"

The pitcher failed, and out in the stand they begin to say, "Take him out! Take him out!"

Oh, I tell you, my friends, sometimes when—God forgive us—we fat preachers, we oily-tongued preachers, peace-at-any-price preachers, preachers who do not hit sin, who cannot lose a friend for Jesus, preachers who never make anybody mad, we preachers that do not know anything about Hell and judgment and repentance; I think sometimes Paul says, "Lord, take him out! Lord, take him out! I have marks on my body where they stoned me and left me for dead! They had to let me over the city wall of Damascus in a basket at night with ropes; I have been in chains over at Rome. Lord, take him out! He has no tears, no broken heart, no power of the Spirit. Take him out, Lord, and get somebody who can preach, somebody who means business!"

How we fritter away time and opportunities when Heaven and Hell are filled with people watching in deepest concern our efforts to win souls. I do not know whether Paul says that, but in Heaven they are wonderfully concerned about this business of soul winning.

* * *

He Missed His Calling. How far has that man missed his calling, and the intent of God, who claims to be a gospel minister but does not win souls! I remember talking to a preacher, a graduate of Moody Bible Institute, a graduate of Wheaton College, and who even then was taking graduate work in Northern Baptist Seminary. He told, me, "Now evangelism is all right for those who like it, but personnally I do not feel led to do that. I want a teaching ministry. I want to be pastor of not too large a church, then there will not be too many calls on my time. Then I can have a big library and spend much time in my study, digging into the Word of God. If you feel called to evangelism, that is well and good, but I choose to be simply a teaching pastor."

I looked at that poor man into whom so many thousands of dollars of God's money had been invested, and I fear without much hope of return, and I said to him:

"There is nothing wrong with you that could not be cured if you simply come back to God as a backslider, like a drunkard, or like Peter who denied the Lord, or like David who committed adultery. God can forgive a preacher who has missed the whole idea of his calling and He can make his life over just like He can others who are backslidden.

* * *

Called to Preach? In West Texas a dear Baptist deacon in a country church said to me, "Brother Rice, I am afraid the preachers around here are not called to preach. They have no tears when they preach. Nobody is ever converted. There seems to be no burden for souls and no power to win them."

I answered him, "Oh, they are probably called, but perhaps they have not been anointed to preach. One needs not only a divine instruction, a clear leading as to whether he ought to preach the Gospel, but he needs a holy empowering to melt his heart, give him compassion and power to win souls."

Oh, reader, I beg you today, set out to win souls, constantly meditating in the Scriptures and seeking the burning heart, praying continually to be filled and empowered by the Holy Spirit.

* * *

People Are Going to Hell. My nephew, Pete Rice, then in charge of the horses on his father's ranch and supervising the rides throughout the summer on the big Cumberwood Christian Conference grounds at Murfreesboro, was asked by one of the preachers at a conference, "What do you plan to do after you are through college?"

Pete answered, "Well, I would like to run the ranch and handle livestock, but I guess I'll have to be an evangelist."

But the questioner persisted, "Why do you say you 'have to be' an evangelist? Can't you be whatever you want to be?"

"Well, with all those people going to Hell, and all that, I guess I'll have to be an evangelist," Pete replied.

And that was a wonderfully spiritual response. That is some evidence of the call of God which God had put not in his mind primarily, but in his compassionate heart.

* * *

The Foolishness of Preaching When my father started out to preach, a man said to him, "Will, you are young and you are making a fool of yourself. You can go far in this world. You have a personality and a good mind, and you could make lots of money, see the world, make a name for yourself; but now you go throw yourself away preaching the Gospel. Will, there is nothing to it."

My father said, "I tell you now, you are dead wrong if you think there is nothing to Christ and the Bible and salvation. There is something to it. I can prove it to you. You come and sit on the front seat in this first revival and hear me preach, and if you are not saved during this revival, I will never preach again, I will lay the Bible down. There is nothing to my call to preach if God won't save you."

The man answered, "I am a mighty busy man, but I think enough of you to break you of this foolishness, and we will get this thing settled if you mean business about it."

So he came and sat on the front seat. The first time my father preached, nothing happened to him. And my father said, "If God doesn't help me, I am ruined. God called me to preach. How can I quit preaching? I told this man I would lay down my Bible if after he had heard me preach during this revival, he was not saved." He said, "Now, God, it is up to You to do it."

The next night the man sat on the front seat. That time he was a little bit more sober, and the third night he came and broke down, came weeping down to the altar.

He confessed how ungodly he was, how great a sinner he was. He said, "God has been good to me to let me live. Will, pray for me." He was saved and so my father did not have to quit the ministry!

* * *

Bold Preaching. My brother, Dr. Bill Rice, also an evangelist, held a blessed revival campaign in a big tent in a city in California known as the "wine capital of America." They grew grapes in that beautiful valley, and in the city they made wine to be sold all over America. Some of the wealthy churchmen, in the wine business, approached my brother and said, "Some of us plan to put $2,000.00 in your love offering if you do not disturb the business from which so many nice people get their livelihood." But he went boldly before that congregation and preached, "Woe unto him that giveth his neighbour drink," from Habakkuk 2:15.

* * *

"Preach It Everywhere!" A young preacher said to me years ago at Toccoa Falls, "Brother Rice, people criticize me. I preach on Hell all the time, and they say I am one-sided about it. I want your opinion."

I said, "When you preach on Hell, do you weep?"

"Yes, and that's another thing they criticize me about. I can't keep the tears back."

I said, "Go ahead and preach it everywhere you go then."

* * *

Sowing the Gospel Seed. Oh, it is so important to keep the gospel seed pure, and not to mix with it any false gospel (Matt. 13:37-39).

What happens when mixed seeds are sown together?

In our West Texas garden once we planted rows of cucumbers, and beside that rows of cantaloupes. It was thoughtless, and how astonished I was when I picked what appeared to be a beautiful cantaloupe, and found that on the inside it tasted like a cucumber, but not a good cucumber! It was no good to eat and the seed was no good for planting.

Once as a lad I picked cotton under the hot Texas sun and thought how nice it would be if I could find a good watermelon and eat it in the shade! I found the watermelon in the patch nearby, but alas, when, with difficulty, I broke it open to eat the red heart of the melon, as I thought, I found it was not a watermelon. Someone had planted watermelon vines and citron vines or "pie melon" vines side by side. The resulting melon had a rind so tough I could hardly break it or cut it, and the inside was not even red and tasted like a gourd! That is the result of mixing two kinds of seeds in the same field.

We should beware of sowing divers seeds side by side "lest the fruit of thy seed which thou hast sown and the fruit of thy vineyard be defiled" (Deut. 22:9).

* * *

From Playboy to President. It is said that Vice-President Chester A. Arthur, when elected as the teammate of President Garfield, was a playboy, and was counted the tool of selfish interests who sought to use him for bad ends in the government. But on the death of President Garfield, Chester A. Arthur suddenly found himself president. And with commendable integrity he suddenly broke away from all the men who would have used him for evil purposes and dedicated himself to the business of being an upright president. He was never a great president nor a great man, but he was greatly sobered by the responsibility thrust upon him so unexpectedly; and he felt the need to watch his step and safeguard every action since he was exalted to such a responsible place.

Every evangelist anointed of God and greatly used in preaching before big congregations will find that the hearts of multitudes are given into his hands. He can lead them right or wrong. How earnestly, then, should he seek the will of God and how holily should he seek to humble his heart and avoid the sins that come with prominence. Every attractive gospel singer will have foolish young women throwing themselves at his head. Unless he walks very softly and discreetly he will fall into grievous sin. The man who reaches a responsible place of importance and fame must watch his step. He will be tempted all the more.

* * *

A Reproach on the Pastor. First Timothy, chapter 3, gives some very strong commands to the pastor about his family. He must be "one that ruleth well his own house, having his children in subjection with all gravity" (vs. 4). And his family is involved in the command of verse 7, "Moreover he must have a good report of them which are without; lest he fall into reproach and the snare of the devil."

In a revival campaign in Oklahoma I walked from door to door, from business house to business house, inviting people to revival services at the First Baptist Church. They were courteous to me and kind but reserved; and they stayed away in great numbers! I did not know why, until one morning I woke to find that the pastor's nineteen-year-old son had come home drunk in the night, had gone into the church basement and lay there in his vomit. A preacher's children may bring great reproach and limitations on the preacher's ministry.

* * *

Preaching Without Tears. When I first began to preach, I was shocked at the difference in preaching and in other public speaking. I had carefully worked out every detail of my speeches, often memorizing them, polishing them, trimming every word to suit. They were logical and well ordered. But when I began to preach, some way the Spirit of God got hold of me and I would oftentimes leave the prepared thread of discourse, with this illustration or that, or with entirely new material that I had not prepared. And I found that again and again the tears ran down my face as I spoke, and my voice would choke with emotion. I was sometimes greatly embarrassed, and I once asked God to let me preach without so many tears. He took me at my word and the next time or two I tried to preach it was cold and barren and powerless as if I knew nothing of God. I had no joy in my own heart; how could I rejoice others? I had no tears over sinners, and why should sinners weep?

On my face I asked God to give me back again the tears, the broken heart, and He did. And I say to you solemnly that all the preaching without tears, without fervor, without a holy abandon such as a man must have if he is possessed and driven by the Spirit of God—all such preaching is a mockery. God forgive us poor, lukewarm preachers!

Revival

Christians: Warn Men

I have learned in these years as an evangelist that one indispensable part of a great and blessed revival is that the people of God begin to join in with the preacher, and join in with the Holy Spirit, and join in with conscience, to warn men and plead with men and invite men.

In Hammond, Indiana, in the Pine Street Presbyterian Church years ago, I preached Sunday morning and God's power was there. Several held their hands for prayer. At the invitation some of them came to be saved, but one woman who held her hand for prayer did not come. At the benediction, I had the pastor lead in prayer and I hastened to see her. "You held your hand that you wanted to be saved," I said.

"Yes, I do want to be saved," she said, "but it seemed such a long way down there, and I was timid!"

"Then don't you want to be saved now?" I asked.

She did. So I turned to the third chapter of John, where I showed her that she must be born again, that Christ died for her and that God loved her, and that if she would only trust in Jesus Christ and rely on Him, He would give her everlasting life. She bowed her head while we prayed. She trusted the Saviour. Then, as a token between her and God and me that she then took Christ as her Saviour and claimed Him as her own, she took my hand.

"Now, would you like for me to tell these people that you have trusted Christ as Saviour, so you can claim Him openly?" I asked.

"Yes," she said, "I would."

So I called the people to attention. I said, "Here is a woman who held her hand for prayer during the services. Now she has trusted Christ, and she said I might tell you that she is saved. Do you want to come and shake her hand and tell her that you rejoice with her and that you will pray for her?" Oh, they gathered happily around to shake her hand.

She was half laughing and half crying, and she said, "I wanted to go during the invitation, but that aisle seemed so long! It seemed such a great way down there! If I had just had anybody to go with me, I would have gone then," she said.

Her brother, nearby, spoke up and said, "Why, Sis, why didn't you come and tell me? I would have gone with you."

I turned rather sharply to him and said, "You have been a Christian many years, a member of this church. You want your sister to come and beg you to go with her down toward the front!" I said, "That is not God's plan; His plan is that Christians should plead with sinners, not the other way around."

Oh, she wanted to come, but no one offered to go with her. Just an earnest word, just the pressure of a friendly hand on her arm, and she would have come then.

* * *

Sufficient Grace. Never will I forget when early in my first full-time pastorate we came to a seeming impasse. I had started revival services. I had, in my own heart, made this a condition: if the church would ask me to lead in revival services so that I would have a chance to get acquainted with the people and God would have a chance to use me in winning souls and in building up a poor, discouraged, divided congregation, I would accept the pastorate. When they had agreed that I should lead in revival services, we were besieged by days of rain and storm. The pitiful handful of people who came were not expectant but impassive, though kindly. Many had vowed never to again attend the little church where there had been bickering, strife and bar-renness. It seemed that even God had turned His face away, and the church building had been struck by lightning and burned to the ground. Now we were meeting in a little board tabernacle, and I had come to the end of my strength.

That morning I walked up the railroad track, anywhere to be alone. I sat disconsolately upon a rock and cried out to God not to let me go back and to face my problems and burdens in the ministry without some assurance that He was with me, that He would give the victory. And I found this blessed passage where Paul learned the secret of grace sufficient for all the weakness, for all the thorns of Satan, all the infirmities, all the persecutions and distresses. God said to me, as He had said to Paul, "My grace is sufficient for thee: for my strength is made perfect in weakness" (II Cor. 12:9). I rose from there determined to have the strength of God in my weakness. A marvelous revival followed. And, thank God, for many long years I have found that always the grace of God, the marvelous, infinite, matchless grace of God is enough for revival, enough for soul-winning power.

* * *

Seek God's Face for Revival

In 1945 I was invited to a citywide campaign in Buffalo, New York, to be held in Kleinhan's Music Hall. About ninety churches, rescue missions and other Christian organizations joined in the invitation. Primarily laymen had pressed the matter for revival and preachers and pastors had somewhat reluctantly perhaps gone along.

After the first Sunday services, with crowds jamming the auditorium to the doors, I attended the meeting of fundamental and Bible-believing pastors on Monday. How shocked I was to find that there was a great deal of disagreement among the pastors. They were divided, it appeared, into three separate cliques. Men from the two largest churches of two denominations, active in the campaign, openly quarreled and derided each other in the pastors' meeting. I was greatly distressed to find there was not the humility, the concern, the spirit of cooperation necessary for the great citywide campaign.

On Tuesday night I preached on "The High Cost of Revival." On the platform was a great choir of 300 voices, and before them 30 or more pastors in a row. As I preached I felt led to turn and say to the pastors, "Oh, how can we have a revival unless God's preachers get under the burden and get right with each other and seek God's face! Why don't you brethren call a night of prayer and pray for God to unite our hearts and bring the power we need?"

I closed the message and asked the congregation to stand for the benediction. But a pastor behind me said, "Wait, Brother Rice! We have been passing notes here and we are agreed we ought to have a night of prayer." Several pastors offered their churches. I selected the one most convenient downtown, a large church, and said, "Tomorrow night at 10:00 o'clock, after the service here, we will meet at that church and spend the night in prayer and confession and waiting on God." On Wednesday night at 10:00 o'clock, some 300 had gathered to pray. The next morning when the sun arose at about 6:00 o'clock, still there were fifty or more people waiting on God who had prayed the night through.

There were immediate evidences of God's moving of the Spirit. Thursday night, though I did not feel it wise to hold the crowd for an invitation, I found that five people immediately spoke up who wanted to be saved and said, "I do, I do." In such a united campaign, with a mixed crowd from far and near and with the general public, in a great city auditorium, I would not have expected to give an invitation before the second Sunday night. Ordinarily, unless God begins to put a burden upon the hearts of Christians and deep concern on the hearts of lost people, one cannot hold the crown together for a continued invitation time, in such a big public auditorium. But since the power of God became so evident, on Friday night I gave an invitation and here they came, I think about fifty people, to trust the Saviour and night after night, through the nineteen days, they came. We had 997 public professions of faith in those days. And each Wednesday night of the three weeks we had the whole night in prayer pleading with God for His blessing and it came!

"If my people. . .shall. . .seek my face," God said. That is part of the price of revival (II Chron. 7:14).

*   *   *

Christians: Turn From Sin for Revival. In Greenville, South Carolina, in the midst of our campaign in the Textile Hall years ago a boy about eleven went into Woolworth's store and almost in tears pleaded to see the manager. He must bring back forty-five cents for nine packages of chewing gum he had stolen! A news reporter who was present chatting with the manager was greatly impressed. At the Belk Department Store he talked to a department head, and was astonished to find that women were coming in bringing back things they had stolen from the department store.

In Decatur, Texas, in the midst of a revival campaign that lasted ten weeks, resulting in hundreds of souls being saved and in a new church of over three hundred members, with the land bought, tabernacle built and a full-time pastor on the field, there was an amazing evidence of people turning away from one current sin. A young druggist stood with tears to testify. When he had inherited a drugstore from his father, he was shocked to find there was not a place in the whole country where one could buy a Bible. He bought a stock of Bibles and Testaments, thousands of dollars' worth. They remained in stock year after year with almost none of them sold until this revival campaign. Now he had sold out the stock, had reordered twice and was greatly impressed that everywhere in town people were reading the Bible and talking about the Bible.

In an Oklahoma city, in I think the third week of a revival campaign, without knowing the reason for the strange truth, the local newspaper announced with astonishment that there had not been an arrest in the town for two weeks and not a person had spent the night in jail, a precedent unheard of.

Oh, wherever God's people want revival they should start family altars. Husbands and wives should apologize to each other for their sharp words. Christians should pay up bad debts. They should give up filthy habits. They should, as I have seen happen again and again, pour their liquor down the sink, and give up their tobacco.

*   *   *

God Melts the Opposition. In a certain revival campaign, the chairman of the board of deacons was shocked and then became incensed at my plain preaching. I would make sinners angry, I would drive people away instead of winning them, he said. He made his plans. They would have a meeting of the board of deacons on Saturday of the first week of the revival effort, and they would insist that the revival effort close on the middle Sunday of the proposed two weeks' revival effort.

However, on Friday night the drunkard son of this deacon was wonderfully converted. Oh, what praises! What rejoicing! What tears! Suddenly that deacon thought I was the best preacher in the world! Why, he thought the revival ought to continue indefinitely! The opposition melted and God gave a gracious revival and many were saved.

*   *   *

God Answers by Fire

In a revival meeting in Oklahoma City I preached for two weeks. I preached in a tent, and I sweated and wept and prayed and God seemed not to answer. The people came, crowds of them, and a few had been saved, but no great breaking out had come. I preached on the subject I am preaching on tonight. I said that night, "We will put no human fire on this altar. If God does not come to move and bless, we will go home without it. I promise you now and I promise God, I will never give another invitation in this campaign unless God begins to work without an invitation. I have pled and tried to get people to move, but I am not going to do it any more. God is going to move or the thing will go down in defeat." I preached that night and poured out my heart, and when we came to the close, I said, "The thing is done. If anybody wants to be saved, you can be. We are not going to stand and sing. If anybody wants to be saved, you can stand to your feet."

One man stood and said, "Brother Rice, I am in torment. I must have this thing settled." I told him to come on down to the front. He trusted Christ.

In a little bit a woman came holding up two fingers. I did not know what she meant. They were stained with yellow.

"Twenty-two years," she said. "Will the Lord save a woman like me?" She meant that for that long she had used cigarettes. I will tell you now, it is as bad for a man to use them as it is for a woman, whether you count it so or not, and it is a sin for either. In my church in Dallas—and down there it is harder to set a standard—in my church no Sunday school teacher teaches a class who goes to moving picture shows or smokes cigarettes or attends bridge games.

Somebody says, "You are a fanatic." All right, but if you are not going to mean business for God, you had as well get out of the pulpit. I gave up a good work as college teacher. There are lots of things I can do. If I didn't mean business for God I would get out.

Then another, a girl, came. She came down the aisle weeping, without any invitation. I was not begging anybody to come. This is what she said, as she covered her face with her hands, "What will mother say? She had such ambitions for me; what will mother think? Oh, Lord, what does it matter what she thinks!" Then she said, "What will Dad think? He has been holding me back, but what does it matter what he thinks? All my friends with whom I have been going out—what will they think? What does it matter what they think, just so my soul is saved!"

I tell you, by this time the crowd was pretty well broken up. "I will give an invitation now," I said.

I tell you, preachers had just as well put it up to God and let Him take a hand in this matter. I believe in a God who answers by fire. May God give it! I am not against human methods, consecrated methods, but I am against depending on them instead of fire from Heaven, the power of God!

*   *   *

First One Down the Aisle! One girl came to me one night in Waterloo, Iowa, and said, "Brother Rice, I am heartsick, and I ought to have come forward before. What do you think of this kind of a Christian: I played for a dance Saturday night; I played the organ in church Sunday morning." This twenty-year-old girl looked up at me pitifully and said, "What do you think of that kind of a Christian?"

I said, "That is pretty bad, isn't it?"

She said, "Yes, and I'll be the first one forward tomorrow night."

She played the piano for the service. After two or three chords on the piano (people were already starting to come down the aisle), she turned and ran so as to be the first one forward, as she had promised.

* * *

God Sends the Fire When We Seek Him With All Our Hearts

I left the University of Chicago where I was doing graduate work and came back to Texas and went into little country revival campaigns. God spoke to my heart in Pacific Garden Mission and told me to preach. I said, "Lord, if You will save souls, I'll preach. If You don't I can't preach!" You need not be a whipped and defeated preacher. The Lord will bless and souls will be saved if you pay God's price. Blessed be God, He has been saving souls everywhere I go.

I remember in one revival meeting, I went with Brother Ross. We went into Corinth community near Decatur, Texas, where there was no pastor and had not been one for a year. They had starved the previous one out. There were only two deacons in this church and one would not come to the revival. Brother Ross did the preaching and I sang and did personal work. Brother Ross preached on Sunday and nothing happened. He preached on Monday morning and Monday night, Tuesday morning and Tuesday night, Wednesday morning and Wednesday night, and on through Friday, with not a soul saved. We did not plan to continue more than ten days. I was discouraged, and as we went down into a ravine Saturday morning to pray, I said to Brother Ross, "This has gone far enough. The Lord did not call me for this kind of a business. I want to see something happen or I want to go home." Brother Ross thought so too. So we agreed to call a day of fasting and prayer. We said, "Let's give God one more chance." We announced that on Sunday we would have a day of fasting and prayer.

To make a long story short, I didn't have any breakfast Sunday. I was burdened. We went before Sunday school to prayer meeting, stayed for Sunday school and preaching, and then we said, "If anybody wants to, you may stay here and pray." Only five people stayed. One of them was the deacon. The others were an old preacher and his wife from another town, Brother Ross and I. We confessed our sins, read the Bible, prayed, and waited on God until three o'clock in the afternoon. Then others came in to hear an afternoon sermon. We prayed more, and I said, "Before we go we ought to claim some promises and say what we want to expect tonight. What do you want tonight?"

Few had anything to say. At last one said, "I would like to see one soul saved but I don't know whether there will be or not."

I asked others, but no one expected a thing. At last the dear preacher visiting from another community spoke. He said, "You young preachers ought to know that there is not going to be anybody saved. That deacon is mad at the other deacon, and they have starved out one preacher, and God is not going to bless people like that."

Then I said to Brother Ross, "Let's get out by ourselves and claim some promises and shake hands on it expecting sinners to be saved in the service tonight."

Brother Ross said, "Why get by ourselves? Why not do it right here? What do you want God to do tonight?"

I said, "I want to see that many souls saved tonight" (holding up ten fingers).

Brother Ross said, "Do you believe it?"

I said, "Well, er . . . well, I *want* to believe it. (My, I was scared!) I will believe it if you will!"

The dear man agreed. We shook hands right there, and he said, "There will be at least ten people saved in this church tonight."

The old preacher got up and said, "Listen here, you boys, you are young and you are making a mistake. There will not be ten people saved tonight and the people will believe that God doesn't answer prayer."

I said, "But God *does* answer prayer, and we *are* going to see at least ten people saved tonight."

One man got his hat and started out the door and said, "If God saves ten people here tonight, I will never do another wrong thing as long as I live!"

The people thought, "Well, we had better go home and feed the chickens and get the cows in a little early. You never can tell what will happen. I want to see what will happen." Everybody hurried off home to do the chores and get back.

I hadn't had any breakfast, and I had stayed there all day and had not had any dinner, and I tell you frankly, I was too scared to eat any supper. I went out to the ravine and said, "Lord, it is up to You. If You don't answer in this matter, I am ruined."

And, my friends, nobody can have a revival unless God takes a hand in it. It is all foolishness trying to save people unless power from Heaven comes. So I said, "Lord, it is Your revival, not mine. I didn't save myself. I didn't call myself to preach, I didn't bring myself here. I didn't start this business. Lord, help us tonight."

I said to Brother Ross, "I am going to do everything I know to do. I will talk to everybody who comes to this place. I will do all I can, then God must save."

He agreed.

In a little while here came a buggy with a woman and a twelve-year-old boy. I talked to the boy and others. When we gathered we sang two or three songs, and the preacher preached, not very long, but red hot with earnestness. And I remember we sang as an invitation song, "Jesus Is Tenderly Calling Thee Home." Sitting in the choir was an old drinking, gambling sinner—how many souls he was leading to ruin! His name was Jernigan. I turned to him and said, "Aren't you tired of this life?"

He held on to the bench, and I said, "Why don't you turn to God tonight?"

And he did come, out of the choir, to the preacher and the front seat. The whole crowd was moved.

I remember a little woman, Mrs Walker. She had been grieving because her boy was following in the footsteps of this drunkard Jernigan. About the time he came this woman jumped and shouted, "My boy! My boy!" I turned around and saw her boy climbing over the benches from the back seat of the choir, coming down to the front!

And that man who got his hat that afternoon and said, "If God saves ten people tonight, I will never do another wrong thing as long as I live," went outside the church after his grown sons. Every window was a frame of faces. He grabbed one of his boys by the wrist like a child and brought him into the building and down to the front and said, "Get down on your knees!" He called for me. I got down beside him, urged the lad to trust Christ, and prayed, and he was saved. We go up. This father wiped his eyes and started elbowing his way back to the door and outside. He had another boy, and brought him in, leading him like a child. He said, "Get down on your knees!" He too was saved.

There was a boy at the back I wanted to talk to, but the aisles were so crowded with people I had to walk on the backs of the benches to get to him.

It was a little country place, and we were using kerosene lamps. One of the lamps flickered and went out. Then another back yonder flickered and went out. Finally, about eleven o'clock the last one went out. Nobody had noticed that others had gone out until we were left in darkness. Somebody went across the road and got more kerosene and filled up one of the lamps and we continued the service and people were saved. If Ross or I would stick our heads out the door, all those on the outside would run for the bushes! After awhile the thing quieted down.

Somebody said, "Let's line them up and count them and show that God answered prayer." So around the entire front of the building they stood, these new converts who found God that night.

One, two, three, four, five, six, seven, eight, nine, ten, eleven, twelve, and on—I didn't remember how many were in that line until I told this incident over the radio one time, and I got a letter from the first man who came out for Christ that night, Mr. Jernigan. He was indignant. This saved sinner said, "It is a funny thing you didn't remember how many were in that line that night. There were twenty-three grown people!" Oh, God proved that night that He is a God who can answer by fire! We do not have any business starting a revival campaign anywhere unless we expect God to speak to hearts and make Himself real. God answers prayer! God answers by fire!

*   *   *

"Sodom, Gomorrah, and Binghamton." In Binghamton, New York, in 1936 in revival services in the Binghamton Theatre sponsored by a number of churches, I preached on "Sodom, Gomorrah, and Binghamton; Three of a Kind."

A group of learned preachers meeting in the city, took heated exception to my sermon subject. A prominent denominational official said that for Binghamton, with its schools and hospitals, art and industry, its progressive and intelligent people, to be compared with ancient Sodom was unthinkable! His remarks were printed in the daily press. However, the same night in a big club, within a block of the theater where I preached, was held a very saturnalia of debauch and sin. Fifty prostitutes were brought in from New York City. The most prominent men in the city bought tickets to the banquet and show. By midnight many of the men were drunk and many of the women were naked, and by 4:00 o'clock in the morning, I was told, officers had to stop the breaking of furniture and had to interfere with the wild carousal. Literally hundreds took part. Many were members of the churches where these pious and complacent preachers held forth. Investigation revealed that such orgies were frequent affairs.

Many of the preachers were openly modernistic, denying the deity of Christ, the blood atonement, the new birth, and the inspiration of the Bible, and yet they were shocked at the comparison of Binghamton to Sodom and Gomorrah. They were rich, increased with goods, and had need of nothing, they thought. But God knew that they were "wretched, and miserable, and poor, and blind, and naked."

I announced the same sermon subject for the following night. Still larger crowds heard me with blessings from God the second night on the same subject, and the revival continued with hundreds saved.

That incident seems to me the more remarkable, in that newspaper men came to me with shocking revelations about the wickedness going on in the city, while most of the preachers either did not know or did not care.

* * *

A Women's Meeting Disbands

I was in the North Akron Baptist Church in 1930. The ladies' missionary society asked me one afternoon if I would come and talk with them, and I went. We had been having a good revival. About one hundred people were saved. To my surprise, the people came in cold weather, in deep snow, in zero weather or lower. I went there and they led me through the pantry, and my, my, there must have been about forty dollars' worth of pretty food prepared by a caterer. There were more Cadillacs and Packards parked in front of that church! I thought, "My, what in the world has happened?" They were members of that church, but they had not been coming to the revival. There were about thirty women in that society. They were having a humdinger of a time, a fine program. "Madam President" had not been to the revival, but they asked the evangelist to speak to them.

I began, "How long has it been since you have had anybody saved in this meeting?"

They looked blank. I went around the line. I began at the other end from the president. I asked one woman, "When have you had anybody saved in this meeting, or through its work?"

She answered, "Well, I have been here one year and I have not seen anybody saved."

"Well," I said to the next woman, "was there anybody saved last year?"

She replied, "I have been here thirteen years, and I have never seen anybody saved in this meeting."

And then I said, "Was there ever anybody saved in this meeting?"

And nobody knew of a soul that had been saved. I asked everybody before I came to "Madam President," and when I got to her she said, "Brother Rice, that is not what this meeting is for."

"Knock it in the head then!" I said. "Kill it! Here I have been in this revival for three weeks, sweating blood, and we have had nearly one hundred souls saved, and you have never been to a service!"

They were afraid we would get some people saved that were poor, and they would have to take care of them that winter if the tire factories closed down. They did not want me to "fill the church up with that kind of trash." I had been hearing about that.

I said, "Why don't you good women get together and have a Bible class and let the pastor teach it? Away with this entertaining and foolishness, and start out to win somebody to Jesus Christ."

One woman said, "I have been hungry for that."

I said, "It would be far better, don't you think, to get out here and get people saved and see lives transformed than to be doing what you are doing? How many of you women want it?"

They discussed it.

One woman said, "I make a motion we disband and have a Bible class and let our pastor teach it, and try to win souls."

I believe all but three voted to disband. They did. They planned to meet together the next Sunday morning in a big Bible class and start out to win souls.

*   *   *

"You Are Ruining My Business."

I was in a revival meeting at Sherman, Texas. One morning early I got on a train to go back to Fort Worth for a radio broadcast. A man came along and said, "Aren't you Brother Rice?"

"Yes."

"My name is Brown."

I said, "Where do you live?"

"I live here in Sherman."

"Well, have you been over to the evangelistic services on the courthouse lawn?"

"No," he said, "I haven't, but that is what I want to talk to you about."

"All right, what about it?"

"I think you owe me $300," he said. (I had just started; I owed him a whole lot more than that before it was over!)

I said, "Why do I owe you money?"

"You nearly busted my business. I own the two shows in town, and you are ruining my business."

I did not cry a bit. In fact I did not even apologize! You are going to have to break up some picture-show businesses or some hog businesses or break up something else if you have revival.

* * *

The Mule Died!

A white man on a plantation had a sick mule. Remembering a Negro friend who had also had a sick mule, he went to him and said, "Mose, what did you give that mule of yours when he was sick?"

"I gibbed him a bottle ob turpentine," said the colored man.

The white man gave his mule turpentine, and the mule died. He came back to Mose and said, "Mose, I gave my mule turpentine like you said, and he died!"

"Yes, Boss, my mule done died, too!"

So our brethren who depend upon special features, outstanding speakers, chalk talks, paintings, the music of whiskey bottles and tumblers and musical saws, will find that they, too, have a still-born revival effort on their hands just like all others who depend on human devices have done. Those things do not bring revivals now, it is true. But then they never did bring revivals before. Revivals only come by the miracle-working power of God!

The Holy Spirit does use human instruments and human devices, but we must remember that all human personalities and human instruments and methods and devices are merely incidental. Revivals come from God, through the miracle-working Holy Spirit working in Christians!

* * *

Saved on Company Time!

I was in revival services in Amarillo, Texas, years ago in a little Baptist church. A carpenter, a contractor, got converted. He was building two houses and had two big crews of men. We were having morning services at ten o'clock. Do you know what he did? He went around to these houses and said to all those carpenters, plumbers, and painters, "Boys, we are having a meeting down at the church." Then he said some good things about the preacher and said, "I want you to hear him. I will tell you what we will do. Nobody will work on my job here from ten to eleven o'clock. We are all going down to the church on my time."

One man said, "I do not care to go to church. I'll stay here and work."

"No," the converted man said, "nobody is going to work on my job while the preacher is down here in my church trying to have a revival. We are all going down there." So they came in their overalls, and some of them got converted. The man's son-in-law and several of his old tough carpenters got converted.

Salvation

A New Heart. I know a man who had been drinking for years, who wanted to be saved, but he feared and feared. "How can I ever get rid of this enslaving habit?" That was the thought in his heart. He had made so many vows and broken them every one! When he had promised his wife to quit, he did not have the will power to do it. He was soon dragged into the clutches of drink again. So when in deep distress of soul he knelt down to pray and call on God, he said, "O God, I don't promise You anything! I promised my wife I would quit drinking but I could not do it. I don't know whether I can quit now. I don't promise You anything, but my friends keep telling me that You can give people a new heart. If You have a new heart for me, I sure need one!"

God did give him a new heart, did help him to turn his back on liquor and the sins that had enslaved him in the past.

* * *

The Church Is the Place for Repentant, Forgiven Sinners. I remember so well when I was pastor in Shamrock, Texas, years ago, that a woman was wonderfully, happily saved. Oh, the tears of rejoicing she had when she knew her sins were forgiven! She came and presented herself for membership to the church. She was received, and I baptized her. I said, "Now you must come to the women's Bible class, and you must come to the Women's Missionary Society and a certain circle that meets near your house." Then I went to a good woman who taught that women's Bible class and who was active in the leadership in the missionary society, and said, "Now, you must make this woman feel at home. You must invite her to your class and to the missionary meetings, and let her get in with Christian people and enjoy the work of the Lord."

What did she reply? "No, Brother Rice, I don't think we ought to do that. She has a bad reputation. She has lived a very sinful life, and it would not be good for the reputation of the church if a woman like that takes any active part. I don't think we could receive her in the class and in that missionary society."

Now I was very plain and sharp, and most of you wouldn't do what I did; but I am sure I was right. I said to her, "She is coming to that Bible class and she is coming to that missionary society. Her sins have been forgiven. She has honestly repented with tears. Now she is God's child, and she belongs to Him and belongs to this church." And I said, "If I hear of any woman pulling her skirts aside and making her feel uncomfortable and unwanted—if I know of anybody who shuns and scorns and ill-treats that woman because of her past, which has been forgiven and is now under the blood, God being my helper, I will brand that woman from the pulpit as the hypocrite she is!" I said, "I wouldn't pastor a church where a poor lost sinner, after he or she is saved and forgiven and cleansed and wants to serve God, can't be happy and can't be received."

* * *

Rest for the Soul. Thank God for the peace He gives to poor sinners who trust in Jesus! On a cold November Saturday night in Dallas, Texas, a man came to me. That morning he had tried to commit suicide by turning on the gas in his room. He was saved by a chambermaid who herself had lived a harlot's life. After he got out of the hospital, he and this chambermaid came to see me. This man who was so frantic—his wife had quit him; no home, no job, health broken with an incurable disease. Now he felt he couldn't go on. As he knelt by my bed I put my hands on his head, prayed for him, and showed him the Scriptures. He trusted Christ.

He sat up and said, "Isn't it strange?"

I said, "What is strange?"

He said, "I was so worried, so fretted. I thought I couldn't live, couldn't face another day. Now it's all gone and I feel so peaceful and happy, and haven't a care in the world! Isn't that strange?"

I said, "No, that isn't strange. Jesus said, 'Come unto me, all ye that labour and are heavy laden, and I will give you rest. Take my yoke upon you, and learn of me; for I am meek and lowly in heart: and ye shall find rest unto your souls.' You have found rest for your soul" (Matt. 11:28,29).

* * *

"Something Sure Has Happened to Me!" In Shamrock, Texas, a big, fighting, drinking bully of a man named Clyde Bar-row was converted. The change in his life was marvelous. He had such a temper and had been a great fighter. One night in town some of his old companions came upon him and urged him to have beer with them. He refused, and one officious, sinful man threw beer in his face and down the front of his shirt, thinking that the smell of it would entice him to drink. Clyde Barrow came to tell me about it and, with tears running down his face, said, "Brother Rice, I wasn't even angry. I said to the man, 'I could break you in two with my two hands and a few months ago you know I would have done it. But I am not mad at you. I am just going to pray for you.' " And then he said, "Brother Rice, something sure has happened to me!"

* * *

As the Lost Sheep Might Tell It

We have the Saviour's account of the finding of the lost sheep in Luke 15:4-7. It is a beautiful story. But to open our eyes to the beauty of wonderful, free salvation as revealed by the Saviour, suppose we contrast it with the way some people teach salvation. Let us suppose that the lost sheep tells the story, and let us see how different is the story told by the lost sheep from that told by the Saviour Himself. These are the imagined words of the lost sheep.

"I was a poor, lost sheep; I wandered far away from the Shepherd, far away from the pasture He had assigned to me. I was self-willed and disobedient and wicked, lost out in the mountains, far away from the fold and the Shepherd. I realized my lost condition and turned to seek the Shepherd. Dangers were on every hand. I might have fallen over a cliff, and have been broken and killed on the rocks below. I might have fallen into a mountain stream which ran beside the slippery path. I might have been caught on the thorns and brush so I could never get away. Or the wolves of that wilderness might have caught me and devoured me. I realized my desperate plight and my pitiful bleating echoed through the mountains as I made my way back to the Shepherd.

"At last I found Him! At first He would not listen to my pitiful cries. He insisted first that I must show more humility, more evidence of repentance. But at last I 'wept my way to Calvary.' At last I was able to 'pray through.' At last the Shepherd agreed to take me, but I must follow Him carefully home.

"So I am following the Shepherd home. I am fully resolved to 'hold out faithful.' I am fully resolved to make the fold my eternal home. I believe that the Shepherd has already done His part and now it depends wholly on me as to whether I get to the fold. The road following the Shepherd is rough, but I intend to be faithful so the Shepherd will not cast me off.

"When I get back to the fold I am going to call all the other sheep together and tell them to rejoice with me because I made it home. By my faithfulness, by my perseverance, by enduring to the end, I shall have safely reached the fold."

How shockingly different is that parable, as told by the sheep! But with a little careful thought many readers will recognize the supposed language of the lost sheep as the usual talk of many Christians.

Many Christians talk about how they found the Saviour, not how the Saviour found them. They speak as if they were getting safe to Heaven by *following* the Shepherd, instead of being carried on His shoulders! They speak as if they expected to get home safe to the eternal fold with the Good Shepherd by "holding out faithful to the end." They talk as if people got saved by "weeping their way to Calvary" and "praying through." You can very well see that the story does not coincide with the story as told by the Shepherd Himself, the Lord Jesus. The sheep seems to think that he did most of it, but the Lord Jesus clearly teaches that He does it all.

* * *

Unexplained Facts. All around us are facts that we certainly accept as facts, but that we cannot understand. William Jennings Bryan used to say, "I cannot understand how a red cow can eat green grass and make white milk and yellow butter. But I can drink the milk and enjoy it, and I like butter on hot biscuits." Millions of people listen to the radio, though they could not make one and cannot explain one. All of us use electricity, and not a man living can explain it.

Once a Christian doctor and an unconverted doctor were talking together; and the unconverted physician said to his friend, "How can you expect me to be a Christian? I am a rational, educated man with a scientific mind. I cannot believe that which I do not understand. And I cannot understand the new birth that people talk about. Therefore I cannot be a Christian."

But the wise Christian physician simply said, "Doctor, you have delivered hundreds of babies, and yet you cannot explain the first birth. Where does life come from? How does God give the tiny baby a soul? You cannot even understand the first birth, but you believe it. How can you expect to understand all about the supernatural, second birth when God changes a wicked heart and makes a poor lost sinner into a child of God?"

*   *   *

The Call of God. I well remember there happened years ago, when I was a boy, a scene that impressed itself indelibly on my memory. It was in a revival meeting in the school auditorium. A school girl friend of mine went to her big, burly brother and pled with him to be saved. Tears ran down her cheeks and I remember how she looked that day as she put both hands upon his shoulders and lifted her tearful face to him. She said, "Charlie, you know how I love you. I want you to be saved. Mother is praying for you. Now is the time to be saved, Charlie. Won't you come tonight?" Charlie stood there and looked at her with a stony gaze. She kept pleading. He told her, "No, Lillie, go on away and leave me alone. I am not ready tonight. No, I say, leave me alone!" Finally, as she continued pleading, he seized her hands and threw them away from him and said cruelly, "Leave me alone, I say, I am not going!" Lillie went away weeping that night and I do not know but maybe the Holy Spirit of God went away too. I know that night God spoke into that young man's heart with all the tenderness of Calvary. It was the call of God!

*   *   *

Better Have the Shame Over With. In Dallas, Texas, in 1932 in an open air revival, a woman in a great crowd sent me a note. She said about this: "Brother Rice, I have been a member of a church twenty-two years. Most of that time I have known I was never converted. I am not a child of God, but I cannot stand the shame of confessing that I have been in the church unsaved. It would break my husband's heart. He would think I have been a hypocrite, and perhaps I have."

I sent her word that both she and her husband had better have the shame over with now, that she had better confess her lost condition and turn to Christ for mercy and salvation now, rather than wait until she faced the Lord Jesus Christ and have Him say, "I never knew you. Depart from me, ye that work iniquity."

The next night she came weeping to trust in Christ. She told me that she had been in the church unsaved. She was baptized and has made a happy Christian.

* * *

Not Saved by Nature. The 19th Psalm tells about nature:

"The heavens declare the glory of God; and the firmament sheweth his handywork. Day unto day uttereth speech, and night unto night sheweth knowledge. There is no speech nor language, where their voice is not heard . . . ."

But that Scripture continues in verse 7:

"The law of the Lord is perfect, converting the soul."

That is something nature never did do. Many a man with a poetic soul has stood sometimes by the seashore with a sense of awe as he sees the grandeur of the mountainous waves. Every man with any sense has sometimes, I suppose, looked out at the stars at night and been overwhelmed with the sense of God.

One evening when I was a boy growing into my teens, I went out into the stack lot and climbed up on a great stack of feed, and far into the night I lay out there and looked up into the stars. My soul was thrilled: I knew there was a God. I know it now. There must be! Nature claims there is a God. But notice this: Nature never saved anybody. Looking at the stars never saved anybody.

I preached the funeral sermon of a man not long ago who had just gone to Heaven. I had been with him before he died, and he told how he was converted. He told how when he was a young man one night a group of children were playing around the door. He heard one little girl say, "Oh, if the wrong side of Heaven is so pretty, don't you know the right side must be beautiful!" And that little girl's words about Heaven went like an arrow to his heart. When he came to himself he was away down in a lane by himself looking up at God's Heaven. But he was not converted until he later heard the Gospel of the crucified Saviour and the blood shed for sinners, and then he was saved!

* * *

Turning a Mesquite Tree Into a Peach Tree

When I was a boy in West Texas, there was in our front yard a mesquite tree. In that semiarid land there were many mesquite trees or bushes, but not many other kinds of trees except on the water courses. Mesquite trees at a distance often look like peach trees. They are small like peach trees. They are crooked and irregular like peach trees. The leaves, blossoms and fruit are not the same; but the general size and shape of a mesquite tree is similar to that of a peach tree. Fruit was desperately scarce in West Texas. How many times I wished that mesquite tree in our front yard was a peach tree! Now suppose that I set out to make a peach tree out of that mesquite tree. Suppose I should buy two bushels of big Elberta peaches and with string I would tie them onto the branches of the mesquite tree. A mesquite tree bears beans by nature, not peaches. But let us suppose that we pull off all the beans and tie peaches all over the tree. Now we have a lovely peach tree!

That sounds silly, doesn't it? Birds would peck the peaches. They would get overripe and fall. And flies and gnats would gather. And next spring that mesquite tree would have again that delicate shimmering green in the fronds of tiny mesquite leaves, the blossoms would come out like fuzzy sweet-smelling caterpillars about an inch and a half long; and when the blossoms turned into fruit, lo, there would be pods of mesquite beans all over the tree, the tough bitter-sweet pods of beans that I have chewed many times and that horses and cows liked. All our tying of peaches on the tree and taking away of the mesquite beans would not change the mesquite tree into a peach tree at all! The *nature* of the tree itself would have remained unchanged.

But in that same silly way men try to make themselves Christians! They were sprinkled when they were babies, or perhaps baptized when they were older; they were confirmed; they learned catechisms, or they took their first communion. They set out to attend church, perhaps to sing in the choir, to give some money, to live a moral life. They pulled off some of the mesquite beans and they tied on some peaches; but actually they did not have a new tree at all! To quit tobacco, to stop cursing, to quit getting drunk, and to start to going to church and saying prayers does not make a Christian at all. "THAT WHICH IS BORN OF THE FLESH IS FLESH" (John 3:6)! You will never be a Christian until you are born of the Spirit.

*   *   *

"When Your Thread Becomes Tangled, Call the Foreman."

In a textile mill a sign before the workers said, "When your thread becomes tangled, call the foreman." A new employee came to work. She soon found her thread tangled. She worked and worked to untangle it and could not do so. At last in despair she called the foreman. When he rebuked her for not obeying the sign, she said, "But I tried my best."

He answered, "To really try your best is to send for me."

So good resolutions are not good enough. They are only inadequate, and more or less insincere, unless first of all you call for Jesus Christ. If you want to be good, He can give you a good heart, can help you to want to do right, can help you to overcome sin. Oh, when you make your holy vow, when you make up your mind as Daniel did, be sure that first of all you take Christ as your Saviour, and trust Him and love Him and surrender to Him and depend upon Him and claim Him as your own Saviour now and forever!

* * *

"I Lied to God."

In the Panhandle of Texas several years ago I talked to the father of eight children. We had dinner in his home that day, a fine chicken dinner, and he told me how in France during the World War, in the front-line trenches, his company was shot to pieces and only a handful of men were left alive. "I prayed then," he said, "and I promised God that if He would get me out of that alive and back to my wife and babies, I would serve Him." I asked him if he had kept his vow to God, and he told me that he had not. "I lied to God," he said. "God kept His part of the bargain. God has been good to me, and I didn't do what I promised."

"Don't you think it is time that you kept your promise to God?" I asked.

He did think it was time, and I remember with what joy and what humility and what confession he turned to Christ and trusted Him for mercy and salvation. The memory of the goodness of God led him to be saved.

* * *

We Need a "Done" Religion!

You say, "Well, but Brother Rice, if a Christian gets drunk, and then gets in a fight while he is drunk and somebody shoots him and he dies in that state, don't you believe he is a goner?"

No, I believe he *deserves* to be a goner. You say, "Will he be saved?" Not *will* he be saved; he is already saved if he trusted in the blood. It is not whether he *will* be saved. You had better not risk anything about what is going to be;

you had better get it done. Too many have a *do, do, do* religion . . . . What you need is a *done* religion. I can look back and say, "On the cross Jesus said, 'It is finished.' Thank God, it is done! Mine is already done! Praise the Lord, it is done!"

A famous prizefighter was converted in a meeting held by J. Wilbur Chapman in Atlanta, Georgia. Mr. Alexander, the singer, urged the preachers to come shake hands with the new converts. One preacher, a very staid, quiet, formal preacher, came to shake hands with the converted prizefighter, and he said, "Well, Brother, I hope the Lord will bless you." This prizefighter jubilantly answered, "He has done done it, Brother!" Already done!

"Can You Face God for Me?"

In one of his books, Dr. L. R. Scarborough tells of being called to face a dying man to whom he had spoken many times about his soul. This dying man turned to his wife and said something like this: "Wife, you've done the church-going, you've done the praying. In a little bit I'm going out to meet God. You have done the rest of it; can you face God for me?" The weeping wife nodded to Dr. Scarborough to answer, and he said to the poor lost man, "No, old man, nobody can answer to God for you. You must yourself take Christ as your Saviour or be lost forever."

Every person who has come to the age of accountability must for himself or for herself accept or reject Jesus Christ. This is a personal question.

* * *

The Rabbit That Didn't Need a Refuge

When I was nine years old my family moved to a cattle ranch in West Texas. Coyotes, the slinking, dog-like wolves of the prairies, had been killing calves, and so my father had sent for a beautiful, thoroughbred greyhound. He was coal-black in color, and so we called him "Coaley." And when the men were busy with the cattle, with crops, or building fences, Coaley chased rabbits. Long-eared jack rabbits were numerous, and how often I watched Coaley chase them and kill them.

There were some other dogs at the ranch, two collie pups and a little bench-legged bulldog. They, too, ran jack rabbits. Yes, they ran them, but never caught them, for jack rabbits are proud and speedy creatures, and very rarely any but the greyhound catches a full-grown jack rabbit. The collie pups would bark furiously, and the jack rabbit would lay one ear back and lope easily away. The little dogs would come back to the house, panting and happy since they chased the rabbit out of the country and had a morning exercise!

I never saw a jack rabbit run into a hole. The prairies were dotted with prairie-dog towns, with many holes, and many badger holes. There were granaries (grain barns), haystacks, and sometimes near the creeks there were hollow logs or little caves, but I never knew a jack rabbit to take refuge in any such place. No, the proud and arrogant jack (sometimes called the "mule-eared rabbit") always ran the race out. It seemed as if his proud and haughty spirit would not admit he needed any help, any refuge. The jack rabbit always depended upon his own hind legs.

But when old Coaley, the greyhound, began to chase rabbits, then business really did pick up. Many a jack rabbit, when Coaley began to bay, galloped languidly away as if this were just another collie pup on an idle chase. But it was not long before that jack rabbit would lay back both ears and run for dear life, for then the dog, like a black fury, like avenging judgment, would be at his heels! How many times I threw my hat in the air and shouted until I was hoarse! I have seen a rabbit dodge, and Coaley's feet would fly out from under him, and he would hit the ground with a bump, but then he was up and gone again until the rabbit was caught. If the rabbit got between cotton rows, it would only take a few yards, for he could not dodge. And in any fair chase, there was always one conclusion; if Coaley tried, he caught the rabbit. Many a time I have picked up a big, heavy jack rabbit, weighing sometimes eight or ten pounds, and all of him running muscles, the big thick back and ham muscles, with tiny front feet. And many times I have thought that a jack rabbit is a gallant runner, but there was never one made that could out-run, in an open stretch, a thoroughbred greyhound. Too proud to hide, too self-confident to run to shelter, spurning the hole in the ground or a ledge of rock, the jack rabbit depended upon himself and lost!

But there is another kind of rabbit in West Texas, the tiny "cotton-tail." He is only about a third the size of the jack rabbit, and lives in the brush. He hops along, waving his little white flag of truce behind him, a timid and defenseless creature. One day my father and I went fishing in the west fork of the Brazos river. As we drove along in the buggy, my father said, "Son, look out for bait. We must have something to bait our hooks or we will have no supper tonight." In the brush of the river bottom a little cottontail rabbit suddenly hopped across the trail in front of us. With a roar of barking, the hound that had been trotting behind the buggy plunged by us and out into the brush after the tiny cotton-tail rabbit. I thought, "Too bad, little rabbit. I've seen old Coaley chase too many long-legged jack rabbits. You have no chance. We will have bait for our hooks tonight."

But suddenly, out to the left in the brush and trees, the dog's bark changed in tone. There was something frantic, disappointed, in it. If a dog could talk, that one would have been saying, "Come out and fight like a man, you dirty coward!" At first I wondered if the dog had run onto a bob-cat, or some other larger game. I jumped out of the buggy, pushed my way out through the brush, and there I found the dog howling and scratching and whining at a rock half as big as a house! But under the overhanging ledge of this rock, not more than four inches above the ground, the little rabbit had run. Down on hands and knees I saw him, far back under the rock. He was trembling in excitement, and breathing heavily. His little eyes protruded with fear, but he was perfectly safe. The helpless little rabbit had the good sense to run to a place of safety! He could not depend upon his own legs. He might well have said to himself, "I am nothing but a little cotton-tail rabbit. I can't outrun a dog, any kind of a dog. My only safety is in finding a hiding place." So he ran under the rock, and there he was perfectly safe. I called the whining, complaining dog away, and later we shot a crow for fish bait. The little cotton-tail rabbit was safe in his refuge!

I did not see it then, but many times since I have thought of these two rabbits, the long-legged, proud, independent jack rabbit, that never seeks a place of safety, and the timid little cotton-tail, who immediately runs to a safe refuge at the first alarm. They picture the two attitudes of sinners. Some men say, "I'll take my chance. I am not afraid." So they try to outrun sin and Satan themselves. They depend on reform, on morality, while sure and certain their sin is on their trail and must find them out. But some others, thank God, see their danger and run to Christ for mercy and salvation.

There was a time when I heard the hounds of Hell baying hard on my trail. I knew I was a sinner. I realized I was lost. Justice would never do for me—I needed mercy. Only the mercy and forgiveness of God could save my poor soul. So I ran to Jesus Christ, a sinner's only refuge. Of Him says Isaiah 32:2: "And a man shall be as an hiding place from the wind, and a covert from the tempest; as rivers of water in a dry place, as the shadow of a great rock in a weary land." Christ is the Rock of refuge! He is my fortress, He is my defense, my safety; the Lord Jesus Christ, who has paid for my sins.

*   *   *

"Seek, and Ye Shall Find." A few years ago a Lutheran woman from Wisconsin had a Catholic friend, and this friend recommended that she go with me on a tour of the Holy Land. The Lutheran woman wanted to be saved but did not know where to go. So she came with us to the Holy Land. In Jerusalem in a little service she trusted Christ. How glad she was! She told me about it, weeping for joy, and the next day she told me again, "Jesus said, 'Seek and ye shall find,' and [triumphantly] I sought and I found!" Oh, the heart that seeks Jesus finds Him. Whosoever calls on the Lord shall be saved (Rom. 10:13).

* * *

Take the Risk. Just to believe that the bank in your city is a sound bank, safely managed and honestly administered, is not enough to do you any good. As long as you do not deposit your money in the bank, but leave it in a sock under the mattress, or in a vase on the mantel, your belief about the bank cannot do you any good. It cannot save or protect your money from thieves. There is no "saving faith" in the bank until you deposit your money with the bank and risk the bank, depend upon the bank.

You may believe that a certain doctor is capable, well-trained, reliable, a skillful physician. But your mental agreement with those facts has nothing to do with getting you well if you are sick. In that case "saving faith" in the doctor would mean that you must call the doctor and turn your case over to him, risk him, depend upon him, rely upon him to get you well, through the skill God has given him.

No matter what you believe about a ferryboat, it will not take you across the river until you get on it.

And no matter what you believe about Jesus Christ, He cannot be your Saviour until you trust Him. Saving faith means that you must depend upon Jesus personally; that you risk Him, rely upon Him, commit yourself to Him.

* * *

God Calls Everyone. In a home in Southwest Texas a wife and her daughter were Christians. The husband and father was not. I said to him, "Why aren't you a Christian?" And he said to me, "I have never been called."

"Oh, yes, you have been called!" I said.

And I showed him the command of Jesus in Matthew 11:28-30, "Come unto me, all ye that labour and are heavy laden, and I will give you rest. Take my yoke upon you, and learn of me; for I am meek and lowly in heart: and ye shall find rest unto your souls. For my yoke is easy, and my burden is light." I showed him II Peter 3:9 that God is "not willing that any should perish, but that all should come to repentance." I showed him Revelation 22:17, "And the Spirit and the bride say, Come. And let him that heareth say, Come. And let him that is athirst come. And whosoever will, let him take the water of life freely." I showed him Isaiah 1:18. "Come now, and let us reason together, saith the Lord: though your sins be as scarlet, they shall be as white as snow; though they be red like crimson, they shall be as wool." And every time I read one of those Scriptures, he would say, "I didn't know that was in the Bible." I pressed the point. "Then God has called you, hasn't He?" And I gave this command of Acts 17:30, "And the times of this ignorance God winked at; but now commandeth all men every where to repent." Yes, God had called. He had no excuse. We knelt together by the divan in his living room and he asked the Lord Jesus for mercy and forgiveness. He was saved and joined his happy loved ones as a Christian.

* * *

God Commands Repentance: Acts 17:30.

Will you notice that God does not "suggest" or "advise." He does not even "plead" in this passage. He *commands* men to repent. In World War I, I was in the army and in the army camp I was sent out to drill with a squad of men as an acting corporal. We had been instructed as a company, and now the squad was scattered over the drill ground, practicing marching and stopping: "Squads right," "Squads left" and so forth. The company captain approached and I called to my shuffling squad, "Halt." They awkwardly stopped and tried to line up, but the captain said, "Did you give the correct order then, Corporal?"

I said, "No, Sir, I did not."

"And why not? What was the order you should have given?"

"I should have said, 'Squad halt!' in two counts."

And the captain pressed the matter: "Why did you not give the correct order?"

"Sir, I was scared," I said.

He gave some further orders, "Button that shirt pocket!" And to me he said, "If you are going to be a noncommissioned officer, hold up your head."

When he turned to go I saluted and I said, "Thank you, Sir!"

He turned to me sternly and said, "Don't thank me. I am not giving advice, I am giving orders!"

"Nothing Against Him!" In my boyhood I visited a Methodist annual conference in Texas. Bishop Dickey presided, I believe. When it came time to review the work of the pastors and appoint them to their next year's stations, I remember what a thrill I got as the roll was called. When a pastor's name was called, all of his fellow pastors would cry out, "Nothing against him!" . . ."Nothing against him!" . . ."Nothing against him!" . . ."Nothing against him!" It was thrilling to me then.

But since then I have thought that if one cried out the name of this poor, unworthy but forgiven sinner in Heaven, all the angels of God would answer, "Nothing against him!" for they can see the wounds of the Saviour, and they can see His loving heart has forgiven and made me God's own. Yes and they can see invisibly that righteous robe of Christ which covers all my sins.

* * *

Now Is the Time. Youth is the time to be saved. I have put it to a test in congregation after congregation in years of public revival campaigning, and by the votes of many thousands of Christians I have learned that over half of all the people who ever claimed to have trusted Christ as Saviour found Him before they were fifteen years old.

I made such a statement in a sermon in Peoria, Illinois, and years ago the sermon was printed in the paper. I went then to Dubuque, Iowa, for a revival campaign and there a lad came forward during the invitation weeping. He had read my sermon. He had read the solemn warning that youth was the time to be saved. With tears he told me, "I read where over half of the people who ever get saved are saved before they are fifteen. I read that over half of the chances that one will ever have to be saved are gone by the time he is fifteen years old. I am just fifteen years old! Oh, I hope I haven't waited too long to be saved!"

He was wise. He trusted Christ that night.

* * *

Why Coolidge Would Not Run. Lost man, what shall you be profited if you gain the whole world and miss Heaven? If you gain the whole world—all the fun, all the wine, women and song, all the primrose paths, all the plaudits of men, all the fame, all the money and pleasures, all the things for your body and none for your soul—and then miss Heaven, miss the joy of seeing your mother again, or your wife, or the little baby God took from you, what would it be worth?

I am reminded of Calvin Coolidge. People said to him, "Why won't you run for President?" The Republicans said, "We need you as the President. We can't lose if you will run." But Calvin Coolidge said, "I do not choose to run." They tried to make him say when he would accept the nomination, but he said, "I do not choose to run." People didn't quite understand. Months later, after the campaign was over there appeared an article in the *Saturday Evening Post* by former President Coolidge telling about his boy. He had played tennis on the White House courts and had blistered his heel. Like a boy he neglected it. Soon it became infected and blood poisoning set in. The doctors were called in, but it was too late. The poison went to his heart and he died. A year or so later when Calvin Coolidge wrote his article he said, "When my boy died, the glory of the Presidency faded away. I didn't want to be President any more."

If you do not make sure about your soul, one day everything you gain in the world will be trash. You had better take advice and get this matter settled. "What shall it profit a man, if he shall gain the whole world, and lose his own soul? Or what shall a man give in exchange for his soul?" (Mark 8:36).

The Enemy Was Not There. Dr. H. A. Ironside told how when his sons were little, he once put on a great fur coat and played bear with his five-year-old boy. Down on all fours he galloped after the child from room to room. The little fellow screamed, half in delight and half in fear. Dr. Ironside told how he hemmed the little fellow up in a corner in the kitchen, and to the five-year-old, the snarling bear seemed very real. Then he screamed and fell into his father's arms and said, "You are not any old bear! You are my daddy! You wouldn't eat me up! You love me and you wouldn't hurt me!"

And the dear, saintly preacher told how, when he was a young fellow, he had felt that God was on his trail with avenging angels and the sword of judgment. He felt himself a sinner and that an angry God was ready to hew him down and send him to Hell. But when he fell into God's arms, he found that God loved him and that He was not his enemy but the best Friend, the best Lover he ever had. The enemy he feared was not there.

*   *   *

"All Is Forgiven." In 1921 when I was in Chicago I read in the daily paper, in the personal column, a sad little item, an advertisement: "Emma, please come home. Mother is sick and calling for you.

All is forgiven." Whoever Emma was and however she had broken her mother's and dad's hearts, they loved her, they wanted her, they forgave her. And so God will forgive you if you will seek Him today and call upon Him while He may be found.

* * *

No True Roman Catholic Is Sure of Heaven

A noble young Catholic man wrote me. He was greatly impressed with THE SWORD OF THE LORD. He appealed to me that I would enter "the true church." How much good I would do, he said, if I would join the Roman Catholic Church and use whatever gifts and training I have in advancing the cause of "the true church."

I wrote him that I could not do that, first of all, because as it is now I have perfect assurance that my sins are forgiven; I have the assurance from the Word of God and from the Holy Spirit who lives within me that when I took Christ as my Saviour and relied upon Him, my sins were all forgiven and there, once for all, as they were paid for on the cross, my sins were forgiven, I was born of God and I am certain of Heaven. I told him I do not deserve this salvation, that it is all of God's grace, but it is certain because the blood of Jesus paid for it; I do not have to go through the church to get this salvation; I have already gone to Christ and when I trusted Him I received everlasting life. I told him that I could not give up this sweet peace and assurance.

I told him that I am relying on the one sacrifice forever which perfected the one who trusted in Christ according to Hebrews 10:10-14, and that now I could not put any confidence in the mass, since, after my sins were remitted through the blood of Christ, "there is no more offering for sin" (Heb. 10:18). And I urged him to find out if his priest, or if any other Catholic he knew, had sweet peace and assurance that his sins are already all forgiven, that he is now already a child of God and certain for Heaven, with all his sins forever hidden under the blood of Christ.

He was indignant. He was sure Catholics had just as much peace and assurance as anyone else did. So he went to his local priest in Tennessee. That priest assured him that no, of course, he did not know for sure that his sins were all forgiven. He hoped to go to Heaven but he would probably have to go to Purgatory for a time first.

The young man was distressed so he went to a bishop and there he received the same kind of an answer. Now, getting desperate, he wrote to a number of archbishops. And again he got the same kind of answer, that none of them could know for sure that their sins were forgiven.

Distressed he went back to the local priest and asked the priest why now there would be the sacrifice of the mass when the Bible so plainly said that Jesus had paid the whole debt by one offering forever, and that "now. . .there is no more offering for sin."

The priest scoffed at him. "Who gave you the right to interpret the Bible?" he stormed at the young man.

The young man, cut to the quick, said to the priest, "Who gave you the right to say that there is need for more offerings when the Bible says that Jesus' offering settled the matter once for all?" The priest, instead of answering him, angrily slapped his face and turned and left him.

That young man went to bed that night but tossed in torment for hours. Could no one then have any assurance of forgiveness? Was there no certainty of salvation through the blood of Christ, to one who trusted in Him? And in his groping mind there came again the Scripture of Hebrews 10:10: "By the which will we are sanctified through the offering of the body of Jesus Christ once for all," and there he put his trust in the Lord Jesus alone and had the peace that he could not have by Catholic dogma.

*   *   *

"The Easiest Thing I Ever Did!"
Thank God, I am accustomed to seeing miracles happen when God's people meet God's requirements. In one campaign I saw a long-time drunkard come to claim Christ as Saviour. When, soon thereafter he joined the church as a candidate for baptism, I saw another man who had been his bitterest enemy, but now a devoted follower of Jesus Christ, rush forward to be the first to shake his erstwhile enemy's hand. He told me, "I thought it would be hard, but it was the easiest thing I ever did!" Thank God, it is not unusual but usual to see drunkards converted and sobered, to see convicts saved and made into decent, good citizens. It is not unusual to see broken homes reunited, to see Catholics and Jews and aged sinners saved.

*   *   *

"I Wanted to Be Sure. . ."
In Dubuque, Iowa, I had revival services in the First Presbyterian Church. One night when I preached on trusting Christ, a fine seventeen-year-old boy came to trust in Christ. How wholehearted and sincere he was!

A few nights later I preached on the words of Jesus to Nicodemus, "Ye must be born again." And when the invitation was given, here came that same seventeen-year-old boy again, at once, to take my hand. He said, "Brother Rice, the other night I trusted Christ to be my Saviour, and now I want to be born again."

I explained to him that when he trusted Christ and when Jesus Christ came into his heart, he got everything that God had in connection with salvation. He got a new heart, he was born again into the family of God, his sins were all forgiven, his name was written down in Heaven, and he had everlasting life. "Well, I wanted to be sure I had everything," he said.

Dear friend, when you have Jesus Christ, you have "everything" in the way of salvation. "He that hath the Son hath life" (I John 5:12).

*   *   *

Out of the Darkness Into the Light.
I remember the story of a man who went across the corner of a pasture through the weeds and stepped on the rotted boards that covered an old abandoned well. The boards crashed through and he fell into the cold water. The well was lined with field stone. He found he could keep himself above the water by holding on to the stones and by bracing his feet. He cried and screamed for help. No one seemed to hear. He called again and again.

Night came on and only a faint star gleamed through the opening above him. He called until his voice grew hoarse. His hands were numb. His strength was failing. He was almost in despair that he would soon slip down the stagnant water of the old well. But at last a passer-by heard a faint cry and came with a lantern. Men let down a rope and pulled the exhausted man to the surface. His cry was heard. He was delivered from his watery prison. He was pulled out of the darkness into the light. He was saved from death.

Oh, quicker than that, the dear Lord Jesus will hear the cry of every sin-sick soul who wants forgiveness and mercy.

*   *   *

Call on the Great Physician, Not a Quack.
In Alabama a man had a running sore break out on his cheek. The sore seemed incurable. It grew larger and worse. Surely, his friends said, it was cancer. He should have gone at once for radium treatment or surgery. But no, he read an ad in a paper where a quack doctor offered to sell a salve that would cure cancer. He bought the salve, boasted that he had saved the doctor's expense and

the pain of surgery, and applied the salve diligently. The sore healed over on the outside, but went on with its deadly work, and after awhile the man died of cancer. He would not call for help though he desperately needed it. So many sinners will not call on the Lord Jesus Christ for salvation though they are wicked sinners in God's sight.

* * *

"First Batter" and "Second Batter!"

In the little cow town in West Texas where I went to school we marched out of the room in somewhat subdued, orderly fashion. But the understanding was that one was free to talk as soon as we got outside the building. So the first of the larger boys to reach the door would shout, "First batter!" and the next would cry, "Second batter!" We played "work-up" baseball.

Well, Paul cries, "I am the chief sinner!" (I Tim. 1:15). If Jesus died for sinners, Paul boldly gets in his claim as early and as strong as he can! And I feel like shouting, "I am second sinner!" The blood of Jesus is for sinners and nobody else. Thank God, I have gotten in. I have confessed my sin and have looked to the blood of Jesus who has paid my debt. I am "only a sinner, saved by grace."

* * *

Experience Proves, by Actual Canvass of Multitudes, That Nearly Everybody Ever Saved Is Converted in Youth.

In a large revival audience of about 800 people professing to be saved, I asked, "How many here were first converted, saved, after you were sixty years old?" One man held his hand, claiming to have been saved after he reached the age of sixty. The man was one out of about 800! So any man living under the same circumstances, unconverted at the age of sixty, would have missed about 799 opportunities to be saved, proportionately to only one chance left to keep out of Hell!

Then I asked, "How many were saved after you were fifty years old?" Three others held their hands. With the one man saved when past sixty, there were four out of 800 who had found Christ after they had passed their fiftieth birthday! So any person living under the same environment and circumstances would have only one chance out of 200 to be saved after fifty years of age.

"How many were saved after you were forty years old?" I then asked. Then about twenty people said that they had been saved after reaching the age of forty years! In that congregation only one person out of forty were saved after reaching forty. Any man under similar circumstances, who is forty years old and unconverted, has thirty-nine chances to go to Hell and only one chance to be saved!

Then I began at the other end, began at the lower age groups and asked how many had been converted by the time they were ten years old and under eleven. Probably one-fourth of the congregation, including more than half of those in the choir and a large percentage of the best personal workers and most useful Christians, held up their hands. Another large group had been saved by the time they were twelve years old, less than thirteen; and before the age of fifteen a clear majority of those 800 people had found Christ as Saviour, they said!

I have made similar tests in principal cities of America now for a number of years. Everywhere the same general proportions are similar. More than half of all the people who are ever saved are saved by the time they are fifteen. In certain areas, notably the South, where there are very active, large Sunday schools and where soul winning is stressed in the Sunday school, often in large congregations half of the people, or more, vote that they were converted to Christ before they were twelve years old. I have never found any congregation where the large group who held their hands as having been saved by the time they were fifteen years old was not estimated at more than half of the congregation who claimed to be saved! And I believe that all over America, seven out of eight of all who have been converted were saved by the time they were twenty-five years old.

*   *   *

Something Better Than Orders

In 1963, the Sword moved from Wheaton, Illinois, to Murfreesboro, Tennessee. The move has been greatly blessed of God. We bought the large properties of the Westvue Baptist Church, which moved to another section of town to build the Bellwood Baptist Church. We spent some thousands of dollars remodeling the building, 80' x 140', two stories, and moved in.

One day in August a salesman for the Sabin Robbins Paper Company came to see Mr. Nevin Wax, head of our four-man printing establishment, where we print the Sword books and pamphlets. He expected to sell some varied small lots of paper, and when he learned that we buy most of our book paper in carload lots, he knew that was out of his class.

But Nevin said, "Now, I want to talk to you about the Lord. Have you been converted? Have you accepted Christ as your own personal Saviour?" No, he had not. But with a few earnest words and some Scriptures, the paper salesman was led to call on the Lord for forgiveness and to trust Him and to claim Him as Saviour. He came around to other departments among our thirty workers to shake hands and tell them how glad he was to be saved, and then he went away. He did not sell any of the small lots of printing paper as he would to a little local print shop. But he got something far better than orders!

That was in August. In November we got from the Sabin Robbins Paper Company an expensive envelope and inside was an engraved card. It told of the sudden death of the salesman who had come to see us and expressed the loss of the company over the going of this useful man, and promised that another salesman would call on us soon.

Oh, surely that man had gone to many a print shop where some Christian could have told him about the Lord but did not. But when he called that day on the Sword of the Lord, God said to him, "To day if ye will hear his voice, harden not your heart." God said to him, "Choose you *this day* whom you will serve." So that very day he decided to choose Jesus and he found salvation. If he had waited it probably would have been too late forever!

* * *

A Proud Heart Finds Peace. In revival services in the Marquette Manor Baptist Church in Chicago years ago, a young woman came to the services who was very bitter. She was unconverted. She had lost her mother. And one night she said to me, "Brother Rice, you may think I am a fool to come and hear you night after night when I do not believe a thing you say."

I answered, "No, you may find out that this is the only time in your life that you ever had your wits about you, that you ever acted with any sense." Then one night the proud heart which had gone as long as it could with no peace, with inner turmoil and bitterness, came to the Lord Jesus and found the peace that her mother had had.

* * *

One Last Invitation

The big jet plane lifted off the runway at Tel Aviv in Israel and headed northwest toward Athens. Some members of the Sword Tour of Bible Lands eagerly looked over the map of the Middle East. Yes, among the many islands off the coast of Turkish Asia Minor was the little island of Patmos. We should pass right over it! We sent word to the pilot, asking if he would call it to our attention. And he did. From six or seven miles above it we looked down on the stony island where John, the beloved apostle, had been inspired to write the last book in the Bible, The Revelation of Jesus Christ.

Ussher's chronology, as used in the Scofield Reference Bible, places the date of the book of Revelation in A.D. 96. Then the Apostle John, the last of the twelve apostles left alive, must have been nearly a hundred years old when he was exiled to this small island. He was "in the isle that is called Patmos, for the word of God, and for the testimony of Jesus Christ" (Rev. 1:9). Here God used the hatred of wicked men to put John alone where He might give to John the words of the last book in the Bible, The Revelation.

At last, the book is nearly finished. I can imagine that the old man of God is exalted beyond measure! He has written the messages to the seven churches, has seen and has written down as the words were given to him, the awesome scenes after the rapture of the saints, these events which will last through the rise of the Antichrist, his reign, "the great whore," the world state church and the false prophet then to be aligned with the Antichrist. He has seen the destruction of the mighty city Rome, restored for a time as capital of the world empire of the Antichrist. He has been given the description of the return of Christ in glory to reign, the battle of Armageddon, and the wonderful millennial reign of Christ, the last rebellion, and then all the sinners dragged out of Hell, and the bodies from graves in the sea brought up for judgment, in Revelation, chapter 20.

Then, no doubt, his soul was transported as he saw the "new Jerusalem, coming down from God out of heaven, prepared as a bride adorned for her husband." He saw the gleaming towers, the walls of jasper, the gates of pearl, the golden streets; he saw the river of life and the trees of life. Oh, how his enraptured soul must have rejoiced as he recorded the words of God, about the city foursquare, the place where there is no death, no sorrow, no sighing, no sin, no night; no need of the sun, for the Lord God and the Lamb are the light of it!

But, "John" (let us suppose that the Lord spoke to the aged disciple), "we must write down one more sweet invitation for sinners, one more loving offer of mercy, one more plain, last call for the thirsty to drink of the water of life. And we will tell them that it is free and that it is for 'whosoever.' "

I imagine that the aging man, with the trembling voice of his years, said in his heart, "Yes, Lord, I have the parchment ready. I have prepared the ink with carbon, with soot from the fireplace. My goose-quill pen is trimmed and ready. Say on, O Lord Jesus!"

And so the Lord gave this last invitation in Revelation 22:17, "And the Spirit and the bride say, Come. And let him that heareth say, Come. And let him that is athirst come. And whosoever will, let him take the water of life freely."

* * *

Not to Russia, but to God. In Indonesia a young man was selected by communists to go to Russia for special training as a communist. As he went out to the airport and was ready to board the plane, he found a copy of my booklet, *"What Must I Do to Be Saved?"* on the ground, carelessly dropped by someone. He took it up, read it. He was startled! He must not go to Russia. He must turn to God. He did trust the Lord Jesus and wrote to tell me about it. Now he is a preacher in Indonesia.

* * *

Interviewing the Prodigal

Suppose I meet the prodigal son of Luke 15 on the way home. I say, "Hey, where are you going?"

He says, "I'm going home to my dad. Don't bother me."

I say, "Wait a minute, I want to talk to you."

"No, don't talk to me, Mr. Rice. I must hurry home. I have played the fool long enough."

"Well," I say, "how do you feel?" (You know, a lot of people say, "If I felt right I would come.")

But this boy says, "I feel like a bum, and a crook, and a fool; that is the way I feel. But I am going home anyway!"

"Well, wait. Don't you think you had better wait until you feel right?"

"No. If Dad will just forgive me, and if I get a good meal under my belt, I'll feel all right. Leave me alone!"

And so he goes home.

I say, "Wait a minute! Why, you look pretty ragged to be going back to your father's mansion. Is he the rich fellow who lives up on the hill in that nice white house with the rolling acres? Is that the man?"

"Oh, yes, that is my father."

"Well, are you going back in rags like that? Don't you think you had better buy a good suit and wait until you earn your way?"

He says, "Oh, no! I can't wait for anything. My father has a good suit of clothes. He has plenty! I'm going home and let my father furnish those things." And so here he goes!

I say, "Where is all that money you wasted? Don't you think you had better stop and earn a little?"

He says, "No, I can't earn it, I would starve to death. But I will go to my father. He has plenty; he will take care of me."

"Well, how do you feel?"

"I feel bad, but I am going home to my father."

A little later I slip up there. Ah, what a good time he is having! I hear the happy laughter of his friends, and the father's great tones as he talks to the boy. I hear the rattle of silverware, and I hear the servants all talking as they gather around the table. I hear the father say, "Son, may I give you just a little more of this veal? It is mighty tender. We have saved this calf and kept him fattened up a year until you got home. Can't you eat a little more?"

"Well, you can give me a little more. Boy, I have never had anything like this before," the boy says.

And maybe the mother says, "May I give you another glass of buttermilk?" (Maybe he was a Southern boy and would want buttermilk!)

So he is having a good time. I slip up by his side and whisper in his ear and say, "How do you feel, old boy?"

"Oh, boy, I just feel wonderful! My father loves me and he has forgiven everything, and my heart is satisfied. I have on a nice robe that represents the righteousness of Christ. I have on the ring; that means I am His son, God's son. I have the shoes on my feet. That means I am clothed with the Gospel of peace, and am very proud of it. I have a message to tell. And I have had the fatted calf of God's richest blessing. I feel fine!"

Don't wait, brother.

> **Let not conscience make you linger,**
> **Nor of fitness fondly dream.**
> **All the fitness He requireth**
> **Is to feel your need of Him.**

Oh, sinner, come on back to the Father's house. Throw away the Devil's apples, and you will find the Father has everything good and sweet for you. And in the long run, oh, how glad you will be that you let Jesus be your Saviour and let God be your Father and had your sins forgiven and washed in the blood.

Separation and Standards

"I Will Die Clean!" Once I had a letter from a dear woman who heard me regularly on the radio. She said she became convicted about the sin of dipping snuff. When some visitors came to her house and rang the doorbell, she had snuff in her mouth and had no time to run to the kitchen to spit it out. What would she do? Ashamed for it to be known that she dipped snuff, she swallowed it, wiped her mouth, and went to the door!

But the nicotine in that mouthful of snuff made her sick. She felt greatly ashamed that she had a habit that she dared not let her neighbors know about, ashamed that she had a secret that she must hide from those who would be offended by it. She had heard me preach about how a Christian ought to keep his body as a holy temple of the Lord and she resolved she would quit the stuff. She had used this form of tobacco for many years. It had a vise-like hold upon her—a habit which it seemed impossible to break.

When she gave up the snuff, she got sick. Lying on her bed desperately sick, she said, "O God, if I die, I will never touch the filthy stuff again! If I die, I will die clean!" But God raised her up and she was free from the habit.

* * *

Christians Who Did Not Stay Steadfast. So many Christians these days do not stay steadfast. In 1932 I preached in Chicago at the Paul Rader Tabernacle on the sin of yoking up with unbelievers in the Lord's work. A trustee of a well-known Christian college heard me and arranged for me to come and preach the same sermon at the college. The founder of the college had taken a strong stand on this subject; it was one they stressed much. Would I preach to the students and faculty? The college paid me for the trip and the earnest Bible sermon. It was well received. But this week that college has joined in with notorious modernists in a revival campaign. It has joined with churches that put on dances, joined with preachers who deny the authority of the Bible and the blood atonement, the virgin birth, and the actual deity of Christ, to sponsor the thing that they once stood so strongly against.

I know an editor who led in the great movement against modernism in his denomination and against the inclusive policy of sending believing and unbelieving missionaries to the foreign field, having Christians and infidels teach in the denominational colleges. But when some noble men pressed the matter and came out of the denomination, he went back to

support that which he once opposed. He sought the favor of those
he once rebuked.

* * *

One Need Not Answer All Problems; Just Get Them to Jesus! The way to get people saved is not by answering all their problems, but by just saying, "Why don't you come to Jesus?"

One woman argued, "But I don't
see any harm in the picture show!"

I said, "I am not talking about
the picture show; I am talking
about Jesus."

"Yes, but you people—"

"Never mind us. Why don't you
come to Jesus, and then ask Him
about it?"

She argued on: "But I don't see
any harm in a nice movie."

I said, "Why don't you just come
on to Jesus, give Him your heart,
trust Him to save you and then if
He says there isn't any harm in the
movies, I wouldn't quit. But if He
says there is harm in them, then I
would quit."

Still she said, "But I don't see
any harm in going to the movies."

"Tell Jesus you don't see any
harm in going. But will you trust
Him and give up the sin in your
heart and then whatever He shows
you is wicked and wrong, will you
turn from it if Jesus asks you to?"
After much argument, and after
bringing her to this question, she
soon was saved.

Then almost immediately after
she got saved she said, "I don't
believe going to the picture show is
so important after all. I believe I
can give them up pretty easily!"
After she was saved, there was not
much of an issue about it.

* * *

Speak Plainly. In Winston-Salem, North Carolina, in a blessed citywide campaign in Liberty Tobacco Warehouse, I preached, as I do elsewhere and perhaps more plainly since it was so needed there in that tobacco country, that the body of a Christian is the temple of the Holy Spirit, that it ought not to be defiled, and that Christians ought not to make money out of harm to others. Some men left their jobs at the Reynolds Tobacco Company, and one of them began at once to be a preacher greatly blessed of God. He sold his stock in the company, trusted the Lord, and went out boldly. But some people were very angry. They protested that half the money that came in the offerings was put in either by those who raised tobacco on their farms or by workers who worked in the cigarette factories. Angry notes were sent to me in protest. As the angry mob turned against Paul because he preached against their idols, so some men resented this evangelist, and at least one church in Winston-Salem

and one in Durham, North Carolina, was closed to this preacher because in the tobacco country I felt I must speak plainly about the harm of tobacco.

* * *

You Cannot Win Souls at the Dance. A preacher said to a girl, "You ought not to go; it is bad company. Your influence will be wrong. You will lose out."

She said, "I don't believe it."

The preacher said, "I can prove it. Listen, when you go to a dance, try to win somebody to Christ."

She said, "I believe I can do it."

So she went with her boyfriend to the dance. On the dance floor that night she asked, "Are you a Christian?"

"No, are you?"

"Yes."

"What are you doing here then?"

She didn't win him to Christ! And you won't win anybody to Christ in that crowd. The crowd is wrong, always has been wrong, the crowd that goes to the dance.

* * *

Fake Separation. There is a fake separation, a fake sanctification abroad in the land today which sets many Christians too far away from lost people. In my great Buffalo, New York, union campaign I asked the congregation how many

thought they could get some person who drinks to attend the services if I would preach on "The Double Curse of Booze." Out of a congregation of perhaps 2,400 there were not more than ten or twelve who thought they could get someone guilty of this sin, afflicted by this craving, damned by this curse, to attend the services! This was a shocking indication that they had separated themselves too far from all such people, that they did not have the close touch with sinners and the compassionate heart for sinners, and the confidence of sinners such as New Testament Christians ought to have.

The Bible doctrine of separation does not mean separation from all unconverted people. Rather it means separated unto God and to live for Him and please Him. And we really cannot please the dear Lord Jesus if we ignore, or if we care little for, the dying sinners around us.

* * *

He Gave Up the Lodge. Stephen Merritt, a Christian leader in New York City years ago, went about testifying for God, preaching the Gospel. Yet he prized most dearly his membership in the Masonic Lodge and the lodge jewels which he wore. But God dealt with him so keenly that he came to see that he had not slain utterly the Amalekites, as God commanded, until he should give up the oaths that were forbidden, give up this symbol of salvation by works and character. Then penitently Stephen Merritt gave up the lodge and its offices and jewels and oaths!

* * *

A Dying Girl of the Streets Asks, "Am I Any Worse Than Society Girls Who Dance?"

How well I remember when I preached one time on the street in Fort Worth while attending the Seminary. We took that big Nash truck and Seminary students and had a service on the street at the corner of Tenth and Main. Either Brother McMurray or I had some word to say about the dance. A young nurse spoke to my wife. "I have a story to tell you. Perhaps you will tell Brother Rice." She told my wife this story:

"I am a nurse in the City-County Hospital here in Fort Worth. A young woman there is dying with a venereal disease. She called me the other day and said, 'Nurse, you say I can't live long.' This girl dying in the City-County Hospital in Fort Worth, this seventeen-year-old girl with venereal disease brought on by sin, of course, said to me, 'Nurse, I know I have done wrong. I know I have sinned. I don't try to excuse myself. I have got to meet God pretty soon. Nurse, do you really believe I am so bad?'"

"I said, 'Of course that is a terrible sin.'

"But this girl said, 'Nurse, do you think it is any worse for me? I went on and plied my trade to make a living. Nurse, do you think it is any worse for me than for these society girls who had their dances until after midnight and the latter part of the night men came down to see me?'

"I didn't know what to tell her. I didn't know what to say."

Yes, I think she was worse. That is, probably she knew she was doing more harm, but actually the women who danced and inflamed the men were guilty of the same sin, and every such night God booked them up as adulteresses and scarlet women, because Jesus Himself said that "whosoever looketh on a woman to lust after her hath committed adultery with her already in his heart." Certainly those who inspire the lust are equally guilty. Brother, put that down!

* * *

He Wanted the Results Without the Standards.

I was in revival services with a large church in St. Louis. Sunday school teachers and others objected to my strong stand against worldliness, Hollywood movies, cigarettes, and immodest dress on the part of Christians. They approached the pastor about it. He reminded them that he did not preach that way, and he did not necessarily agree, and each one must decide for himself. He thought I was a little extreme. They came to tell me that. I prayed a night about it and the Lord seemed to clearly show me the answer.

The next day I asked the pastor, and he sheepishly admitted, yes, that he attended the movie theatre, too, "but only the best pictures," and he never reproved worldliness in the pulpit. He wanted the results of evangelism without the reproach which always goes with Spirit-filled, bold preaching. He wanted members for the church, but he did not want the plain preaching that goes with revivals in the power of God. I reminded him that he had long known all about my doctrinal position and my position on worldliness before inviting me. For years he had taken THE SWORD OF THE LORD, of which I am editor. He wanted the attendance, the numbers, and whatever prestige might come from having me in his church. But he thought I was too strict in my standards for Christian living, particularly for young people.

I gave him a day in which to either openly back me up in Bible preaching against sin or else I would leave the meeting. And I did. I was sad to learn later that his daughter married a drunkard, lived a worldly life, and broke his heart.

* * *

Native, Maidenly Modesty Disappears in the Dance

A preacher named Jenkins some years ago preached in the First Baptist Church in Amarillo on the dance. The dance then was not nearly as bad as now. But Brother Jenkins said that a girl doesn't stay as modest after dancing as before; that a girl who has this man's arms about her and then that one's, and wears the evening clothes and all that sort of thing, doesn't stay modest, doesn't stay where she can blush, where she has the same virtuous reticence of character and mind. He said that she is not the same girl after she has had every man's hands on her; that such a girl doesn't stay the same.

A man got red in the face, as some of you are getting tonight. He got hot under the collar and said to himself, "This preacher is going to eat that. My girl Molly is as good a girl as any in this town, as good as she ever was, even if she does dance. That preacher is going to eat that. Dancing doesn't make any difference with her modesty."

He planted himself out at the front door of that Baptist church at Amarillo. But before the preacher got out to the front, Molly stopped him and said, "Brother Jenkins, you are right. I am not the Christian I used to be. I am not as spiritually-minded as I used to be. I am not the same girl I once was. Pray for me. The dance has done it."

Nearly everybody was gone. The preacher went on to the front, not knowing what was about to happen. Then the father said to Brother Jenkins, "I want you to know, you have got to take back what you said tonight. My girl is the same after dancing as before. Molly is as clean and modest and virtuous as she ever was. That is a reflection on my girl's character."

The preacher said, "Let's see what Molly has to say about it. Molly, come here."

The girl, with red eyes, came, and the preacher said to her, "Molly, I want you to tell your daddy what you told me."

She said, "Dad, I am not as modest as I used to be. I don't pray like I used to. I don't feel God's presence like I used to. The dance has been a curse to me."

The father said, "God help me! If I had known that, I wouldn't have let you go!"

I say now, there is something about the modern dance that breaks down conventionality, and makes a girl's virtue not safe and man's integrity not safe!

Service for Christ

Finish the Fight. When I played college football I found that the best football player might not be the most brilliant athlete. He was often the man who never stopped running until the whistle blew. He would "follow the ball." How many a tackle I have made when the opposing runner had cut all the way across the field and I seemed too far away to have a chance at him, when suddenly finding himself cut off on that side of the field, he would reverse his field and I would meet him coming back! Blessed is the man who keeps on and finishes the race!

I saw a boxing match the other day. One of the contestants was knocked down twice in the first round. It seemed that he must prove a quick loser to the energetic fellow he faced. But he learned how to deal with that left uppercut and catch it on his glove. He kept on. In the third round he was pretty well in control. At the last of the ten rounds, there was no doubt that he was the best man. All three judges gave him the decision. He finished the course and finished strong.

Oh, God give us men who are not necessarily brilliant, not necessarily spectacular, but faithful men who finish the fight.

* * *

A Renegade Jew!

A friend of mine who was an orthodox Jew, born in Russia, came to America to get away from the pogroms in Russia, where his father, a Jewish rabbi, was slain. He himself had spent eight years in study of the Talmud, planning to be a rabbi. So he taught in the Chicago Hebrew Institute. The Holy Spirit sought this Jew, led him from Chicago to Dallas and from Dallas to Fort Worth, where eventually he could not get away from the Hebrew Scriptures that foretold the coming of the Saviour. I saw him stand one day in the Southwestern Baptist Theological Seminary chapel to tell how at two o'clock that morning he had surrendered his heart and life and all to the Lord Jesus Christ.

With childlike simplicity this Jew set out to serve the Lord. He came to my home often. I remember the day when he brought me a letter. His face was gray, his hand trembled; it was from his baby sister whom he had brought from Russian Poland and had supported in America. He translated the letter from Yiddish for me, and this is about what it said:

"Dear Louis:—

"Sister and I are greatly distressed at the insane thing that has happened to you. Who ever thought that you would become a traitor to your father and your father's religion, a renegade Jew! Oh, leave your bastard Christ and come back to us and be happy again!"

He had been a father to those younger sisters, but with trembling lips and hoarse voice he said, "Brother Rice, I cannot give up my Saviour! I love my sisters—I have supported them ever since my father died. I have given them all my money and tried to make them happy. This breaks my heart; but I cannot give up my Saviour!"

Later he brought me another letter from the same sister. He had written his two sisters urging them to accept the Saviour. The reply was something like this:

"You are no longer a brother of mine. Already we have counted you dead. The rabbi has conducted funeral services for you. We have gone through the apartment and sought out everything that had your name on it and every gift you ever bought for us, and have destroyed them. The only thing that remains is this fountain pen you gave me on my last birthday. When I have finished this letter and signed my name, I will stamp the pen to pieces on the floor and throw the pieces in the garbage. You traitor Jew, you may have your bastard Christ! You are no brother of ours any more!"

That was hard for my Jewish friend to bear. Remember that a Jew is not received very warmly even by Christians. They never forget that he is a Jew, they never forgive him his idiosyncrasies and peculiarities. The average Christian is not very kind to a Jewish Christian; yet my friend steadfastly refused to go back to his family. His surrender to Jesus was voluntary. He had counted the cost and he, having put his hand to the plow, did not look back! I believe that that is the kind of service God wants.

* * *

Bargain With the Lord. In 1926 I had a little bargain with the Lord. I said, "Lord, from this time forth I will look after Your business and You look after my business." I gave up a regular salary, and have never had one since, nor make any bargain wherever I should go for the Lord's service. I gave up my life insurance. I do not think salaries nor life insurance are either wrong. This was a matter of trust where I had clear leading from the Lord.

How wonderfully He has kept up His part, though poorly I have done mine. Oh, the giving, provident hands of Jesus! How He has given millions of dollars to get out the Gospel! He has given houses and cars and food and open doors and power and souls saved and friends by the thousands. The hands of Jesus are provident, giving hands.

* * *

Anxious to Please. How eagerly we ought to seek to please God in everything! As I grew up, how continually anxious I was to please my father. We raised horses in West Texas and how anxious I was that my father should not think me a coward about riding a bucking bronc! Sometimes if a horse seemed unusually strong and wild, he would say, "Son, you don't have to ride him unless you want to. But if you get on him and he throws you off, then you must climb right back on." And so I did. It was no disgrace to get thrown: I did get thrown more than once; but it would have been a great disgrace if

I should play the coward and my father would be ashamed of me!

Sometimes when my brother or I would ride away from home Dad would say, "Remember whose boy you are now." And now and then he would remind us that not one of the family had ever been arrested.

And when I came back to my hometown of Decatur, Texas, as an evangelist, my father hitched up his Chevrolet car onto the block and tackle to help set up the big 800-pound center poles for the tent, and then he brought his cane-bottom chair and leaned back against the tent pole and heard me preach, his eyes misty with tears. He had named me John for a Baptist preacher friend, and, I think, for John the Baptist; and how he delighted that God had laid His hand upon me to preach! I wanted to please my father. He was worthy of the reverence I gave him, and it had a profound influence on my character.

* * *

Just to Please People! How carefully a young man dresses for his date—clean shave, freshly dressed, pressed suit, a mouthwash, hair well combed, teeth brushed. And when one goes to apply for a job, how careful he is of his grooming, of his language, of his attitude!

The cosmetic ads go to ridiculous lengths to stress how one may please the senses of another. Unpleasant breath is pictured as something horrible: the reason for not making a sale or getting a good-night kiss. Even a little dandruff on the shoulder is pictured as a subject of gossip! And ladies are warned to use hand lotion that makes the hands "kissing soft." And "dishpan hands" are shockingly displayed as reminding one of a lobster's claw, of a prickly cactus, or worse! I say those extremes are silly. But they illustrate how anxious we are to please people. Oh, then, how anxious we ought to be to please God and have His smile upon us!

* * *

When You Love Someone. . . I remember when I fell in love with the girl who is now my wife. When springtime came on, I tried to find and bring to her the first wild flowers. When the peaches were ripening on the trees I waited and watched so carefully to find the first ripe peaches for her enjoyment. I read a lovely book and enjoyed it, but I could not enjoy it alone; so I marked page after page, then sent it to her. I wanted to please her in everything I could.

Likewise, should we not set out to try to be attractive to God, to please God day by day in the smallest details? Oh, what could be more important in this world than pleasing the dear Saviour who died for us and who loves us and keeps us and is preparing a home for us in Heaven!

* * *

Find Something to Do for the Lord

Years ago my Uncle George N. Rice of Gainesville, Texas, who has gone to Heaven, said to his pastor, "I wish there was something I could do. I feel so useless."

"There is one thing you can do," the preacher said. "I like to shake your hand. I know how you love people."

It was amazing how everybody loved Uncle George. Let me illustrate.

When my father's first wife died, he left two children with his brother, my Uncle George, and he reared Jimmie, my older sister. All the youngsters in town piled into his big house. Half the town pretty soon called him "Uncle George."

I went to see him before his death, and there came in a middle-aged woman. She stooped over his bed and kissed him, and said, "How are you, Uncle?" though she wasn't kin to him. She was a former member of a fine big class of 100 girls he had had in Sunday school. She had been kissing Uncle George all her life, and when he was seventy years old and sick, she came in and kissed him.

I was at his house for dinner one day and an old fellow came by with a load of wood. Uncle George bought the wood from him, though he didn't need it, and made the man get down off his wagon and tie his horses and come into that nice dining room with its beautiful silverware, and the gleaming white linen cloth. He brought that man in with his overalls and sat him down at the table. Aunt Gertrude had everything as fine as could be. He would bring in any chicken peddler to eat dinner with him. He didn't just give them some food in the kitchen, he brought them to the dining table with the family. Everybody loved Uncle George. This is the point I started to make—everybody loved him.

He said, "I wish I could do something for the Lord."

The preacher said, "You can. There is one thing you can do. You love people. Get out in the vestibule and shake hands with everybody that comes in the door, then shake hands with everybody that goes out."

And my Uncle George did. Soon he was teaching a class of 100 young women. Later he was partially paralyzed and everywhere he went he had to be in a wheelchair. They would set that chair in the vestibule by the door, and it got to be a custom that hardly anybody used the other doors at all. Everybody went in one door and they would file by and shake hands with Uncle George as they went out.

Now God wants every Christian to have a job and fill that job happily, successfully, prosperously. If you do not do it, you are a seat-warming Christian, a parasite, growing without any roots.

* * *

Doing the Impossible. During World War II Winston Churchill said to engineers in England, "Prepare me a harbor on the coast of France. Prepare me a floating breakwater so that we can make a harbor where there is not any."

They said, "It is impossible; it would be beaten to pieces."

"Impossible nothing! Go and do it!" he said.

They insisted, "There is not any way to do it."

"Go and find a way to do it; we've got to have it!"

And they made it and landed tens of thousands of allied soldiers in the invasion of Europe, because they found a way to do what was impossible.

Listen to me! There are not any impossible things with God.

Got any rivers you think are uncrossable?

Got any mountains you can't tunnel through?

God specializes in things thought impossible

And He can do what no other power can do.

Jesus Christ said, "I have promised to be with you; go ahead and do it." He ignored the difficulties.

* * *

Does God Have to Drag You? My brother Joe had a model T Ford. He told me he always knew how to start it: "Any time you jack up both hind wheels and crank it until the water boils, it will start."

If you go at it that way, you can get some Christians to teach a Sunday school class. You can get them to tithe, or get them to come to prayer meeting, or get them to testify. If you really jack both hind wheels up ·and crank until the water boils, you can get them to do something for God. Is God content with the kind of service that comes always with a grudge, always with the brakes on?

I was in a revival meeting down in Southwest Texas. I went to Hico, near Lampasas. They have live oak trees and white limestone everywhere. I was in a hurry. I went in my car. I was going back to the revival, and I came to a fellow whose car was out of gas, or something was wrong with his car. I tried to help get his car started, but I couldn't. So I told him, "If you want me to, I will pull you in." I hooked on with a tow chain. Over those rough, rocky roads we went, driving about thirty miles an hour. The man in the car behind me couldn't see. He sat back there and kept putting on the brakes. Finally I stopped to see what was the matter. He said, "I will just sit here if you don't mind. Just unhook the chain and I will send my boy after the car later."

Do you think God wants to take you anywhere when He always has to drag you? when you always have the brakes on?

* * *

"Indian Giver!" When I was a ten-year-old boy we lived on a ranch in West Texas, and Christmas time to us was wonderful. For instance, we got an orange at Christmas. We very rarely had any at any other time in the year. We would get twisted candy and a few nuts, and we had a good time. It didn't take much to make a happy Christmas. Every one got an orange. We didn't have orange groves in Texas then. They all came from California, and were rather expensive and we were poor. I wonder how many people

remember when you didn't get an orange except at Christmas? (Many held hands.) So at Christmas we each got an orange.

My stepmother said, "Now children, I can make a fruit cake and I will have to make the citron with the orange peelings. I will candy the orange peelings if you will give yours to me."

So every one agreed. That may seem a little funny to you. Why should children object to giving the orange peel? But if you got just one a year, you could eat the peel with a little sugar and it was delicious, and we hadn't had an orange since last Christmas. We used to get bananas and we not only ate the bananas, but we scraped all the inside of the peeling. You don't do that now. Yes, the orange peel is really wonderfully good with sugar. Now my stepmother said if we would give her the orange peelings she would make a cake.

We agreed, and she put the orange peels up on top of the kitchen safe. We didn't have any refrigerator, of course. It was a safe with tin doors and nail holes punched in the doors. So she put the peelings up on top of that so we couldn't see them. They were to be left there several days, then Mother was going to candy them. I got to thinking about the orange peels. That orange was given to me for Christmas and I didn't have to give it, did I? Why did I give it all? I ought to have kept a little bit, one good section. I could have eaten it with some sugar. I thought, "Well, I don't think she needs that much," so I went back, reached high on the safe and got one piece of the orange peeling and ate it with some sugar. Boy, it was good!

A day or two later as I thought about it I decided I could have one more piece. It was mine anyway, wasn't it? So I took another section from the top of the safe. You know, I lost count of how many times I went back. One day when I reached up there for one piece of *my* orange peeling there wasn't anybody's up there!

And you know, I have told God many times, "Lord, You can have me. Take me anywhere You want me to go. I will give up anything in this world. You deserve it and You can have it." I have said that and meant it; but the first thing I knew, I felt myself reaching back on top of the safe to take myself back and have my own way instead of God's way. I was an "Indian giver."

* * *

Lessons From Plowing

Some of us have worked on a farm and have driven big teams of four or six horses or mules. I assure you, many lessons can be learned from horses.

What a task it is to drive four horses to an empty wagon when they are hitched with two as a lead team, and two as wheel horses. If the driver does not watch, the lead team will slow down too much and the singletrees will hit their heels, or the tongue of the wagon will poke them in the rump and there will be a startled horse kicking in surprise and the whole team upset! Or, if the lead team goes too fast, they will pull the wagon up on the heels of the wheel team and they will bump their legs on the singletrees. Or, the wheel team will not follow the lead team exactly and so there may be a mix-up. But just put several tons of weight on the wagon and in a moment all the difficulties are gone. Each horse buckles down to his job and automatically stays in line. The wheel team cannot pull the wagon fast enough to run the tongue into the lead team. The lead team cannot pull the wagon up on the heels of the wheel team.

So it is that a great goal and a tremendous occupation with the most serious and blessed thing in the world can straighten out everything in the life of a Christian.

As a youngster I once worked a team of four horses and mules abreast to a big double-disk turning plow. Two of the team were wild young mules and as I drove into the field, before I got the plow into the ground, those two young mules got excited and bolted. They dragged the other team and the plow and me right along with them, and there we went, cavorting across the field! But I reached quickly for a lever and let the plows down deep. What a change! As the big disk-breaking plows caught hold, they began to throw the soil in great arching streams. The wild mules suddenly found they were doing all they could do, going zigzag across the field, pulling a plow that normally all four were needed to pull. That took the wind out of their sails mighty soon! Soon, sweating and panting, they were glad enough to stop. I drove back to the edge of the field, got my furrow running straight and had no more trouble with the young mules.

You see, many a young mule of a Christian gets off the track unless he gets some consuming passion for which it is worth giving up everything else. Soul winning is the one greatest thing in the world.

* * *

"If Any Man Hate Not Father and Mother," Jesus Said (Luke 14:26). A man was talking with me about his lovely daughter, the only one left at home. Oh, how they loved her! But she fell in love with Jim. Jim was a nice fellow, but he didn't have much of an education, and he didn't have much money. And their daughter wanted to marry Jim. Father said, "Now, Honey, you stay here with us."

"No, I can't."

"I will tell you what we will do. I'll send you through college."

"I don't want to go to college. I want to marry Jim!"

"Well, I'll buy you a piano and pay for piano lessons."

"No, Dad. All I want is Jim. I've been dating him for a year or more and I know what I want to do."

So this father said to me, "She doesn't care for us. Look at all the money we have spent on her all these years. Now she despises me and her mother."

No she didn't. She just loved Jim so much that it didn't matter too much about Dad and Mother.

Now sometimes it has to be Jesus, and everybody else out of the picture. I don't mean you wish them ill. I don't mean you do them wrong! I don't mean you hold any malice! I don't mean any lack of filial loyalty! I mean sometimes God just has to be first, above everything else. That is what He wants. You must leave everything—father and mother and all.

* * *

Can You Not Trust God Blindly Without Seeing Where the Road May Lead? A certain horse my father used to have is a great lesson to me. This horse was blind. You could get on him and ride him and other people couldn't tell the difference. You could hardly tell it yourself. He was blind, but you could ride down the road and this horse couldn't see a place he put his foot before him, yet he trusted the man riding him and he went right ahead.

The truth of the matter is, the way my daddy got him, he traded for him a horse that had the heaves. He rode beside a fellow one night and this horse had such a wonderful gait my father said, "What about trading horses?"

"All right, I will trade with you."

My dad said, "No questions asked and we will trade for good?"

This fellow said, "All right," and he got down and they changed saddles and my father got on this blind horse and rode him home that night. The next day my dad discovered he had traded for a blind horse, but a horse that trusted his rider.

My friend, listen to me, wouldn't you like to be able to say, "O God, I can serve you blind"?

Oh, friend, if God comes to borrow $1.00 from you, would you ask Him to sign a promissory note? We ought not to. If God wanted to buy something from you on credit, would you look up and see if His credit was good?

* * *

"Me Give It to Jesus." I am told that an Indian chief heard a preacher earnestly plead as he told the story of the Gospel. The Indian chief came and gave his blanket (and giving a blanket means something for an Indian).

That preacher said, "What is this?"

The Indian replied, "Me give it to the Lord; me give this blanket to the Lord."

The preacher went on talking. The Indian went off. After awhile he came back with his gun and laid it down and said, "Me give this the Lord. Me give it to Jesus."

The preacher took it, and went on preaching. The Indian went and brought his pony and gave it to the Lord.

The preacher kept pleading. Finally with tears streaming down his face, this Indian came and said, "No more got to give. Give myself to Him."

My friends, can you say tonight, "God, do not hold back Your hand. Take what You want—all I have, all I am"? It is a sad thing for a Christian to be left alone. Can you say, "Lord, have your way tonight"?

* * *

God Opens the Doors. Once in Fort Worth, Texas, a committee waited on me to tell me that if I did not give up a certain radio broadcast, my name would be blackballed in every Baptist church, I would be named at the association meeting as one unfit to hold revival services in churches. I would be denounced in *The Baptist Standard.* I had taken a plain stand against evolution teaching in my own *alma mater.* I was standing for the fundamentals of the faith. But after prayer I decided that the God I serve could look after His own. I ignored the threats of these men (good men but misled) and went on with my broadcast. Thank God, more doors have opened, wider usefulness has come my way, as I disregarded men and tried to be true to Jesus Christ.

God takes the part of every Christian who is true to Him. Go on, my brother, my sister, and win souls at any cost! Take your plain stand against sin anywhere and everywhere. God never leaves one alone and ashamed and forsaken who is true to Him. Trouble may come in the will of God, but thank God, always God allows only what is best and then delivers His servant who is faithful! So Paul and Silas got out of jail in a wonderful intervention of God.

* * *

To Retire or Not to Retire? I boarded a plane at Greenville, South Carolina, for Chicago, with a stop at Cincinnati. On the plane to Cincinnati was a man who boarded at Knoxville. He sat beside me. We talked. He said, "I got two weeks' vacation but it rained every day but two! I didn't get to fish but two days! I have a little place down here. I am sixty-five; I'll retire in January. Then, I'll fish all the time."

I thought, The poor fellow! Anxious to retire! I'd rather have somebody working for me who liked to work, wouldn't you? Don't you think the Lord would, too?

This man got off at Cincinnati, and another man sat beside me, a missionary Catholic bishop in the Solomon Islands. In that wild country he had gone and taken some monks and priests and set up little Catholic churches and they were preaching to those people. He was very approachable. "I am sixty-six," he said.

I said, "Well, in that wild, dangerous country, Jesus could be just as near to you there as anywhere."

He said a thing that seemed strange to me, and I was so glad he said it, "He may be nearer, since we need Him so much more down there." He said, "I am sixty-six, and have diabetes (and he mentioned some other trouble) and I am coming home to Minneapolis to a friend there. Then I am going to see my buddy, Cardinal Cushing, at Boston. He and I were in school together. I am going to have an operation and treatment up there. But they want me to come home and retire. But I don't want to retire. So they asked me to take a charge in the United States. But I want to go back. I wish you would pray (a Catholic bishop asking me, a Baptist preacher, to pray) that I can get back to my field."

* * *

Followers of Christ. One day in the Galilean Baptist Church in Dallas, I preached on this Scripture, "If any man will come after me, let him deny himself, and take up his cross daily, and follow me" (Luke 9:23). At the close I asked the people who wished to make a new dedication of themselves to the Lord and to say that wherever God led they would follow Him, to come and take my hand. It was a time of tearful reconsecration and of great blessing. One woman came weeping to take my hand and say, "Brother Rice, I am going wherever you go." That sounded strange to me, but after prayerful thought I saw that it was to be expected. She trusted me to find the will of God. She trusted me to explain His Word. In following her pastor, she would only be trying to do what

Paul plainly commanded people to do when he said, "Be ye followers of me, even as I also am of Christ" (I Cor. 11:1).

* * *

Crooked Sticks. We should remember that the only kind of men God has to use are imperfect men. Dr. J. B. Gambrell, famous Southern Baptist of a generation ago, used to say, "God can hit some mighty straight licks with some mighty crooked sticks." And I am glad that God in mercy puts His treasure in earthen vessels. I am glad that He calls people to preach and counts them worthy who are unworthy, as Paul said he was.

* * *

Twist Satan's Tail! Christians may expect trouble when they go out and out into Spirit-filled, aggressive soul winning and into any aggressive fight against Satan and wickedness and unbelief.

One preacher said to me, "You talk about the Devil as if he were a person. You speak about Satan being against your work. Why do you think Satan does not attack me and bother me?"

I answered in the familiar cowboy language of my boyhood, "If you twisted the Devil's tail as much as I do, he would hate you, too."

* * *

No Loved Ones in Heaven?

Sometimes friends say, "Brother Rice, wouldn't it be wonderful to have a vacation?" But I just can't get away. If I have an opportunity to preach somewhere, to conduct a revival, how can I go away and spend two weeks just fishing and walking and riding and sight-seeing?

Somebody said: "Wouldn't it be wonderful to take a three weeks' trip, go up through the Rocky Mountains, see the Garden of the Gods, go on into the great parks, into Wyoming and across the ranges and see the great Sequoia trees in California and go on up into Washington State—wouldn't that be wonderful if you could take a trip like that?"

I said, "No, no, that wouldn't be wonderful to me."

"Why, what would you like if you had a three weeks' vacation?"

I said, "I have already seen Washington, D.C., with the cherry trees in bloom. I have seen Santa Catalina Island and Carlsbad Cavern and the Grand Canyon. I have seen the high Rockies and the verdure and beauty of the Smokies and the Alleghanies. I have seen Washington's monument, Mount Vernon, the Betsy Ross house, Independence Hall and the Liberty Bell. I have seen the Battery and the Statue of Liberty, and the Little Church Around the Corner and Wall Street. That isn't what I want."

"What would you want, then? Where would you go?"

"I would go home and eat my wife's cooking. I would sit at home, study and read the books I haven't time to read. I would play with my own children—I'm almost a stranger to them. I would sit around and talk, and play and sing at the piano. I never get to sing with my children."

One of these days I am going home. But if someone should say, "I will give you a lovely home and a big bank account, but you must leave Mrs. Rice and your children out," I would say, "You can have your mansion. You can have your money and your bank account. You can have everything else. I want somebody who loves me. I want those whom I love." What a tragedy if some of you get to Heaven and the ones you love the most have gone to Hell! Someone wrote a little song, "I Dreamed I Searched Heaven for You." What will Heaven be like if those you love the most are not there? In view of the glories and blessedness of Heaven, Christian friends, how much is the soul of your boy or your girl or your neighbor or your friend worth? How much is a soul worth? Oh, God help us to see the value of a soul as the Lord Jesus saw it—He saw it enough to die for it—then help us to go in tears and bring them in.

*   *   *

The Secret Is in the Heart! In Kansas City during the great Gipsy Smith revival years ago, an old preacher came into the room where the Gypsy was sitting after the service. Thousands were being blessed and hundreds saved. The older minister placed his hands upon the evangelist's head and felt about it. "I am trying to find the secret of your success," he said.

"Too high! too high! my friend, you are too high," Gipsy said. "The secret of whatever success God has given me is not up there but down here," and he placed his hand upon his heart!

I heard this man preach, this Gypsy, born in a tent, won by his Gypsy father, who never had a day's schooling from men, and yet who has preached to the multitudes for sixty years. And as he preached, again and again the tears coursed down his cheeks, and my own heart was stirred and warmed and blessed. The Word of God must be in the heart.

* * *

Emptiness for God's Filling. I have failed God so many times. But one time I provided lots of empty vessels when it seemed surely there was no oil to fill them. I accepted a revival invitation in Binghamton, New York. A man who habitually slanders preachers in his paper secretly prevailed upon the pastor to cancel my engagement as he has jealously attacked many other sound and useful preachers. But I felt that God wanted me to go for that revival campaign. I sent ample evidence of my doctrinal position to the pastor.

Then I drove away in my car, from Dallas to Binghamton, New York, in mid-winter, without money enough in hand for the return trip, planning, if need be, to rent a hall and have an independent campaign in the town where God had so clearly led me to accept an invitation. Oh, the heart-searching during those days of winter driving and praying!

But when I arrived in Binghamton the Grace Baptist Church had widely announced the revival campaign and received me with open arms. Within eight days the campaign had blossomed into a city-wide campaign in the big Binghamton Theatre, seating twenty-two hundred people, with eight or nine churches cooperating. During the month in the theatre there were nearly four hundred public professions of faith, most of them adults, and the city was profoundly stirred. Oh, I have found out that if you furnish the empty vessels according to God's commandments, you may be assured He will multiply the oil to fill them!

* * *

Ignore the Odds. When, in World War II, there came the break-through at Lo, in France, and the American armies planned their dash toward Berlin, it is said that some of the generals talked about the number of German tanks that roamed the south of France. Would they cut the supply line? General Patton considered the matter earnestly for a bit, then said, "We'll just ignore them!" Well, they that are for us are more than they that be against us. "If God be for us, who can be against us?" If sin abounds, then, thank God, grace does much more abound. And God is "able to do exceeding abundantly above all that we ask or think" (Eph. 3:20).

Sin

Enamored of Sin. I talked to a young woman who loved her fast crowd and particularly she loved the dances. Not just these rock 'n' roll dances so much, but the waltzes, and the embraces and the promiscuous necking that goes with it. She didn't want to be saved. She knew she ought to, and the Lord seemed to reveal to me her trouble; she had waited and waited and said, "I know I ought to. I'm going to, but not now. I'm not ready."

So I said, "You dance, don't you?"

"Yes, how did you know?"

"Isn't that keeping you away from God?"

"Well," she said, "Yes, but. . . ."

She would have her good time, then some day she was going to seek the Lord, but not now. You may become enamored of sin. Sometimes it is the habit of drink and sometimes it is the love for money that gets the mastery of a man's ambition to be somebody in business or in politics. I say, seek the Lord while He may be found, before your heart gets hardened, before you get enamored of sin, enslaved by sin.

* * *

The Greatest Sin. At Olton, Texas, in a revival service some 200 or 300 people gathered one morning to confess their sins. For two hours men and women confessed their drinking, their cursing, their dancing, their grudges, their neglect of duty. In the midst of these confessions, a man arose trembling to his feet to say, "I have been guilty of all the sins other people have mentioned. I drank, I cursed, I lived in revelry and sin.

But the meanest thing I ever did was that all my life until three o'clock this morning I rejected Jesus Christ; I did not surrender to Him nor love Him nor serve Him. That is my greatest sin."

He was right, exactly right. Only a rotten heart full of sin and love for sin can keep anybody away from Jesus Christ! If you today are not a Christian, if you did not run to Jesus the first time you ever heard about His love and mercy, then you are a blackhearted sinner. You love sin; you choose sin; and you purposely, deliberately turn your wicked heart away from the light of God, away from truth, and away from righteousness, and walk into the darkness and wickedness of sin! Nothing in the world shows a wicked heart like staying away from Christ.

* * *

Fortunetelling—Heathen Idolatry. In Fairfield, Alabama, I saw on a certain street a number of places with a fortuneteller's sign outside each. Usually the sign included a picture of a palm and the name, "Madame So-and-So." I was surprised to find so many women in the trade of fortunetelling. I looked inside a door. Later I inquired of a preacher friend as to why there were a number of beds in the small rooms which were visible from the door, and I was shocked to hear that most of the palm readers were also prostitutes.

It is not surprising that, in many cases, fortunetelling should be linked up with other evils because fortunetelling itself is heathen idolatry which the Scripture says is an abomination to God. For these very sins the heathen nations were driven out of the land of Canaan and destroyed. God warned the Israelites not to take up the same abominations.

* * *

Hidden Sin Revealed. While I was in a revival in an Oklahoma town some years ago, a wife discovered in her husband's pocket a letter which proved he had been untrue to her, had committed adultery with another woman. Her heart was broken with grief and shame. Eventually she told her husband what she had found. With a horror of shame he admitted his guilt. Then he said, "If you will forgive me, let us both get right with God, trust Him for salvation and then live true to each other and God." She agreed and they both were happily converted and she told my wife the story. That sin was uncovered and forgiven. But what about the sins hidden through all these years, unforgiven, unconfessed, unlamented? What about the sins that are kept secret now but revealed on the judgment day?

* * *

"Good-Bye, Daddy." When Grace, my oldest daughter, was three or four years old, she rebelled at some command. Sadly I spanked her very hard and made her do what she was told to do. Then I left, and when I left, I did not tell her good-bye. She still sulked for a little bit over her spanking, but then she was penitent and she began to say to her mother, though I was already gone, "Good-bye, Daddy! Good-bye, Daddy!" And when she took her afternoon nap, half-asleep, with tears running down her little face, she would say, "Good-bye, Daddy!" She was tired of her own way. She was sorry for her rebellion. She wanted to make right what she had done wrong.

So your stubborn will must be given up if you would have the fullness of God's blessing. Do not hesitate to pull that idol of self-will out by the roots and let God have His way in your life, if you want to live at the place of blessing.

* * *

"Ministerially Speaking." In a leading religious magazine when I lived in Dallas, Texas, I saw a report of the Gipsy Smith revival in Dallas. It was a great revival. I attended a number of services. The crowds were really enormous and the results, I believe, were blessed.

But the reporter of the meeting stated that the First Baptist Church seats 6,000 people, when in fact it seats considerably less than half of that. I counted the opera chairs in the various lengths of rows in the entire balcony, then the number of such rows very carefully. I counted the number in the choir. I carefully counted the number of persons closely packed in the Gipsy Smith meeting in a row of seats across the entire auditorium and multiplied by the number of such rows in the entire lower floor. I estimated that way that the building seated 2,540 people. A church auditorium actually seating 2,500 people, as that does, is a magnificent auditorium. Why stretch it to the enormous and mythical capacity of 6,000? I do not know who made the report, and I was in the heartiest sympathy with the great Gipsy Smith revival. The crowds were really enormous. But I know that whatever preacher reported that revival ought to have taken five or ten minutes and found out at least the approximate capacity of that wonderful church building before making such a terrible blunder; a false statement that will bring reproach upon preachers and churches.

* * *

How Can You Escape a Wasted Life?

Let us suppose for a moment that later in life you may be saved. I think it is unlikely, if you neglect salvation in your youth. The vast majority of all the people who are ever saved are saved when they are young. Far more than half of those saved are saved before they are fifteen years old. And the vast majority of all those who wait until they are grown before accepting Christ, never accept Him and die and go to Hell. But suppose, for the sake of argument, thay you may be later converted, born again, and that you may thus miss Hell. I am afraid you will not do it, but if you do, what then? Still you cannot escape a wasted life, if you neglect your soul's salvation.

Go with me back to my boyhood in West Texas. An old farmer-ranchman was wonderfully converted when he was nearly sixty years old. His face was lined and weather-beaten with the Texas sun and wind. It was lined also with the marks of long years of sinning. But he was wonderfully saved. I recall with great joy how he used to stand in the little Methodist prayer meeting and, with tears running down his face, tell how gracious God had been to him to save an old sinner so long gone in sin. It was sweet to hear.

But that was not the end of his testimony. He never sat down before he pleaded with the people, pleaded with tears, that they should pray for his unconverted sons. One daughter he was able to win to Christ. His sons all remained unconcerned, unconvicted. They never sought the Lord, they never repented, they never trusted Christ.

Out in the cemetery lay the body of one boy who had died at fourteen, I believe, unconverted. He died before the father turned to God.

Another son of the old converted stockman stood in the last row at the Baptist church one Saturday night in a revival campaign when I went to plead with him to turn to Christ and be saved. "Roy, you ought to go," I said. "Roy, if you will go maybe others will turn to Christ and be saved. Think of your brothers. Think of your friends." But Roy shook his head and said emphatically that he was not going.

That happened on a Saturday night. One week later, on Saturday afternoon, Roy drove a bronc colt to a breaking cart to town, a little West Texas cow town. Some jugler friend sailed a Stetson hat under his belly and the colt plunged and ran away. Roy fell off the cart backward. A rider soon caught the colt, Roy got up and dusted off his clothes and laughed at the joke with the others. But as he drove home he fell off the cart unconscious from internal injuries, and the next day he died. I was at his funeral on Monday. The old cow-man came and stood beside the casket after the kindly Methodist preacher had brought a gospel message. The father patted the cold face and said, "Good-bye, Roy." Then he said it again, "Good-bye, Roy." He was loathe to leave. The tears rained down his face and his lips quivered. He brushed back a hair from the cold forehead with trembling fingers and said again, "Good-bye, Roy." I knew what he meant. Everybody else there knew what he meant. He was saying, "Good-bye forever!"

Oh, yes, God in His mercy saved that old stockman. All the years of his neglect did not wipe out the great mercy of God, and at last he was saved, like a brand from the burning, after he was almost in Hell. But, alas, when the father was saved he could not win his boys. His life's influence was wasted and gone!

I was at the funeral of another son of the same father. After a weekend of drunkenness, he was smitten with intestinal paralysis, was rushed to the hospital and died on the operating table. Later, as a young preacher, I went into the homes of the two remaining out of five sons. Now they were married men with grown children, yet they never would go to church, they were not interested in the Gospel, they went on their way of blasphemy and rejection of Christ. God was merciful to save the old stockman, but, and I say this as reverently as I know how, even God Himself, being just and holy, could not undo all the wasted years and influence of the man who was saved in his old age.

I solemnly warn you today that you cannot escape the ruin of a wasted life, if you neglect this great salvation. Even if you should later be saved you will have nothing but tears and heartache over the years that are wasted and gone, which can never be redeemed.

*   *   *

"Touch Not Mine Anointed."

A world-famous evangelist, a marvelous soul winner, whose long life in the white light of public gaze had been spent without a reproach, lost his beloved wife. His hungry heart had long been starved for the companionship which other men have in their homes, but which he was denied by his worldwide service for the Lord and his constant travels. So after a year or two he married again. His sin was only that his bride was a *young* woman, though most devout and blameless.

With critics it mattered not at all that his life was blameless, that his influence over millions was only for good. Many Christian know-it-alls criticised and said, "It's too bad!" and prophesied, "You'll see—it will be the end of his great ministry." The more "fundamental" the ministers sometimes the more catty were their gossipy remarks. Meantime this magnificent man of God has gone on with his blessed ministry in the marvelous power of the Spirit.

We are reminded of God, "Touch not mine anointed, and do my prophets no harm" (Ps. 105:15). It is a special sin to speak evil of preachers.

* * *

The Harm of Critical Tongues.

In a revival in West Texas, one night I preached on the sin of divorce. Unknown to me, two men active in the church work had been divorced and remarried. One of them had married a divorced woman. These two hotly resented my sermon; one threatened me with physical violence, and they talked bitterly in their homes about the preaching. But in a few days the power of the Gospel broke the hearts of these men. In tears, humbly and ashamed, they came to beg my forgiveness and asked me to pray for their families.

One man was particularly concerned over his teenage daughter who had shown some interest in her soul early in the revival. However, as he had raved angrily concerning the preacher, this girl's convictions had all seemed to leave her. Now she could not be reached, it seemed. Her angry father had broken down her confidence in the preacher. Later, when her father and I together earnestly tried to win her to Christ, the child, with set face and hardened heart, resisted every appeal. The man went away convinced, as I was, that he had blocked the salvation of his own daughter by his criticism of the preacher.

No doubt there are multitudes in Hell who went there because of critical tongues of Christians who spoke evil one of another and particularly of preachers and Sunday school teachers and Christian workers.

* * *

The Truth From a Sinner.

I remember only one man who ever told me the truth about why he was not saved. In a country revival service I asked a man, "Are you a Christian?"

"No!" he bluntly answered.

"Don't you want to be?" I said.

He answered, "Well, if I wanted to be a Christian I could be, could I not?"

I answered, "Yes, of course you could. Christ is willing to save you tonight."

"Then I guess I don't want to be, or I would be," he answered insolently.

Yes, he was right. He was not a Christian because he did not want to be. You, poor sinner, poor unconverted enemy of Jesus Christ, are not a Christian because you do not want to be. You want your sin. You may lie about it, you may cover over your sin, but the fact remains you do not love Christ, you do not want Him; rather you want your sin and hold onto it.

Poor sinner, that course will take you to Hell, for "he that covereth his sins shall not prosper," says the text of Proverbs 28:13. You must uncover that sin, open up that wicked heart, confess your sin and repent of it, if you would be saved.

* * *

Sin Enslaves. I talked to Bob Silver after he and a man named Stone had shot down Roscoe Wilson in Fort Worth as he came from the Majestic Theater with $5,000 in a bag. After shooting Wilson, these two got in a Chrysler coupe and sped away. Over by the Baptist Hospital they changed cars and got in another Chrysler of another color. They started out toward Oklahoma. The officers thought they had gone down toward Houston. They combed every road looking for a certain kind of a Chrysler. As these two hold-up men drove over into Oklahoma, they breathed a sigh of relief. "We got away!"

Bob Silver told me, "We breathed a sigh of relief, but there had been a rain, and a car had slipped off the highway. And some other cars had stopped to help them out, blocking the road. We stopped the car and got out. A deputy sheriff came along. He had heard the broadcast, 'Look out for two fellows from Fort Worth, Texas, in a gray Chrysler coupe.' The car we had stolen was of a different color, but the sheriff said to us, 'Wait a minute, boys; I want to talk to you.' "

He told me that they tried to slip back in the car and get their guns, but the sheriff pulled a gun quickly and covered them. He found in the car the $5,000. The sheriff put handcuffs on the two and brought them back to Fort Worth. Bob Silver said to me—that young man whose face was pale because he had been in solitary confinement, and whose hand was as palsied as a man of eighty—"I turned to Stone and said, 'It is God! We can't get away from God!"

I tell you, my friends, Bob Silver never intended to go that far. "I do not know what made me shoot him," he said. "I did not mean to do it."

Nobody else ever intends to go as far in sin as they go. It enslaves you. Somebody may have started to take a shot of dope but nobody intended to be a slave to dope.

* * *

The Faithlessness of Friends in Sin

In Prescott, a country church near Decatur, Texas, I was preaching on the story of the crucifixion and how Judas betrayed Jesus and sold Him for thirty pieces of silver. I reminded the congregation of how Judas brought the money back, burning with shame and a guilty conscience, and pleaded that they undo the bargain, that they release Jesus and take the money back. The chief priest refused. Judas said, "I have betrayed the innocent blood." He had betrayed the only innocent blood this world ever saw; now in shocked amazement, in heartsick mortification, he lamented his sin. He did not repent. A godly repentance would turn him to Christ for salvation, but his heart had gone too long for that. But he was ashamed that he dropped to such depth of sin. He wished he could undo it.

The heartless chief priest said to the brokenhearted, distraught, crazed Judas, "See thou to that!" Grasping the thirty pieces of silver, he left them ringing on the marble floor and went out and hanged himself.

In that country church I reminded the people that the enemy could lead you into sin, then have no sympathy with you when you are distressed and ruined. I reminded them that the bartender who sells the drink and makes the drunkard, pauper, or harlot, then does not want the drunken bum hanging around begging for a handout after his money is gone.

I found a sudden shock go through the congregation. Some woman began to weep visibly and audibly. Others had tears; many had downcast faces.

When the sermon was over and the pastor and I were alone, I said, "What happened to the congregation this morning, when I spoke of Judas and how the chief priests forsook him in his sin?"

The pastor told me that a young woman had only last Sunday morning come forward to confess her sin. A man had made her fair promises of marriage and happiness, then led her into the deepest sin. Now pregnant and in disgrace, she came to the church to beg forgiveness, beg for restoration, have their love and fellowship. "But the young man," the pastor said, "has already gone to another community and has ruined another girl." All his promises to marry this girl show that one's friends in sin cannot help one when sin's ruin comes.

*   *   *

"I Ought to Be in Hell Right Now!" A young woman in Chicago heard me preach on the Christian Business Men's program broadcast over radio WJJD from the Grand Opera House, some years ago. She wrote to tell me that she was almost in despair. Other preachers, she said, either had not had time or did not know how to help her. I wrote her and she came to see me. Sitting in the hotel lobby, she told of her training in Bible institute, how she had preached the Gospel on street corners, professing entire sanctification, how she had gone to be a missionary in the mountains. But strangely, she had seemed to become devil-possessed. Every kind of blasphemy and cursing ran through her mind, continually, she said. She was tempted to curse God, tempted to go out into the vilest sin. God seemed a million miles away, and she could not find the way to peace—could I help her?

After prayerfully asking a few questions, I said to her, "In Bible institute you were praised for your sweet voice, for your devotion to Christ. After hearing your testimony, many people told you they wished they could be as consecrated, as holy as you were. You took it upon you to preach, though the Bible clearly forbids women

preachers to mixed congregations. Now, I do not know whether I can help you. It will depend altogether on your answer to this question. Do you realize what a wicked sinner you are in God's sight?"

The poor girl looked at me a moment and then dropped her face in her hands and began to sob. I saw the tears falling between her fingers. "A sinner!" she said. "I am the greatest sinner that ever lived. I ought to be in Hell right now! I wonder why God lets me live, anybody to whom He has been so kind and who has been so wicked, so vile, so self-willed. Yes, of course I am a sinner," she said.

"Then I can certainly tell you how to have peace and joy and the whole thing settled happily," I said. And we turned together to I John 1:9, and she claimed and received the perfect cleansing and forgiveness promised to all who will confess their sins.

* * *

Sin Hurts Your Children. When my first baby was born, I was much interested when I saw the doctor and nurse dropping some antiseptic solution in each eye of the newborn baby. I said to the doctor, "Doctor, you don't need to do that with my baby, thank God!" But he, an old friend of the family, said, "I know that, John, but the state law requires that every new-born baby must have an antiseptic, equal to one per cent silver nitrate solution, dropped in each eye." Then I learned that sixty per cent (six out of every ten, sixty out of every hundred) of the children blind from birth are blind because they were infected by the mother at birth, infected with venereal disease and blinded on account of the sins of fathers or mothers.

Sin is always horrible, but how horrible it is when it comes to light in our beloved children! Some one has said that one who has children has given hostages to fortune.

* * *

The Slavery. of Sin. After I preached on the street at Fort Worth, Texas, years ago, I talked to a ragged man, with filthy clothes and unkempt hair, about the Lord. He told me he had once owned two farms, had $10,000 cash in the bank, had been a respected citizen, a member of the school board. When I quoted Scriptures to him, he often knew the wording of a verse and would quote it. He told me how he had regularly gone to church with his wife; but when she died and the restraint of her sweet influence was gone, he drank more and more, and ceased going to church. Drink had so enslaved him that he drank away all his property, was now a bum on the street asking for a handout. Sin took him farther and farther away from the Gospel and Christian influence.

* * *

Find a Target and Shoot! Everybody is against sin in general. Few are against sin in particular.

In the paper I saw a small cartoon of "Country Parson." And he said, "No attack on special sins is like fighting a whole army without killing a single soldier."

I had an uncle who was a scout in the Civil War. He started when he was sixteen and had many a hair-raising tale to tell of battles and escapes. Someone said to him, "In a battle, did you shoot at the enemy line or did you pick out individual soldiers to shoot at?"

He replied, "Every soldier who was any good picked out particular targets and aimed at them." And then he told how some soldiers frantically fired and loaded, fired and loaded without pointing at anything! He told of walking through a battlefield after a battle (I think it was at Bull Run) and found that many a soldier had forgotten to remove his ramrod before he pulled the trigger and there was many a ramrod shot halfway through a tree! Indefinite, vague references to sin are not enough.

* * *

The Ending of Sin. Dr. Bob Jones, Sr., the mighty evangelist, said in my hearing that he read with astonishment in a daily paper that a certain pastor was accused of murdering the woman choir leader in his church. Dr. Jones said to a friend, "That is a lie! That preacher never did anything of the kind! He is one of the purest, best men I ever saw. I have preached in his church. I have been in his home. He is a good man. He might make minor mistakes but he is not a murderer. I know he did not kill that woman as the newspaper reports indicate."

But Dr. Bob tells us that the next day the newspapers carried the confession, signed by the preacher. He had fallen in love with the choir singer. They had carried on an affair long years. At last when exposure was threatened and the man's entire ministry was at stake, he killed her. He did that which he never dreamed he would do. Sin had a different ending to what he expected. And so it always is with sin.

* * *

Someday You Will Wish You Had! A well-to-do banker had a wild and reckless boy. The banker had sense enough to make money but not sense enough to whip his boy and make him mind. At last the rebellious lad ran away and joined the Navy. On shipboard he got into one scrape after another, landed "in the brig" again and again. Finally he was called before the captain of the ship. He told me later that the captain sat quietly and talked in a soft, smooth voice, and said, "Son, I hear you are having some trouble. You don't seem to want to obey the rules." The lad was silent. He had threatened that they could not make him do things. They could not boss him. The captain continued, "Son, you are in the Navy now. It is true we cannot make you do anything. We can't make you into a good sailor if you don't want to be. We can't make you keep the rules, if you have no sense of loyalty. No, we can't make you do anything." And then, as the lad himself later told me, the captain's eyes grew steely and he said slowly, "No, we can't make you do anything, *but we can surely make you wish you had!*"

You are right, sinner; nobody can make you come to Christ if you do not want to. Even Christ Himself will not force an entrance into your rebellious, wicked heart. But, oh, I warn you now, the time will come when you will surely wish you had—had accepted Him, had loved Him, had claimed Him openly as Saviour and Lord. You will wish you had!

* * *

Sin Starts Small. When the Devil wants to take a man to Hell, he starts on him as a child and has him reject salvation for a time. He will say, "You are young. You have plenty of time." And little by little Satan leads him on, and the man burns in torment. One day he was a tenderhearted child, and it would have been so easy to be saved. "I will sometime, but not now," he said. Everyone who goes to Hell was one time so near salvation and Christ. Sin always starts small.

Back yonder before World War I, nobody expected it would start when a half-crazy student and anarchist shot dead the Archduke Francis Ferdinand at Sera Seva, Austria, June 28, 1914. Nobody supposed that would embroil the world in war around the world, when thirty nations would be involved with war, millions would die and multiplied billions of treasure spent. Nobody believed that. But it happened. Sin always starts small.

*   *   *

Chains of Sin. It is said that a Greek tyrant, or king, of a certain Grecian city, was jealous of a certain great blacksmith in his town. Perhaps he was not loyal to the king. The blacksmith was brought before the king, and the king said, "I am told you can make a chain that no man can break." The man said he could. The king asked him to make one for him. So he made a chain so fine and welded every link so carefully—that was not so easy to do then—and when he got through, he brought it back and held it up before the king and said, "It is so strong that if it had an elephant on each end pulling, they couldn't break it."

The king said to one of his officers, "Bind *him* with it."

So it is. We make the chain that binds us and enslaves us as Ahab did when he let down the bars and gave way to sin and sold out.

*   *   *

Sin and Fear. When I was a boy teaching in a country school, I spent a night in a home where there was a young man. He was one of the vilest cursers and heaviest drinkers in that community. He was loud-mouthed and guilty of all kinds of sin.

One night we were left at the house alone. To my astonishment, as soon as the rest of the family got away, this young fellow who was a loud-mouthed, drinking, cursing bully, a roughneck, a fighting man, got up and barred all the doors, putting chairs against them. I said, "What's the idea?" "You never can tell what might come along," he said. He sat there and every time he heard any kind of a noise outside, he jumped and trembled. He was scared.

Sin does not help people, sin

does not bring contentment, but puts fear in the heart.

A thirteen-year-old girl I had the joy of winning to Christ said, "Now I won't be afraid to go to sleep any more."

If you are not saved, all your days you will have fear. You know it is your guilty sins that bring you remorse of conscience and make you fear. You think you can go on in sin. But it will cost you remorse of conscience if you do. You think you can go on in sin and never have to give an account. But you are going to give an account to yourself. Your own conscience will accuse you. One day you will pay for all your sin in remorse. Sin never does pay. Sin does not bring contentment.

* * *

Sanctified Only in Spots! How many great and noble saints of God have tried to be perfect and have, for a season, thought that they were completely sanctified, and done with the old nature, and made perfect in love! Charles G. Finney thought so, and, oh, the darkness that came over his mind when he discovered that after all he was not perfect and sinless before God, not completely sanctified!

I remember hearing Dr. H. A. Ironside say that, when he was in the Salvation Army and most devotedly believed and claimed complete sanctification, that again and again he came to pray for the complete eradication of the carnal nature. Again and again he claimed that he had received the blessing he sought. But always, he said, "I found that I was sanctified only in spots, instead of completely sanctified!"

It is true that Christ died and atoned for all our sins. But the complete results of the atonement have not yet taken place. We have saved souls, when we believe on Christ. We have received the firstfruits of the Spirit. But the rest of the wonderful harvest of salvation has not yet come in. The redemption of our bodies, and the change of this old tainted nature into the perfect likeness of Christ, awaits the rapture.

* * *

Drawn Into the Desert of Sin. Once I had a sad, sad letter. A young woman wrote to tell me how for months she led young men on and allowed some kissing and fondling and petting, and then when they were aroused, she must suddenly go home. And she thought she had perfect control of herself, she could play with sin and make men miserable over her. But she became more and more affected by sex desire, more and more a victim of her own disregard for God's laws and disregard for the happiness of the men she played with. Then, overwhelmed, she was swept on into the sin she had never meant to commit. Then she lived for months a life of promiscuous immorality.

But she found it more and more a desert with no real satisfaction of heart. She turned and sought the Lord and God in mercy forgave her. Now she earnestly longs to please God in everything and tries to live a holy life.

But she asked me, "How am I ever going to have a normal Christian life as a modest young woman? How can I resist any advances in love-making and keep things on a pure, clean basis until I become engaged and then married to some good man?"

She knew she had played with sin so long and there was a fire in her bosom that she feared to trifle with.

I trust God will give her grace to stay straight and to love without any undue familiarity until the marriage bond gives her the freedom that no one has a right to outside of marriage. But she was only saying that the more you drink of the waters of this world the more they lead to disappointment, disillusionment and heartsick trouble.

*   *   *

Sow Not Among Thorns

Fallow ground, barren ground, unbroken ground, brings forth weeds. As my father and I rode horseback along a road in West Texas years ago, he said to me, "Son, that man will lose his cotton crop if he doesn't watch out."

"Lose it?" I said. "How could he lose it?"

"If he doesn't kill those weeds and that grass soon," my father said, "they will get higher than the cotton plants, will overshadow them and crowd them out and there will be no cotton crop."

Sure enough, it turned out as my father said and that field was abandoned as that farmer desperately tried to kill out weeds in another patch and save what he could of his crop. It is almost useless to sow among thorns and weeds on fallow ground. So are religious services with hearts unbroken, hearts preoccupied with the thorns of worldliness and sin. One reason for breaking up our hearts, plans, and hopes and breaking up our wills is that we may root up these absorbing thorns of sin.

One day when I was five years old my bare feet pattered down the furrow following my Uncle Tom. To my distress he plowed up some beautiful flowers among the corn rows. I asked him, "Uncle Tom, what are these pretty flowers climbing on the fence, and on the cornstalks?" He told me that they were morning glories and I liked the name then, as I do now.

I said, "Aren't they pretty, Uncle Tom?"

He answered back, "They are not pretty to me. I wish every one in the field were dead. If I grow morning glories I can't grow corn."

Some of the things in which you delight seem sweet as a morning flower; but I wonder, dear reader, if they can prevent your growing corn for the Lord? Are the things you love and hug to your bosom like thorns on a barren field, an abomination to the Lord of the harvest?

About the hardest work I ever did as a boy was "grubbing." In West Texas the mesquite trees do not grow high, but have gnarled and twisted roots growing big and strong, deep into the ground. What digging with the mattock, what tugging with team or stump-puller or tractor before the land was ready to be put in cultivation! But it would be useless to try to cultivate the soil otherwise. Roots would break the plow. The sprouts would shoot out of the ground, the bushes would take the ground again if they were not dug out.

"Sow not among thorns" (Jer. 4:3) if you want fruit for God. Dig out that sinful habit! Confess and forsake that wicked grudge against your neighbor or loved one—forgive today and be forgiven! With penitence, with confession and tears give up that amusement that seems "no harm." Break up your ground, dig out the thorns, and then God will make your ground fruitful.

*   *   *

One Little Gate for Sin to Go Through.

My brother, Dr. Bill Rice, and I were discussing the problem of what any sin, when consented to and unrebuked in the heart of a Christian, will do. And he said, "If you leave one little gate open, every cow in the pasture may get out." And he meant that a man who consents to a little "white lie," as you might call it, will go deeper in lying. And one who is intemperate in his speech may grow to cursing. One who allows hate and malice may become a murderer. There is no safe course for one who consents to some sin and lets it go on unrebuked, unconfessed, unrepented in his life.

*   *   *

Once He Was Tender, Once He Wept. . .

You who turn down the Gospel, do you know that your heart is growing colder and colder toward God? Do you know that you will be less likely to go to church tomorrow than you are today? Do you know that soon you will not be moved at all by the teachings of the Bible, nor stirred at all by the pleadings of a godly mother or wife or sister, or the preaching of a plain sermon? Oh, when you neglect this great salvation, how can you escape hardening your heart?

I take you to the scenes of my boyhood in a little West Texas cow town. In a small Methodist church a godly woman asked her class of boys to pray for her son to be saved.

I was a member of that class. A revival campaign began in the Methodist church. The first Sunday morning I went to Clyde and said to him, "Clyde, your mother and the whole Sunday school class agreed to pray that you would be saved in this meeting. It is time to be saved, Clyde. All of us are praying for you. Won't you come today?"

I remember so well how he held onto the back of the seat before him, and how the tears dripped down his nose and onto the mahogany-stained pine pews. With trembling lips he said to me, "John, I am glad you are praying for me and I want you to keep on. And I am going to be saved, too. I am not quite ready, but I sure am glad you are praying for me."

His heart was stirred and tender. Yet he did not surrender that day.

Another year came around and another revival campaign. Still Clyde had not trusted Christ as Saviour. A second time I went to talk with him and pled with him to accept Christ. This time he was polite and friendly. He thanked me for speaking to him but said he was not ready. And this time there were no tears. The fatal effect of procrastination was taking place in his heart.

Another year, two years went by. Clyde now was about grown. He went into the Panhandle of Texas and worked away from home. When he came back he wore long trousers and was now a man. I was a year or two younger. Another revival season came on. This time Clyde sat with a rough crowd of unconverted young men in the back. When the invitation came I went to him again and urged him to accept Christ as his Saviour. He was no longer a boy. Now, buttressed by his wicked companions, he sneered at me and said, "Don't you think I would have sense enough to know if I wanted to go, without anybody telling me? I am not going!"

Again I reminded him of his mother's prayers these years. I reminded him that he and I had talked this matter over and he had intended to be saved. I pressed upon him that now was the time to be saved. I urged him and took hold of his arm, but he refused. Finally he turned to me and said aloud, so that all around could hear it, "No, I am not going, I tell you! Damn it, leave me alone!"

I had spoken to Clyde many times before. I do not remember whether I ever spoke to him again about salvation.

The years passed and 1918 came on. I was drafted and so was Clyde. I understand that he never came back from the war.

Once he was tender. Once he wept over his sins. Once, with trembling lips he thanked me for urging him to be saved. But as he neglected his soul's salvation through the years, his heart became hardened, the door was closed so that he could not, even if he would have, turn to Christ to be saved.

*   *   *

Coolidge Goes to Church. It is said that President Coolidge, with a great reputation for brevity of speech, went to church. When they returned Mrs. Coolidge said, "How was the sermon?"

"Good," the President replied.

"What was it about?" she continued.

"About sin," he replied.

"But," she continued, "what did he say about sin?"

"He was agin it," said Mr. Coolidge.

That is as definite as many a preacher ever gets on the sin question.

Sorrow

Sorrow Is of God. Sorrow is often of God. It is one of the schools through which God puts the choicest servant. It is one way that the dross is melted out of the gold and one is humbled and taught compassion.

My mother died when I was less than six years old. Without a mother, how many times in the rough West Texas country I grieved and thought, "I could have been a better man had my godly mother lived!" When Mother's Day came, I would wear a white flower and spend a lonely day realizing my loss. I did not know that God was preparing me to minister to multitudes.

Oh, how many deathbeds, how many open graves have I stood by! How many broken homes have I tried to mend! How many drunkards and fallen women have I told that the mercy of God offers peace and pardon! How long have I held open wide the door of salvation for sinners and pleaded with them to come! I know God has given me some compassion. I thank God that I early learned to weep.

Dr. George W. Truett had a heartbreaking tragedy. His dearest friend was the Dallas Chief of Police. Once they went hunting together. Going through a fence, I believe, the gun was accidentally discharged and his friend was killed. Oh, it put long pain into his heart, pathos into his magnificent voice, and a seriousness and compassion that all who knew him felt.

Charles H. Spurgeon once preached in Surrey Music Garden in London when some 22,000 people crowded to hear him. Oh, he might have been greatly exalted but some fool in jest cried, "Fire!" and a plunging, frightened tumult came as people tried to flee. Some were trampled to death in that useless and foolish tragedy. Spurgeon was so broken by it that his mind tottered for days. He thought at first he could never preach again! But God puts gold through the flames to refine it.

* * *

The Comfort of God. In Fort Worth, Texas, years ago I saw an example of the comfort of God and the peace of God that comes to one who is in great distress. It was in depression times. A husband struggled to get a job but couldn't. He seemed only a burden to his family, so he left home. He didn't tell a soul where he was going. He just disappeared, leaving his wife and two little children, a boy and a girl. This poor woman settled down to work hard and to make a living for her children. She did the best she could with all kinds of work. Her work was so hard and her body so frail that she took T.B., then she was bedfast. That was before antibiotic drugs, and there wasn't any immediate cure.

There she lay on her bed day after day. And she had to go on relief. I felt so sorry for her.

Finally it seemed the crowning trouble came. Her little fifteen-year-old girl got sick and died. I was asked to preach the funeral service. I thought, "What shall I tell that poor troubled woman whose husband has forsaken her, and her body is sick and now finally her little daughter is taken away? What will I say to this woman on her sickbed?" We had to carry her so she could look in the casket and see the face of the girl whom she had borne and raised and loved so well. What shall I say?

But when I came near her bed she reached out both hands and said, "Brother Rice, Jesus said, 'I will not leave you comfortless: I will come to you,' and He came."

In trouble, in poverty, in confusion, in war as well as in peace, Jesus said, "Let not your heart be troubled." There is Heaven waiting and eternal blessedness. So you can have peace.

* * *

Saved in Sorrow. I well remember a man who came into the Tabernacle in Dallas, Texas, one Sunday night with a despondent face. I had announced in the papers I would preach on *Broken Hearts and Broken Homes—The Call of God.* He saw the subject and came. After a little tender probing in private conversation he told me this story. "I am leaving my wife. She has been an invalid for years. I spent all my money on her. I never looked at another woman. I spent no money for clothes. I gave her everything she asked for. I loved her so I put up with everything that she did. She scolded me, nagged me and quarreled but I excused her because she

was sick. Finally she got to where she would slap my face and pull my hair and scream, but I never lifted a hand against her. Yesterday I gave it all up. I don't hate her, I don't wish her any ill, I just don't ever want to see her again!"

I never saw such despair written on a man's face as was on his. But little by little his heart seemed to open to the truth and I told him that all the troubled and weary in heart should come to Jesus and find rest. I told him that the Master had come and called for him in this sorrow. To hear that anybody loved him seemed to him too good to be true. Finally the doors of his sad heart opened and he, by faith, let the Lord Jesus come in. Then he led me to his fourteen-year-old son and together we told the boy about the Saviour who loves all the brokenhearted and who seeks those who are in trouble and woos them and takes them to His bosom!

* * *

Trouble Is From God. I remember the night Chuck and Mary Lloys married. We came back to the living room after they had gotten away. After changing to traveling clothes and the tossing of the bride's bouquet and the good-byes, one of the other girls came and said, "Mother, I will put away Mary Lloys' things." And Mrs.

Rice said, "No, you won't! You leave them alone! Mary said I could put them away." And Mrs. Rice began to sob. I said, "Now Mother, Mary Lloys is happy and you must be happy. Never mind, don't be crying." She said, "You don't care! She is out and gone and you don't care!"

I said, "When I first held this baby in my arms, held her very close and saw how black and dark was her hair, and how round and chubby her face," I said, "from that hour to this I have known it was coming, that sometime somebody would come along, maybe riding a white charger, and maybe just a boy working his way through school, and she is going to fall for him. This good-bye I thought of a long time ago and shed my tears about it."

I am saying that God planned separation, pain, disease, old age, failure, disappointments, loss of friends and after awhile death. That is in the will of God for people—we had just as well face it. Trouble is from God.

Soul Winners

God Wants Volunteers, Not Draftees

Do you really want to serve God? Read Romans 12:1, "I beseech you therefore, brethren, by the mercies of God, that ye present your bodies [offer, volunteer your bodies] a living sacrifice, holy, acceptable unto God, which is your reasonable service."

Volunteer your body a living sacrifice. I was doing graduate work at the University of Chicago. I had a contract to teach in a college another year. I went down to the Pacific Garden Mission to sing and help where I could.

One night Holland Oates preached. He had been only to the fifth grade, and he butchered the king's English. He told how he had worked hard as a stone mason and had bought a stoneyard. He drank and cursed with the fellows. Then God saved him.

After he got saved, he began to do personal work the best he could. Then one day he dropped a big stone on his foot and mashed his toe pretty bad. He went to his office, shut the door and prayed. "Now, Lord, if you are trying to tell me something, go ahead. Lord, is there anything else of mine You want? You have my boy. I told You that You could have him for service. Do You want me? I don't have much of an education, but if

You want me, You can have me. If You want me to sell this business, I'll go to preaching." Fifth grade education now, and just an old stone mason.

He unlocked the door and as he did, a man came in. He asked him, "Would you like to buy a stoneyard?" Yes, he would. So the stone mason sold the place in half an hour, for half of what it was worth. He sold out for Jesus.

Holland Oates bought a three-quarter-ton truck, put a set of chimes and a little organ in it, and got a cornet for his boy, and they went out on the street corners in Chicago. His son played the cornet, his wife the organ, and they sang. A crowd would gather, and Oates would tell them the best he could how to get saved. Then he would give them a little mirror. On one side it read, "Want to see a sinner? See the other side." When you turned it over there was the mirror. He would hand these out, then say, "Now if you want to know more, go down to the Pacific Garden Mission. I have told you all I know."

This uneducated stone mason went all over Chicago doing just that.

As he preached that night at Pacific Garden Mission, my heart was so stirred. He quoted Romans 12:1 and 2. He had volunteered to serve the Lord. He had offered himself. He told about Isaiah. "In the year that king Uzziah died I saw also the Lord sitting upon a throne, high and lifted up, and his train filled the temple. . . . And the posts of the door moved at the voice of him that cried, and the house was filled with smoke. . . . Also I heard the voice of the Lord, saying, Whom shall I send, and who will go for us? Then said I, Here am I; send me." He said, "All right, you go." And Holland Oates went.

I too said, "Lord, send me." That night I won a drunken bum to the Lord. Oh, it was such a joy. I said, "Lord, college teaching never was like this! If you will let me, I'll do this for the rest of my life." And the Lord said, "John, go to it!" And I have been going now for these many years.

* * *

This Father Was Won at 1:30 in the Morning! In services south of Detroit, Michigan, after I had spoken on soul winning, I urged people to tell who it was that they loved, that they ought to win but they had not yet won. Some mentioned a sister, a brother, a neighbor, a son. One preacher, college graduate, noble, sound young man, stood and said earnestly, "It is my father. He is the best man I ever knew. I never knew him to tell a lie. He will not owe a debt. He raised me strictly. He was such a good man, I was always timid about pressing on him the matter of salvation, but I know I must. I will."

He left the service that night, drove forty miles north of Lansing, Michigan, to see his unsaved father. He woke up the family, got the father out of bed.

The father was somewhat astonished. "Why, Son, don't you believe I am a good man?" the father asked.

"Oh, yes," the son said, "but you need to be born again. You need a new heart. Your heart is not good until it is changed by letting Jesus Christ come in and trusting Him." The fervent entreaty and the Scriptures the lad used won the father, and at 1:30 in the morning the young preacher called back to the pastor of the church where we were to tell us that his father had just accepted Christ!

* * *

She Brought Her Neighbor. I was at Danville, Virginia, for the New Year's services in 1963. On Sunday I preached on soul winning. Monday night we had the watch-night meeting. After I preached on soul winning a woman came greatly concerned and said, "I have an unsaved neighbor, a lovely woman. Oh, I want her saved."

"Bring her to meet me," I said. And the next night they came. After the service she brought her neighbor, a beautiful and gifted woman, to meet me. She said in the presence of the other woman, "This is my neighbor I mentioned to you."

I said to the lost woman, "Your friend here told me she was burdened about your soul. Did she tell you she wants you to be saved?"

The woman modestly dropped her eyes. "Yes," she replied.

"Then don't you want to be saved now? May I show you how to trust Christ as Saviour?" Yes, she did want to be saved. And there near the pulpit she trusted Christ and took Him as her own Saviour. Oh, we ought to win our neighbors.

* * *

"They Are Lost!" Dr. J. L. Ward was president of Decatur College, Decatur, Texas, when I attended there. He had been a roommate of Dr. George W. Truett in Baylor University, and often went to visit with Dr. Truett in Dallas.

He told me how one time he had gone to visit with Dr. Truett and from the First Baptist Church they went out to lunch. As they crossed Akard Street, with its sidewalks filled with people at noon rushing here and yonder, and cars in the streets everywhere, they stopped at a corner. Dr. Truett stood, he said, oblivious to the changing of traffic lights, and gazed. At last he turned with quivering lips and said to Dr. Ward, "Ward, they are lost! They are lost! Look at that crowd! They are lost!"

*   *   *

Unceasing Labor, Sacrifice, Door-to-Door Visitation Bring People. In one church, where thousands of people are brought in on buses to Sunday school and church every Sunday, a church that has baptized more converts in a year than has ever been known since the days of the apostles, the First Baptist of Hammond, a certain woman was a bus captain. She worked diligently week after week, to invite people, to organize and plan, so that every Sunday she could have a bus load to come to Sunday school to hear the Gospel.

Then one day she had the good news that she was going to have a baby. But she went on with her bus work. Then there came tragedy. For some time there was no movement. She went to the doctor. They found that the unborn child was dead. This was on Friday and the doctor said, "You must come tomorrow morning for an operation to remove the dead baby."

But she demurred, "Doctor," she said, "I am bus captain. I must go out all day tomorrow and get people ready for my bus. I must be with them on Sunday and bring them to the services. We will have a lot of them saved. I cannot come for the operation now. I will come in Monday morning."

So against the doctor's protests, she did help get the bus full; then on Monday she came to the hospital for the sad ordeal of delivery of the dead baby.

My own heart feels a holy indignation against those who would criticise this kind of devotion of those who work long hours week after week. Never mind the doors being slammed in their face; never mind the critics and the objectors; they go on getting people to hear the Gospel. And some silly, thoughtless, unspiritual critic thinks that any device they may use on the bus, such as singing choruses, or giving a hot dog or roll to take the place of breakfast, is something worldly and unspiritual!

*   *   *

Be a Soul Winner Now! Brother Robert Hughes said to me one time, "Brother Rice, pray with me." He had not won a soul, but he was told that was all right, he would later on, that he had to grow in grace. But he did not feel that was right; Robert felt he should win souls now.

I said, "Robert, you go to a private place and pray now and

ask God to take all hindrances out of your life and pour out His Holy Spirit on you so that you can win somebody to Christ today."

After praying, Robert went up to the courthouse and met some fellows sitting on the courthouse lawn. Robert was in despair and was distressed. He got it on his heart to talk to some of the men. He talked to one of them, but he did not win him to Christ. Robert came back disappointed to tell me.

Robert saw the man the next day and stopped to talk to him again. Lo and behold, he found the man had already been saved!

I said, "Robert, the reason people are not soul winners is because they do not make up their minds that they can be and ought to be. They have no business waiting about this matter and hoping later to grow into it."

Some people think they are not called to win souls and are not supposed to have blessings like others.

One preacher not long ago said, "I want to have all the power Moody had." And somebody said, "God does not want many people to be Moodys." Maybe He does not want everybody to be a Moody, but He wants us to have as much power and love as Moody had, as much of the Holy Spirit working in us as Moody had.

* * *

One Who Seeks the Heavenly Burden Must Forsake the Earthly One. Jesus said, "Where your treasure is, there will your heart be also" (Matt. 6:21). Earth competes always with Heaven. The body competes with the soul. Time competes against eternity. One who is too much concerned with the affairs of this world will not be as concerned as he ought to be about poor, dying souls and their eternal welfare.

An associate of D. L. Moody, a famous evangelist, won thousands of souls, but felt that as age came on he must set aside some kind of an estate to care for his family. He bought nine hundred acres of land and hoped that it would care for his old age. But in a revival campaign he felt frustrated and hindered in his prayers and limited and powerless in his preaching. As he and his song leader prayed together much about the revival and counseled as to what could be wrong, the song leader kindly suggested, "I wonder if a diamond can shine as well as it ought with nine hundreds acres of black dirt on it?" That godly evangelist felt immediately convicted that he had set his heart too much on the things of earth. He sold that great farm and gave himself wholly to the business of keeping sinners out of Hell.

* * *

Her Heart Ran Over

Nobody ever asks me if I am a Christian, though I am always asking other people. No one ever asks me if I am saved. I ask, "Are you letting your light shine? Are you reading your Bible? How are you getting along with the Lord?" No one asks me if God is good to me and if I am getting along all right with the Lord. Do you think I am an angel from Heaven? Do you think I am not made out of the same dirt you are? I need somebody to help me along.

I think of the time when I tried to win a twelve-year-old boy to Christ in a barber shop here in Dallas. I said, "Son, where do you go to church, and do you go to Sunday school?"

He said, "I go to Sunday school."

But his dear mother who was sitting there said, "Friend, let me tell you that just being a member of a church isn't all you need. Just going to church isn't enough."

I said, "No, that's right."

But she didn't give me a chance to say more. "Listen, what people really need is to be born again and have their hearts made right. There is something real about this business. Going to church is not enough." She said, "I know there is something to this business of being a Christian."

I sat there, and my heart was like a desert that just took in the rain. It blossomed as she talked on.

As we came back through the desert from California I was surprised to see how bright green everything was. They said they had had more rain out there in ten days than in the past twenty-eight years. Half a mile of road was washed away in places—in the desert. The desert was blossoming. That is the way my heart was. It just drank it in as that woman talked to me about the Lord.

She said, "Mister, I was sick and about to die. The doctor gave me up. He had a consultation with other doctors. They told me they had done all they could do. 'Then I will call another Doctor.' They said, 'We have already called five of the best.' I told them: 'But the best One you haven't called yet. I am going to call Him. If you can't get me up, God can. I am going to call Him. I want to live for my children. You can go on away. You needn't leave me any medicine.' "

And she said she turned her face to the wall, so weak that she couldn't pray much, but she asked God, "Lord, let me live today! Lord, keep me alive today. I am too sick to pray, but just keep me alive today." And then the next day she prayed, "Lord, you kept me alive yesterday, now keep me alive today."

She told how she didn't feel like agonizing in prayer; she was too sick. But it wasn't long until she began to feel better, then she prayed, "Lord, now get me well." She said to me, "I want you to know God answers prayer. This is real."

Oh, I have thought about that a thousand times. My heart is hungry to hear people talk like that, who have really talked with the Lord and know what it is all about. You don't have praises like that because your heart is not running over with it inside. "Out of the abundance of the heart the mouth speaketh" (Matt. 12:34).

*   *   *

Difficulties Need Not Prevent You From Winning Souls. In Dallas two women, Mrs. Middleton and Mrs. Crawford, one time went to do soul winning. They went down Tenth Street where there were many nice houses, a lovely residence district, the nicest in our end of town. Up and down the street they went. When they came back they were so discouraged! "Well," they said, "we did win one woman, a maid. Nearly always we were met at the door by a maid. The maid would say, 'Madam doesn't have time to talk to you today,' or 'She is out,' or something else. Most of the time we couldn't even get into the house. In a few cases we got to talk to the colored maid, but that was all. We have walked until our feet are sore—we have walked half a day—and we have won just one soul."

"Well," I said, "if you won just one soul and could do that every half day, hallelujah! That would be over seven hundred in a year's time! And if you could keep one soul out of Hell for a million years by a half a day's work, why that would be wonderful. You shouldn't feel bad about that! But if you cannot win one, try another. Did they turn you down? All right, go down here on Elm Street, down by the park where there are a lot of little shotgun houses on little twenty-five foot lots. [The houses had rooms right behind each other because they did not have room to spread out any other way.] Go down there. The maid will not come to the door, because they do not have any maid. The Madam will not say she is busy, because nearly all of them are on relief and the whole family will be at home. They go down on the railroad track and pick up a few extra pieces of coal that fall off the coal cars in the wintertime."

I knew how it was because I had been down there just a few nights before to take a pair of shoes to a girl so she could come to Sunday school. They called in the neighbors next door and said, "Wait, Brother Rice, you and Mrs. Rice sit down." They went and got the neighbors on either side and said, "Brother Rice is over at our house. Come over and hear him talk." And they got the whole house full of people for me to preach to.

So I said, "They won't run you off. You may not win the hoity-toity and the up-and-outs. But down there where they are poor, where they are on relief, where their floors are uncovered, where they do not get to go to church much because they have only shabby clothes and are tickled because a preacher pays them some attention—I say those people will listen to you." Listen! You can always get somebody. You cannot win everybody; but, thank God, you can win somebody. If you cannot get one, go and get another.

Soul Winning

How Jim Got a Prisoner

It is said that in the last years of the war between the states, a farmer was drafted into the Confederate army. He did not know the drill manual. He did not know how to keep step on the march, nor how to salute. He knew none of the bugle calls. But he brought his squirrel rifle and when the command was given to attack he charged the Yankee lines, joining in the rebel yell. However, the grey-coated Confederates were outnumbered and were soon driven back. The bugle blew "retreat" and the thin grey line withdrew to safer ground. As the battered soldiers treated their wounded, prepared their camp and threw up breastworks in the late afternoon, some one said, "Poor old Jim! He was either killed or taken prisoner in the first battle he was in! Too bad he didn't know the bugle call to retreat and ran right into that nest of Yankees." But about sundown they saw two tired fellows coming over the hill. The one in front had on a blue uniform and the man behind wore a grey. Somebody had taken a prisoner! As he saw the camp, he prodded his prisoner with a bayonet and somebody shouted, "It is Jim! It is Jim! Jim's got a prisoner! Where did you get him, Jim?" The farmer recruit drew up angrily. He felt they had all deserted him in the first battle! "Where did I get him?" he said, "Why, the woods are full of them! Why don't you get one yourself?" So the world is full of sinners, and you can take them alive for Christ, if you only go after them.

My dear Christian friends, somewhere near you is a poor, lost soul, someone who would listen to you, someone who is burdened, someone who realizes he needs Christ. That soul is not saved because nobody has gone to tell him the message of salvation. "Go" is the first command of God to the soul winner. He that goeth forth is the man that returns with sheaves. If you want to be a soul winner then commit yourself to this holy business and go after sinners. Other things are necessary, but this is most necessary. If you would be a winner of souls, then you must go forth.

* * *

Preparation by Prayer. Sometime ago I was called to a funeral of an old man that I did not know, yet one who had plainly told his loved ones he was ready to go to meet Christ, his Saviour. I had never seen the man who died, I did not know one of his relatives or friends who were present at the funeral. I did not know a single pallbearer, except one that I took with me, yet my heart was greatly moved and I felt led to preach on John 3:16. I thought that surely these dear troubled souls, most of whom were unsaved, would be comforted by the thought that comforts my own heart, that God so loved them as to give His Son. At that funeral I preached a gospel sermon, almost as I would preach it in a revival campaign. I asked those who needed Christ to hold up their hands for prayer and most of those present did. I asked those who would take Christ as Saviour to claim Him openly, and tearfully a number of them did. When I returned from the cemetery (where I had the joy of winning two others), I thought back to the early morning when in my private devotions I had asked the dear Lord to help me win somebody that day, and tried to set my heart on soul winning. Through the mercy and help of God I had in a small measure shod my feet with the preparation of the Gospel of peace.

* * *

Big Business Before the Sermon. At Danville, Virginia, in 1963, on Sunday I had preached on soul winning and had urged people to win their loved ones and neighbors and if they could not win them themselves, to bring them to meet the pastor or to meet me. So on Monday night at the watch-night meeting three boys came in and sat near the front. Before the service started I met them. The first boy told me he was twelve years old. Yes, he was a Christian. He told me his name. The second boy told me that he, too, was twelve years old. Yes, he was a Christian, and he told me his name. When I spoke to the third boy, he said he was eleven years old and gave his name. When I asked, "Are you saved? Are you a Christian boy?" the other two boys spoke up immediately and said, "No, he ain't. We brought him tonight to get him saved." I found they had talked to him and he came expecting to get saved.

So when it came time for me to preach, I stopped and said I would preach a sermon all right, but first we had some big business to attend to. I had everybody turn to John 3:16 and we went over it carefully together for a few moments. I asked this boy in the presence of all if he knew that his friends wanted him to be saved. Yes, he did. And did he want to be saved? Yes, he did. And did he understand from John 3:16 that God loved him and that Jesus died for his sins and wanted to save him? Yes, he understood.

And was he ready now for us to pray and ask Jesus Christ to forgive his sins, change his heart and make him a Christian? Yes, he was.

We prayed, then he came to stand beside me and his friends with him that we might tell everybody that he was then and there taking Christ as his Saviour. That came before my sermon!

*   *   *

A Thirst Satisfied. I stopped in a little filling station at Whitesboro, Texas, and had a bottle of orange-ade. I asked the attendant where he went to church. He said he was a Methodist, was once a member of the Methodist Church. I asked him if he was saved.

"I don't know."

"Have you ever been born again?"

"No, I guess not. I don't know."

I talked to him awhile. He told me he had lost his wife, or that she had lost her mind. He had two children, but both had gotten married. He did not have anybody left, so he moved into town and it was so lonely. He was living in the filling station. We talked about the Lord. I asked him if he would mind if I prayed before I left.

"No, I would be glad for you to."

So in that filling station we prayed, and when I got through and looked up he was weeping. He said, "I am so glad you came by."

I said, "I want to meet you in Heaven."

"I want to meet you, too."

I asked him if he was willing to trust Jesus Christ and depend upon Him now. "Are you willing to do that?"

"Yes," he said.

I said, "Here and now will you shake hands with me and put your trust in Jesus Christ and depend on Him to take you to Heaven and satisfy your heart and give you comfort for your sorrows?"

He said, "Yes, I will."

He stood there and wept as I went away.

If you are thirsty, God has water for you (see John 4:1-42).

*   *   *

The Lost Opportunity. In Dallas, Texas, I preached in a great open-air revival campaign and at the same time carried on a daily radio service. A card came from an old man past eighty, dying with cancer. He said, "Brother Rice, I won't be here long and I'm afraid to die. Would you come and pray with me?" The days were filled with more duties than any man could do. I hardly had time to eat or to sleep, for preaching, answering radio mail, advertising the campaign, leading the singing, interviewing burdened souls. Two weeks went by and I did not go to

see the dying man. Then I sent a young preacher to see him, and alas he found that his loved ones were even then gone to the funeral. How I wish now that I had gone without my food and rest and made sure that dying man had peace with God before he died! I neglected my opportunity. I can never have it again in that one case.

*   *   *

"About All I Have Ever Done Is to 'Cuss' a Little Bit." In the first revival I ever attempted to conduct, in a little country church near Decatur, Texas, I remember a man for whom his wife and daughter prayed. One night as the invitation song was being sung under the little brush arbor, I heard someone call for me. In a thicket of plum bushes beside the tabernacle, the daughter and a girl friend knelt beside the gray-haired man. He said to me, "Brother Rice, tell these girls to leave me alone. I am all right."

I told him that if he was really all right it was strange that his wife was so burdened about him, it was strange that his daughter was continually praying and crying about his salvation.

He replied, "Why, Brother Rice, I used to be superintendent of a Sunday school. I have prayed in public. I am as well off as these other church members."

"But that does not make a Christian," I said. "Praying in public, doing church work, living a good moral life is not enough. You are a lost sinner if you have not been saved."

"I have never done much of anything wrong," he said. "About all I have ever done is to 'cuss' a little bit. I am as good a Christian as the others are."

I told him that he might just as well say that he had only killed a few men as far as being a lost sinner was concerned. That seemed to astonish him, and I asked him plainly the question, "Now I am not asking you whether you live a good life, whether you are a moral man. I am asking you whether you have ever been born again. Did you ever trust Jesus Christ to change your heart and to forgive your sins and make you a new creature?"

Very gravely he looked me in the face and then he answered, "No, I guess I never did!"

"Then don't you think it is time you got that settled?" I asked him.

He assented and came with me to the front. There he kneeled down on the oat straw under that simple brush arbor, and by the light of gasoline torches he lifted up his face and with tears said, "O God, if You will forgive me and save me, I will do anything You want me to do!" He was happily saved and had the assurance in his heart that God had forgiven him just as He promised in His Word to forgive all who trust in Christ. But I have often wondered if he might not have gone until death and then have discovered himself eternally lost if I had not pressed the question into his heart that night!

* * *

"It Will Do No Good to Help Him"

When my father was a young preacher, he went to Louisville, Kentucky, for a year at the Southern Baptist Theological Seminary. And during that time he was a student pastor at a little Baptist church in a small town, I think in Campbellsville, Kentucky. It was about 1890. Once he started to the church where he would preach on a winter's morning. As he walked by a lumber yard, he saw a drunken man lying on the snowy ground where he had fallen, unable to walk. He spoke to some men about him! They scoffed at him. "It will do no good to help him. He is drunk all the time. There is no use to bother about him. Others have tried and couldn't do any good." But my father was afraid the man would die from exposure. He lifted the man up and helped to get him home. They helped undress him and cover him and give him hot coffee until the shivering limbs were warmed. They called a doctor to wait on the man. Then he went back a little later when the man was more sober and went again until he won the man to Christ. This drunkard made a good, sober Christian.

More than thirty years later a man came from Kentucky to Texas looking for a preacher named Will Rice. That father, saved years ago, had lived a good Christian life, then on his deathbed he told his children again of the man who had saved his life and then won him to Christ and helped to make him a decent citizen, a godly father and husband. He said to an older son, "If you get a chance to see that man in Texas, tell him that I lived for God and died in the faith and went gladly to Heaven. Tell him that in Heaven I will wait for him."

So the son looked forward to the time when he could see and thank the man who had won his father. He got to be passenger agent for a railroad. He traveled as he wished. He came to Gainesville, Texas, where had been the home of my father. He inquired there and they told him, "He lives now in Decatur, Texas." So he came to Decatur and looked up my father to thank him for blessings long ago.

I cannot tell how the godly influence of my father, not only his teaching but his example, not only certain acts that I noted but the general influence of his heart in doing right, in looking out for others, his moral integrity and his spiritual devotion, has influenced my life.

* * *

Can You Tell God When to Save People? One day a Conservative Baptist pastor in Chicago Heights phoned me and said, "Dr. Rice, a Catholic woman was saved in our services. I gave her your book on *Prayer*. She has been reading it. She came to me and said, 'Pastor, why can't we pray for my husband to be saved this weekend? I believe God wants him to be saved.'" The good pastor said to her, "I feel that way, too."

So on Wednesday night they mentioned it to the congregation for prayer. Another preacher present said, "You can't tell God when to save people." Others said, "You can't be that definite and say you want it done right away."

The pastor called me to ask about it. I told him, "If God led you and the wife to pray that way, go ahead and pray for his conversion this weekend."

So the pastor and this woman prayed. He called me on Saturday. After the Sunday services the pastor phoned me again and said,

"The man was saved fifteen minutes to midnight on Sunday. His wife went home and won him to Christ. She is on shouting grounds." He said further, "We had three others saved, and sixteen young people rededicated their lives. A real revival is on here at the church."

Then the woman herself called me and said, "Dr. Rice, I have only been saved four months. After reading your book I saw we could ask big things from God. So I asked for my husband to get saved this weekend, and he was saved fifteen minutes to midnight Sunday night! Thank God for your book on *Prayer*, which taught me to ask."

*   *   *

The First Soul of the Year

The holy sense of obligation, the high aspirations and hopes of the new year are a wonderful argument for turning to Christ. Some years ago I preached at a New Year's watchnight meeting in Buffalo, New York. A great group of youth meeting from all over the city packed the hall seating some 1200. As I recall, a number were saved at that midnight hour and past. But as I went to my hotel for a little sleep before flying back to Chicago and Wheaton, I earnestly prayed, "O dear Lord, help me to win my first soul for the year today, on New Year's Day!"

I took a morning flight from Buffalo to Chicago. No opportunity presented itself to win a soul. But as the plane stopped at Detroit a young man in the armed services, I think it was the Air Force, got on the plane and took the seat beside me. I tried to start a conversation but he was morose and retiring. He had said good-bye to his young wife and baby and on New Year's Day was starting back to the West Coast to his base in the services.

But when I brought up the subject of his family he became interested. Yes, he had a wife and a baby girl. Was the wife a Christian? Oh, yes, she was a good Christian. She attended a Methodist church at Albion, Michigan, I think he said. He had just bidden her good-bye. About this time the hostess came and said, "Are you ready for lunch?"

"No," I told her. "I am going to eat New Year's dinner with my daughter. All the family will be there. I will get to Chicago a little after twelve and we will have dinner about two. Thank you."

I continued my conversation with the young man. "You say your wife is a good Christian. Wouldn't she be pleased if you could write her and say that today, on New Year's Day, you have decided to trust Jesus

Christ, to take Him as your Saviour, to be a Christian husband and father, and to join with her in having a Christian home? Wouldn't that please her very much?"

He was deeply touched. Evidently he loved his wife very much and she evidently impressed him as a very earnest and sincere Christian.

"Yes," he said, "I know that would please her very much. I have often thought about it and I know I ought to be a Christian."

So I opened my Bible to John, the third chapter, and showed him how Jesus said, "Ye must be born again." And then Jesus told Nicodemus how to be born again: "For God so loved the world, that he gave his only begotten Son, that whosoever believeth in him should not perish, but have everlasting life."

I said to him, "Wouldn't you like for us to bow our heads here and I will whisper a prayer and ask the dear Lord to come into your heart and forgive your sins and save your soul? And down in your heart you may tell the Lord earnestly that you admit you are a sinner and you want Him to forgive you, and that you will trust Him now. Will you do that?"

He nodded his head. We bowed our heads for our quiet little prayer as the plane flew on. And then I asked him, "If you will take Christ as your Saviour today, relying on Him to forgive you and save you, and setting out to live for Him now, will you take my hand as a sign between you and me and God that here and now you trust Christ to forgive your sins and save your soul?"

He took my hand and said that he would write his wife right away to tell her of his glad decision.

Then the hostess came to our part of the plane and said, "We've been circling for twenty minutes above Chicago. The fog has closed in; Midway Airport is closed. We will have to go back to Detroit." So the plane turned back east to Detroit.

I called the hostess and said, "I won't get to eat New Year's dinner with my daughter. Do you have lunch left for me?"

She brought me the lunch and I ate it very happily. We deplaned at Detroit. I said good-bye to my young Air Force friend and got a taxi over to Lansing, Michigan, where I caught a train, getting back to Chicago and out to Wheaton about midnight, as I recall. But, oh, wasn't it wonderful that God answered my prayer and brought me in contact with that young husband so that I had the joy of teaching him to trust the Saviour on New Year's Day?

I had the trip from Detroit to Chicago and back on the plane, it seemed, all in vain. But it was not in vain. The Lord had that trip to Chicago and back so I would get to talk to this fine young man and win him to Christ on New Year's Day. New Year season is a wonderful time to be saved.

* * *

Something Happened at His House!

In Lewistown, Pennsylvania, we had a blessed united revival campaign sponsored by a number of churches. Dr. Harry Clarke, the song leader, was with me, as was my daughter Grace and an advance man and my secretary. On a Sunday afternoon when I preached to men only I was led to bear down heavily on the responsibilities of men; they must give an account for their families.

A tall, gaunt man was present who reminded me of Abraham Lincoln. He was about 6 feet 4 inches high with a lined face, dark eyes, austere face. He looked at me solemnly throughout the service. There was no inkling of what was going on behind that poker face.

After the service, this man put on his topcoat, went out on the steps, reached into a side pocket, pulled out a meerschaum pipe and threw it violently to the icy street where it broke in pieces. From the other pocket of his topcoat he took out a can of Prince Albert tobacco and sailed it in the street. It bounced a time or two, hit the curb and went down the gutter spewing tobacco. Then he drew his sleeve across his eyes and started vigorously down the sidewalk.

I watched him as he stepped about four feet at a stride. There was a determination in his look. I said, "Something surely is going to happen at that man's home!"

This was on Sunday afternoon. The next Friday night he came insisting that my entire evangelistic party come to his home for dinner on Saturday evening. We went and had a lovely dinner. But best of all, here were nine of his people— brothers-in-law, sons-in-law, daughters and sons—who had been saved in the six days. And the next day two more were saved. When we moved from Wheaton to Murfreesboro, I found a picture of the nine new converts in a snapshot taken that night with Dr. Clarke and me.

Oh, a man ought to get his family saved!

* * *

Whose Business Was His Soul?

There are a good many homes where they don't want to hear me tell them about God. Sinners turn a cold shoulder. There are a good many who think they have no need, no hunger; they think they have plenty of time yet. But, thank God, some places I go know they need God.

I went to talk to a man who had been drinking. "How are you getting along with God?"

"Well, that's my business," he replied.

I looked him square in the eye. "It is my business, too. I love you. I mean good, and it is my business, too."

He broke down and began to cry. "If anyone ever needed help, I do," he said.

"You can get help then. God loves you." I read Isaiah 1:18 to him, "Come now, and let us reason together, saith the Lord: though your sins be as scarlet, they shall be as white as snow; though they be red like crimson, they shall be as wool."

"That doesn't mean me," he said. "That is somebody else."

"Yes, it does mean you," I said.

"No, that is for somebody else. I don't mean to say you are telling a lie. But that just isn't for me."

I said, "Yes, it is for you." I told him I would pray for him. I urged him to get right with God.

"Not when I am full of beer," he said.

I went back two days later and asked him, "How is it with you and God?"

"I believe it is fixed up," he said.

When I went to see him, his face was shining. We had prayer. His wife was happy, and so was he.

*   *   *

"I Will Never Darken the Door of This Church Any More!"

My father who is now in Heaven told me long ago about his conversion. It was in Gainesville, Texas. He was a young man, I suppose about thirty. A revival was on and he attended a few evening services to hear the preaching. An old cowboy friend of his came one night at the invitation time and, with an arm about his shoulder, said to him, "Will, I am praying for you. I am anxious about your soul. God has saved me, and I want you to take my Saviour, too." My father said that he drew himself haughtily erect and said something like this: "I am a grown man and I know what I want to do without anybody telling me. I came to enjoy the sermon, but if I have to be disturbed and embarrassed by people coming to me publicly and urging me to become a Christian when I am not yet ready, then I will not come to the meeting any more. If anybody talks to me again, I will never come back to this meeting."

His friend went away, but a few nights later the urge of the Holy Spirit in his heart, his born-again heart that longed to see people saved, compelled him to go to his friend. He approached my father again and said, "Will, I didn't intend to come back, but something compels me. I am burdened about you. I cannot get any peace, and I am so anxious for you to be saved." My father said that his anger mounted, and he spoke quickly and sharply, "I told you that if you didn't leave me alone I wouldn't come to this meeting any more! I will never darken the door of this church any more as long as I live! Maybe it will be some pleasure to remember that you have driven me from the house of God!" And with that he got his big Stetson hat, marched out of the church, and went angrily to his room.

I am sure that the Christian friend must have grieved greatly, but if he could have seen what happened, he would have rejoiced in heart. My father was rooming at the time with his brother and wife. He arrived home, of course, before others of the family, for the service was not yet through. He said to himself that unless he wanted to hear talk, talk, talk about the preacher and about the revival and about people being saved, he had better get to bed before they returned from the service. So to bed he went, but not to sleep. Hour after hour he tossed on his bed and could not find slumber. He got up and smoked, and then tried to sleep, but it was all in vain. No rest came through the long night. Bit by bit he began to see his sins, his folly. He said to himself, "What a fool I am! The best friend I have in the world came to me because he loved me, wanted to see me saved and keep me out of Hell, and I, like an ill-bred wretch, insulted him and drove him away. Now nobody else will come to talk to me, and it will only serve me right if I go to Hell!" His burden got so heavy, that about four o'clock in the morning he got out of bed and fell on his knees beside it. He confessed his sins and begged God to forgive him and have mercy. And finally sweet peace came to his heart and he found rest in Jesus Christ.

At the church services the evangelist had announced a sunrise prayer meeting the next morning. When the janitor came at five o'clock to unlock the church door for this prayer meeting, he found sitting on the steps outside the man who just the night before had sworn he would never again darken the door of that church! My father told it with the deepest of pleasure as an evidence that whether men like it or do not like it, we must talk to men about their souls. We who are saved bring the voice of God to sinners. We will be guilty before God, unworthy of our friends, unworthy of our salvation, unworthy of our profession, if we do not earnestly, urgently press upon men that they are lost and need Jesus Christ as a Saviour!

* * *

Sowing the Supernatural Seed.

Psalm 126:5,6 gives us this great rule for soul winning: "They that sow in tears shall reap in joy. He that goeth forth and weepeth, bearing precious seed, shall doubtless come again with rejoicing, bringing his sheaves with him."

Every one who would win souls, then, must carry the Word of God. All the sower's labor is wasted, all his tears are fruitless, unless he sows the precious seed!

When I was nine years old my father moved us to a ranch in West Texas. I was soon put in a field a mile square, driving six big mules to a plow. We broke the ground, then harrowed it, and then sowed the field to grow feed for the wintertime. I remember driving the six big mules to the long grain drill hour after hour. It was a tremendous experience to me to have day after day the responsibility of that big team. I could not harness them alone, but after they were harnessed I could hitch them to the drill, stop when the sun was straight over my head to water them and feed them and eat my lunch under the wagon; then hitch them again to the drill and sow.

After a certain number of rounds on the portion or "land" we were sowing I was always to fill up the big seed box of the grain drill. But once as I drove happily along watching to overlap the wheel track every time all along, and yet dreaming of great things of the future, I entirely forgot to fill up the seed box! Suddenly I remembered. I stopped the team, looked disconsolately in the box which was now empty and wondered how far I had gone with the empty grain drill, actually sowing no seed. I made a wild guess and after filling up the drill, I went back over much of the land. But I did not guess right and when the grain came up there was a strip a mile long and perhaps fifty feet wide which was barren! I was the laughingstock of the countryside. And many a Christian who seeks to win souls will find himself the laughingstock of Heaven if he does not use the supernatural seed of the Word of God in his soul-winning efforts.

* * *

"If They Stay, I Go!" A certain

large church put out buses to bring in from far and near all the underprivileged children and young people, families without cars, and all they could get to come and hear the Gospel. The children had a tendency to make some noise in the sedate Sunday morning services. They were not all well dressed. The preaching was fitted to *"the poor, and the maimed, and the halt and the blind"* that were brought in from everywhere, and many were saved. A haughty millionaire, seeing the throng about him after the service, said to the pastor, "What are we going to do with all these dirty kids?"

The pastor answered, "I am going to love them with all my heart!"

The Pharisee answered, "If they stay, I go!" And go he did, and the church continued to win multitudes in a record-breaking fashion.

Some modern Pharisees and scribes want the pastor to spend all his time visiting and catering to the church members, and they resent what time he takes to seek out the lost and win them and counsel with them, get them saved. And some fashionable singers resent it when into the choir come some of these not well-trained, not very well-dressed but earnest and believing souls who have found Christ. Some Pharisees and scribes criticize revivals and evangelists. How all must grieve the heart of the Saviour who do not want those to be loved and sought and won and taught, for whom Christ died, the publicans and sinners, who are so dear to Christ's heart.

* * *

Saved While We Prayed!

I once preached on faith in Dallas, Texas, in a conference. I was so blessed of God and so moved, and the power of God was so obvious as I spoke. I was about to close the message, but the people were so moved and I was so moved that I said, "We can't leave here without asking God for something. It would be a sin. What can we pray about?"

I thought of a woman at 812 West Jefferson in Dallas who had written me just a few days before about her son. She had said, "I have never heard you in person, Brother Rice, but I listen to you on the radio every day. Will you pray for my twenty-four-year-old son who has TB. The doctors don't expect him to live long." (Since we have the antibiotics, TB is often curable now. But then many people died with it.) She said, "He is not saved. Will you pray for him?"

So I told my people the story, and I said, "Let us pray that God will save him."

We knelt down and fervently prayed for this man. Finally we got up, and I said, "I feel I have to go see him now. Perhaps God wants me to do something about it."

I got my Bible and I went to 812 West Jefferson, rang the bell. At the head of the stairs a woman said, "Who is it?"

"This is Brother Rice."

She said, "Oh, Brother Rice! I know your voice! Come on up. I hear you so many times on the radio."

I went up the stairs, and I said, "You wrote me about your son, and I wanted to talk to him about his soul."

"All right. He is in the back bedroom, but I will bring a pillow and he can lie on the couch in the living room while you talk to him."

He came in. I said to this young man, "I want to read some from the Bible. May I read to you the third chapter of John?"

"Yes."

I read John, chapter 3, and I said, "Now don't you see that Jesus said, 'Ye must be born again'?"

"Yes."

"All right, have you ever been born again?" (Of course he was supposed to say no).

"Yes, I think I have."

I said, "You have? When?"

"Well, just a little bit ago. Mrs. Moore, 'Mother Moore,' who works for the Radio Revival, was out here. She talked to me and showed me the Scriptures, and we prayed together. I believe I was born again."

I said, "When was she here?"

"Oh, fifteen or twenty minutes ago. She had just left when you came."

I said, "Old boy, while we were on our knees praying for you, a woman came to see you and won you to the Lord!"

Let me tell you, I had rather "have faith in God!" Why don't you read your Bible and find out how God is supposed to do things, and what God promises to do, and what He has done for others, He will do for you. "Faith cometh by hearing, and hearing by the word of God" (Rom. 10:17).

*　*　*

I Have Found the Harvest Always Plenteous. The fields are white unto harvest. Bless God, I have found it always has been true.

I was in the Holy Land again in 1976 and I won our Arab guide, a university graduate, to the Lord. After he was saved he said, "I have been wanting to hear more about this for a long time." Yes. He had guided lots of Christians, but I suppose nobody had time to talk to him about being saved. Here in Atlanta the academic dean in the Southern Baptist University, Dr. Trachian, came from Lebanon. He was principal of a Lebanon high school. Someone had gotten me to speak at that Arab high school in Lebanon. When I asked, "How long do I have?" he said, "Everybody else has only thirty minutes. I take THE SWORD OF THE LORD. You can have as long as you want." When I preached and gave an invitation, fifty-two were saved. Arabs? Yes.

In an Arab high school in Old Jerusalem there were fourteen senior boys. We got five of them saved. One of them has already been to America to train as a preacher.

"The fields are white. . .to harvest" (John 4:35).

* * *

Is a Mule Worth More Than a Soul?

Years ago in West Texas we raised fine horses and mules. I remember that one spring we had forty-four mule colts. Well, when wintertime came on, we brought those mule colts to the home pasture where they would be fed and looked after and the mares were taken out to the big ranch pasture, and so the colts were weaned.

One day Dad sent me to round up those young mules and drive them to the house and they would have some hay.

We had put a dam across a little creek, and as the mules were going across this dam heading home, I waved my arms to drive them and a wild young mule jumped into the creek to wade across. But the mud had silted in until there was about two feet of mud and perhaps two feet of water in there. He bogged down. He was weak and young and he struggled and struggled. It was a cold November day. The water was cold. He struggled until he wore himself out.

I stood on the bank and hollered and tried to get him to get out. He could not. At last he gave up. And when his head went down under the water, I went in to him quickly, got his head out of the water. He shook the water out of his ears, then I placed his front feet out in front of him like a mule or a horse gets up, and placed his back feet well under him and I got down chin deep in the muddy water and got him by the tail and I lifted and got my knees under his back end and I hollered and encouraged him and lifted and pushed and he struggled.

By great effort, he pulled his legs out of the mud and struggled to the bank. He was a muddy, disreputable-looking mule colt! I was wet and muddy all over. It was cold in November and a half mile to the house. I nearly froze, I thought, but, my, how my heart warmed! I had saved a $50-mule colt!

Is not a poor soul worth more than that?

Then let me say it again: The one great business of soul-winning churches and evangelists is to go get the people for God. May God raise up thousands of churches whose sole aim is to reach people at any cost, love them, warn them, teach them, bring them in, sympathize with them, bear their burdens, and in some way get their confidence and bring them the Gospel that Christ died for sinners, and get them saved. Then we will meet them all in Heaven.

*   *   *

Many Would See Jesus. I preached in the Evansville Rescue Mission, Evansville, Indiana, one Sunday afternoon on the duty of soul winning. A registered nurse went to the Welburn-Walker Hospital to night duty and said in her heart, "Brother Rice says I have blood on my hands! Oh, I have sinned in not warning people. I must try to win somebody tonight." In the first room she went to and asked, "Are you a Christian?" the woman sat bolt upright in bed and began to weep. She had had a major operation, but her fever did not go down. She would not sleep at night and the night before she had not even allowed the nurse to turn out the light in her room. Now she told the nurse that it was not the operation, it was not her health, but that her heart felt so guilty that she was afraid she would go to Hell if she went to sleep. "Oh, if I only had somebody to pray for me!" she said. I came the next morning, and have never seen a more eager case. How gladly she seized on the story of salvation, as a drowning man clutches a straw, or as a starving man reaches for bread! She was wonderfully saved, as soon as she could understand how simple it was to trust in Jesus Christ.

No doubt there are thousands, some of them very near to you, whose hearts cry out, "Sir, we would see Jesus" (John 12:21).

Stewardship

Money's Friends. I remember a rich man whom I visited and with whom I had prayer. He begged me to come back again. He said, "A man with money never knows who are his real friends. I have lots of preachers come to see me, but always they are building a church or they have a program that needs some more money, and they hope I will support it. I can't tell who is my friend and who is not."

He found out only what the woman at the well of Sychar had learned, "Whosoever drinketh of this water shall thirst again." And so it is with all the water that this world can give

* * *

Take Time for God. Once I was assistant pastor of a fine church, and in my hands were placed some of the financial arrangements of the church. A well-to-do Christian man in the church instructed me to simply write a check on his account each week for a certain amount for the church budget. For some weeks I followed that plan, then I quit it. I thought that any man who wanted to give money to the Lord's cause ought to give more attention and time to the matter than that. After the first of the month he approached me, saying, "Brother Rice, I find that no checks have been drawn on my account this month for the Lord's work. Go ahead and write a check for me each week. I am glad to give the money. I just simply do not like to take the time to think of it each week and give attention to the matter. I am glad for you to write the checks and I am glad to give the money."

I replied, "If you cannot give God enough time to even write your own checks for His cause, I do not think He wants your money. You can write your own checks, or the church will do without your offerings." Why should God want anybody's money when He doesn't have enough of one's interest and time to even write a check or to turn the money over to the Lord's cause?

* * *

The Blessing of Giving. Once a committee from a church was calling on the members, trying to collect money for the church budget. They came to a poor widow's bare home. She washed clothes to make a meager living for herself and her children. When the committee saw her poverty, they were embarrassed to tell why they came, but she brought $5 from a hiding place and gave it to the committee—a good deal more than many wealthier members had given. Embarrassed, the leader of the committee protested that she could not afford to give so much, and that they must not take the money. She thrust it into his hands and began to weep. "You want to take away my blessing!" she said. "I love the Lord as much as the rest of you! It is my church and I love it and I want to do my part. You want to take away my joy!" Greatly humbled, the committee went away with the gift.

* * *

God Still Answers Prayer!

A few years back I came home from a revival, and I had such a pile of work to do—a book to finish, a subscription campaign on, all the mail to answer. So I thought I would just stay at home two or three months and not have any revivals. Now I get no salary from the Sword of the Lord Foundation. I get no income at all from the Foundation. I get no pay for my sermons, no commission on subscriptions.

In my study I talked to the Lord. "Lord, it seems that I used to have such wonderful answers to prayer. Lord, do you think I wouldn't trust You now. Lord, try me and see." I told the Lord that for a month or two I would stay at home and I would try Him and see if He still answered prayer. I said, "I believe You and trust You just as I did in days gone by."

I had just $200. I sent $100 to Dr. Billy Graham at Northwestern Schools where I was on the Board and he was then president. I sent $50 to a Wheaton College student for a suit of clothes and some other things he needed. I had brought a colored boy from British Guiana to study at Moody Bible Institute; so I sent somebody with $50 to buy him a nice suit of clothes. I had left enough incidental money for Mrs. Rice to buy groceries for a week, so I gave her that. I walked up and down in my study in the Sword building in Wheaton. As I felt of the few coins in my pocket, I said, "Lord, I have that much between me and You for some months. But, Lord, I am not afraid to risk You." I sat down in my chair and the tears rained down my face.

It was funny. A letter came the next day or two, and it said, "Brother Rice, I feel strangely impressed to send you this $10 for personal use. Now this gift is for you and your family." Somebody else wrote, "I never did it before, but here is $5 I feel the Lord wants you to have." That went on and on!

It was a strange thing. When I was in revivals all the time, no one sent me money to use for myself. Now God began sending in all I needed. And when I left for revivals, the special gifts stopped. I had given away all that I had, and here it came back again!

*   *   *

You Can Never Get Ahead of God.

May I tell you a little personal experience? I once was in three conferences—four days at Dumas, Texas, and four days in St. Louis. Dr. Jones was with me in Dumas, Texas. And then four days in Chicago with Dr. Bob Jones, Sr., and Dr. Beauchamp Vick of the great Temple Baptist Church of Detroit, and Brother Jack Hyles, and singer Bill Harvey—five of us. We had a blessed conference and lots of good was done. If we had had enough time to have a man on the field to work it up we would have had a bigger attendance. But we did have a good time.

However, at St. Louis I paid the hotel bill and meals for three of us—$105 I paid out of my own pocket. By the time I paid the hotel bill, and airline transportation for Bill Harvey all the way up from Texas, then I got almost nothing more than expenses there.

Then in Chicago, with three tremendous speakers, I had to take care of their expenses. Dr. Bob Jones had to come from Greenville, South Carolina; Jack Hyles drove from Garland, Texas, 1,000 miles. And there were hotel bills and a $95 printing bill. So I got almost nothing more than expenses out of that conference. Of course, some of you gave some here in the church, but it took about all that came in for me, the pastor, to pay the supply preachers a very modest amount.

But do you know what happened? There came a letter from a man who reads THE SWORD out in California. He had an envelope with an offering of $40 and he marked on there, "Designated for Brother Rice personally." Then another man who is going to school wrote me a note and said, "God has in a wonderful way provided so I can go to school another year and I felt I must share; so I am designating it for you." He sent me a check. It turned out that I had money for my needs and my family.

You can never get ahead of God if you put Him first. God will take care of you. Why don't you prove God?

*   *   *

Preacher Proves He Can Tithe With Family of Fifteen, on $125 Per Month

Years ago I was in a revival campaign in a country community in West Texas. In a daytime service I set out to teach people gathered under a brush arbor that God demanded first place in everything, that He wanted tithes and offerings from the loving and believing hearts of His people. Present in the service that day was a dear country preacher, Brother Kuykendal. He was then, and had been for years, county missionary in Palo Pinto County, preaching in churchless communities, building up weak churches, selling and giving away gospel literature as a rural missionary. He asked if he might tell how God had dealt with him about tithing. I gladly asked him to proceed. He arose and told his story about like this.

Some years ago when I was county missionary of this county, the famous Baptist businessman, H. Z. Duke, who founded the Duke and Ayers Nickel Stores over a wide area, came to this county and, speaking as a Christian layman, urged the men and women everywhere to try God and see if He would not make good His promises to bless them in material things when they gave tithes and offerings to His cause. After Mr. Duke had spoken in one community, I took him in my buggy to another community. Mr. Duke said to me, "Brother Kuykendal, do you believe in tithing?"

"I certainly do," I said. "I believe in tithing and I preach it myself."

"But, Brother Kuykendal, do you *practice* tithing?"

Sadly I had to answer, "No, I do not. I believe in tithing, but I cannot practice it. You see, I have thirteen children at home. Every meal fifteen of us sit down at the table. I receive only $125 a month, $1,500 a year as salary. I have to maintain my own horse and buggy for constant traveling. It is just impossible to take care of all the needs of a family of fifteen out of $125 a month and have money left to tithe. So I believe in tithing, and I preach it, but I cannot practice it."

Mr. Duke was a very kindly man. He said, "Brother Kuykendal, would you like to tithe? Would you tithe if I would back you up financially so you could be sure you would not lose by it?"

"Nothing would please me more," I said.

So Mr. Duke made me the following proposition:

"I want you to set out to give God at least $12.50 every month, as soon as you get your salary. Then as you feel led, you may give more. I promise you that if you need help, I will give it. Simply write me a letter and say, "Brother Duke, I am giving a tithe but I miss the money. I need it for my family. I have given this year so much." I promise you that I will send you a check by return mail. Are you willing to try tithing on that basis?"

I hesitated a moment, moved with emotion, and Brother Duke said, "I have thirty-two stores. I have plenty of money to make good my promise. I will be glad to do it. Will you risk me and start tithing on my simple promise that I will make good any amount you have given, any time that you find you miss it and need it? Will you trust me about it?"

I gladly accepted his offer. I said, "Yes, Brother Duke, I have long wanted to tithe, but I felt I simply could not do it. Now, thank God, I can tithe and I will be glad to. And I will not feel like a hypocrite when I tell others they ought to tithe."

So I started tithing for the first time in my life. Every month I took out first of all one-tenth of my salary and gave it to the Lord's cause; then as I felt led, I gave more. In the back of my mind I always had this thought, Mr. Duke promised me that he would make it up any time I need it. He will send me the money if I simply ask him for it.

But a strange thing happened. It seemed our money went farther than before. I would preach in some country community and somebody would tie a crate of chickens on the back of my buggy. Somebody would put a ham under the seat. Or a godly woman would put some home-canned fruit in my buggy.

A neighbor farmer said, "Brother Kuykendal, God has blessed me so that I cannot get all my corn in the crib this year. I have a big wagon load extra that I cannot keep. May I put it in your crib for your buggy horse?"

Another neighbor drove over with a great hay wagon full of hay for the cow.

It was very strange, but that year we had no doctor bills. The children's clothes seemed not to wear out so badly. It was a happy, happy time. I never did have to call on Mr. H. Z. Duke to make up the money I had given to the Lord in tithes.

Then one day, when the year was about gone and the test was about over, I suddenly realized with shame that I had believed what H. Z. Duke said. He promised to make good anything I lacked because of tithing, and I believed him. But my Heavenly Father had made the same promise, and I had not believed Him! I had taken the word of a man when I did not take the promise of God! Now I had proven God's promises and found that He took care of me and my big family on a small salary. I found that $112.50 per month took care of our family better, with God's blessing, than $125 did without being under the blessed covenant which He has made with those who seek first the kingdom of God and who tithe.

That godly country preacher stood there before the congregation weeping. With the deepest emotion he said:

Now I have tithed for many years. My salary has been increased year after year. We have always had enough. We have never been shamed. The greatest spiritual blessing of my life, aside from my salvation, has been in learning to trust God about daily needs for my home and a big family.

"Prove me now herewith, saith the Lord of hosts, if I will not open the windows of heaven, and pour you out a blessing, that there shall not be room enough to receive it."—Mal. 3:10.

The Will of God

Leaving All for Jesus. A man's ship is very, very dear to him. Nearly all ships have names and are spoken of as if they had personalities. On the island of Grand Manan, in the Bay of Fundy, I spent two weeks among the fisher folk and saw them repairing their boats. The boat was not only the means of livelihood; it was the dearest thing that a man possessed. The boat was called by a name, was patted affectionately, was repaired and scraped and cleaned and painted again and again. Fishing people love their boats. But James and John left the ship. They, with their father, owned the ship and were with him in business.

And they left their father, left him with servants.

I can imagine that the old man said, "John, you're not leaving me, are you? I can't do without you. We have built up a good business. James, you have been a loyal, good son. You can't leave me now. I'm getting old. I need your help."

I suppose the boys would say to their father, "Father, you have the servants. They'll help you. But Jesus has called us and we must go. We must win souls."

I can imagine that John said, "I looked into His eyes, and I loved Him. I promised to follow Him till I die. I cannot give Him up. I'll go with Him anywhere He says."

I imagine that the father might have said to James, "Son, you always were level-headed—not so dreamy and idealistic as your brother. Surely you have enough practical sense to see that you'll not get anywhere going with Jesus. Sure, He is a good man; maybe He is a prophet. Maybe He is even the Son of God, as He says. But we are practical folks; we have to carry on the business. Don't leave me, Son!" But James, too, had determined to leave everything for Jesus.

I can imagine that the father and mother said, "You don't love your old dad and mother. You are not obeying the first commandment with a promise." They did not understand it, but Jesus had plainly said that unless one hated father, mother, brothers, sisters, wives, children, houses, land—even his own life—one could not be a disciple of Jesus. And they set out to be disciples. They forsook everything!

* * *

Obey God's Will to Have God's Strength.

Years ago in Dallas, Texas, a young man in the church of which I was pastor felt the call of God to preach. A business opportunity came his way, a good job, fast promotion, a good salary. He tried the newspaper business and seemed to prosper in it, but he did not prosper spiritually. Preoccupation with his work, missing church services, neglect of Bible study and prayer, a heart growing cold toward soul winning followed, and then, finally, drink and the consciousness that he had drifted far from the will of God and the blessing of God.

I remember when he came forward in a public service to lay down his life again upon the altar. With many tears he said to me, "Brother Rice, I cannot even be a good Christian if I do not preach the Gospel as God has commanded me!"

He had learned the hard lesson that if you do not obey the will of God you cannot have God's strength, God's victory, and God's help in overcoming temptation.

* * *

"All Things Work Together for Good."

Dr. Ironside loved Southern biscuits, I guess because he lived up North among Yankees and didn't get many of them. So when he came to my church in Dallas I took him out to chicken dinner, hot biscuits and cream gravy. Dr. Ironside said, "I am afraid I ought not to eat another one," but he would butter another biscuit and eat it, then he would say, "Listen, I am afraid this is a sin," but he would butter another biscuit and eat it. And Dr. Ironside said once, "Do you like lard?" Did you ever taste just lard? "Well," he said, "You wouldn't like that." "Do you like dry flour?" No. "Did you ever taste baking powder?" That tastes awful; baking powder does. He said, "Do you like that? Well, you just wait till God mixes them all up together and gets His biscuits in the oven and gets them to rise good, and brown good; when God gets His biscuits brown you are going to like them. You might not like the lard by itself, nor the baking powder by itself, nor the dry flour by itself, nor the salt by itself, but when God mixes them, "all things work together" in God's oven and turn out good biscuits. And so "all things work together for good" (Rom. 8:28).

* * *

Open Your Heart to the Will of God. I wonder if the reader is really eager to know the will of God in his life, whatever it may cost him? Luther Rice and Adoniram Judson together had received a great vision of the need for foreign missions and had surrendered themselves to the call of God for foreign missionary work. So, with some support, they went out, hoping to do missionary work in India.

Luther Rice sailed on one boat, and Adoniram Judson on another. The long weeks at sea gave them time to study the Word of God. Each of them knew of the work of William Carey, the English Baptist in India, and they knew they would face the problem of this form of baptism. Both were pedo-Baptists, and the only support promised was from pedo-Baptist sources. Yet each of these godly missionaries who had been willing to give up home and country and comforts and, if need be, life itself for the Lord, with an openhearted study of the Bible came to the conclusion that Bible baptism should be by immersion and of believers only instead of unconverted babies. When they met on the coasts of Asis, Judson went on to Burma but Rice must return to America to organize support among the Baptists.

I am not here arguing the question of the mode of baptism. I am illustrating the fact that one can not really learn the will of God until his heart is open to try to do the blessed will of God.

*   *   *

Put It on the Altar. In a great conference where many had been moved to a step of rededication, a businessman, well-dressed, distinguished, with graying temples, came with many others to take my hand. He said, "It is my business! I love my business more than anything else in the world. I don't need it. I could retire and have all the money I could ever spend. I do not need it, but I simply love to make money! But today I put my business on the altar. Christ and souls will be first and business will be secondary and incidental to pleasing God. I make my vow today!"

A young woman came in the same service weeping. "It is my mother. Today I am giving up my mother to God." She told me how ten years before she had felt the call of God to go as a missionary to China. Her father and mother had demurred. She was the only child left at home. The father said, "If you will stay with us, I will deed this place to you and you will have security and provision when you are old."

"But I must go to China! God has called me," she cried.

Then the mother, accustomed to

having her own way, had a "heart attack." She insisted that the daughter didn't love her. "If you loved your mother like you ought, you wouldn't go off and leave me sick and with no one to care for me."

So the young woman had given up her dream, had turned a deaf ear to the call of God. Ten years had gone by and all the time the burning was in the young woman's heart. Now she said, "I may be too late for China. I don't know what God wants me to do, but I promise Him now that He shall be first, whatever He wants. I give my mother up to God whether she is pleased or displeased, whether she weeps or faints or accuses me."

* * *

All the Keys but One.

You cannot put a fence around a little lot and put God inside that fence. You cannot say, "Lord, you stay within that little part of my life." You cannot reserve part for yourself. You cannot invite God into your heart and life and say, "Here are all the keys but one little key."

F. B. Meyer tells us that in a vision he knelt in his room one night and gave Christ the ring of his will with the keys on it but kept back one little key, the key to a closet in his heart. The Lord said to him, "Are they all here?"

Dr. Meyer said, "All but one."

"What is that?"

"It is the key of a little cupboard," said Dr. Meyer, "in which I have something which Thou needest not interfere with; it is mine."

Then Dr. Meyer said the Lord put the keys back into his hand and said, "My child, if you cannot trust Me with all, you cannot trust Me at all."

"I cried, 'Stop,' " he said, "and the Lord seemed to come back." Dr. Meyer held the little key in his hand and said, "I cannot give it, but if Thou wilt take it, Thou shalt have it."

* * *

Forsake All.

I knew of a Christian wife who prayed faithfully for her unsaved husband. With broken heart she cried to God. At long last the husband was saved. Then he became more and more concerned about soul winning. At last he gave up a profitable business and laid his life on the altar to preach the Gospel. Was the wife pleased? No, she was not! She wanted her husband to be saved. She wanted him to quit his drunkenness. She wanted him to quit following after lewd women. She wanted him to bring home his paycheck. But she did not want him to be a preacher. She did not want him to be counted a fanatic and a fool. She did not want poverty for Jesus' sake. You see, many people would be glad to have you be a Christian and be moral and honest, but they will not want you to be an out-and-out Christian, a "fanatical" Christian, a radical Christian. But what the world does not want you to be, Jesus Christ demands that you be. "Whosoever he be of you that forsaketh not all that he hath, he cannot be my disciple" (Luke 26:33).

* * *

One May, for Salary or Business, Choose Against God's Best. Dr. Lee Roberson tells of a man who, moving out of Chattanooga to another city, came to plead with Dr. Roberson. "I hope you will pray for my children. There is not a good church where I am going. There is not a good Christian school. My children will be in great temptation. Oh, pray that they will live for God."

Then Dr. Roberson said to the man, "If the situation is as bad as that, why move away from Chattanooga? You have a good job here; your children are in this church and are serving God. Why move away?"

"Because I get $20.00 more a week on the new job," the man said. He was willing to jeopardize his Christian testimony and the Christian lives and influence and happiness of his children for $20.00 more a week!

* * *